Building Emotional Resilience in Black Boys

Building Emotional Resilience in Black Boys

How Families, Schools and Neighborhoods Protect Against Racism, Poverty and Adversity

OSCAR A. BARBARIN, PhD

OXFORD
UNIVERSITY PRESS

Oxford University Press is a department of the University of Oxford.
It furthers the University's objective of excellence in research, scholarship,
and education by publishing worldwide. Oxford is a registered trade mark of
Oxford University Press in the UK and certain other countries.

Published in the United States of America by Oxford University Press
198 Madison Avenue, New York, NY 10016, United States of America.

© Oxford University Press 2025

All rights reserved. No part of this publication may be reproduced, stored in a retrieval system,
transmitted, used for text and data mining, or used for training artificial intelligence, in any form or
by any means, without the prior permission in writing of Oxford University Press, or as expressly
permitted by law, by licence or under terms agreed with the appropriate reprographics rights
organization. Enquiries concerning reproduction outside the scope of the above should be sent
to the Rights Department, Oxford University Press, at the address above.

You must not circulate this work in any other form
and you must impose this same condition on any acquirer

CIP data is on file at the Library of Congress

ISBN 978-0-19-774749-0

DOI: 10.1093/oso/9780197747490.001.0001

Printed by Marquis Book Printing, Canada

This book is dedicated to Black mothers, especially my mother Inez, my wife Angela, my sister Sylvia, and all the devoted Black women who have cared deeply and sacrificed so much of themselves to provide and make a life for their sons. Through weariness and worry, heartaches and disappointment, they have had our backs and have been steadfast with love, guidance, and encouragement. They are our heroes and deserve much credit for whatever successes we, their sons, have had in life.

Contents

Acknowledgments — ix

Introduction: Stigma, Adversity, and Worry — 1

PART I. FACING ADVERSITY

1. Less Than Human — 15
2. Barely Making It — 29
3. Racism and Poverty Matter — 40

PART II. FOUNDATIONS OF EMOTIONAL RESILIENCE

4. Emotional Development — 55
5. Development of Social Competence — 67

PART III. DIVERGENT BEHAVIORAL DEVELOPMENT

6. The Golden Age of Childhood — 81
7. Growing Up Fast — 96

PART IV. ORIGINS OF SERIOUS PROBLEM BEHAVIOR

8. Loss, Trauma, and Problem Behavior — 113
9. Lives in Distress — 127

PART V. STRUGGLES WITH ADVERSITY

10. Denying Emotions and Losing Self — 143
11. Becoming a Knucklehead — 157

PART VI. SOCIAL ASSETS AND EMOTIONAL RESILIENCE

12. Emotional Resilience	175
13. Social Assets Build Resilience	188

PART VII. HOW FAMILIES, SCHOOLS, AND NEIGHBORHOODS HELP

14. Preparation for Racism and Adversity	203
15. Strengthening Schools and Neighborhoods as Social Assets	216
Conclusion: Reimagining Black Boys and Youth	229
Bibliography	237
Index	253

Acknowledgments

I wish to thank John Henry Smith and Felix Laniyan for their assistance in reviewing research literature and Thomas LeBien and Amanda Moon for their editorial feedback in finalizing this manuscript for publication. In addition, I want to acknowledge my wonderful colleagues in the Boys of Color Collaborative whose stimulating conversations were of immense value in helping to shape the ideas presented in this volume. Finally, I wish to thank the Robert Wood Johnson Foundation for its financial support of my research.

Introduction

Stigma, Adversity, and Worry

Each year about 300,000 Black boys (BB[*]) are born in the United States into households where most are fortunate enough to receive the affection and care they need to thrive. However, some will grow up in households that are not as fortunate. These households experience chronic stress, food insecurity, homelessness, and other hardships that can impede boys' development.[1] Some BB rise above their difficult circumstances, but others are overcome by them. Insights about why some thrive and others languish under adversity may be gleaned from the lives of Black men who grew up with similar challenges but whose lives took a different direction by the time they became adults. Such is the case of two Black men, born about three years apart in Baltimore, MD and who coincidentally were given the same name, Wes Moore.[2] Both were raised in a household with an older sibling led by a solo mother who struggled financially and relied on the help of others to make ends meet. Both were close to their mothers, but their fathers were absent from their lives. Both displayed academic skills in the beginning that suggested they could be very successful in school. However, by middle childhood both grew bored with school, skipped classes often, and sought companionship, excitement, and freedom in their neighborhoods away from the watchful eyes of adults. It did not take long for each to earn a reputation as a boy headed for trouble. As pre-teens, they befriended and hung out with older boys. As young adolescents they experimented with smoking, drinking, and partying. Lacking money, they became adept at shoplifting to get the things they wanted. By the time they were adolescents, they had progressed from petty crimes and misdemeanors to more serious property crimes. Their increasing encounters with police were a source of emotional pain and frustration for their mothers.

If we paused their developmental clocks at adolescence to project into their futures, it would be hard to be optimistic that either one would turn out

---

[*] Three acronyms will be used throughout this book: BB to refer to Black boys 12 and younger; BY for Black youth 13–18 years old; and BBY for Black boys and youth, birth to 18.

Building Emotional Resilience in Black Boys. Oscar A. Barbarin, Oxford University Press.
© Oxford University Press 2025. DOI: 10.1093/oso/9780197747490.003.0001

well. Fast forward to their forties, both could be found in State of Maryland institutions, albeit different ones. Their lives had diverged in stunning and puzzling ways. One Wes Moore followed a predictable path. He was convicted and serving a life sentence in a Maryland state prison. The other Wes Moore made a dramatic turnabout and was elected to serve as Governor of the same state and has been talked about as a possible vice-presidential candidate. What happened along the way leading one Wes Moore to lose control over his life to the state penal system and the other to win control over the executive branch of state government? Sadly, such divergent outcomes occur over and over in countless neighborhoods. Many accomplished Black men can often point to peers who were even more gifted and talented than they, who would never escape the downward pull of their adverse environments. Examining the outcomes of the two Wes Moores may provide clues about how the numerous divergences occur for BBY.

How Social Sciences Account for Divergent Outcomes

Social and behavioral scientists have wrestled intellectually with this issue and suggested ways to think about the influence of social environments on individual development. For example, economists have highlighted the role of chronic poverty and economic disinvestment as a way of understanding the development of BBY.[3] Sociologists and anthropologists have pointed to the use of racial stereotypes and discrimination to oppress Black males and assert White superiority. They have argued that White-dominated social structures (e.g., in government and education) define BBY as a social problem to justify punitive practices and harsh control.[4] Psychologists have focused on the impact of deprivation and trauma on boys' development and behavior. They have argued that poor mental health, limited self and social awareness, conflict in interpersonal relations, academic disengagement, pessimism, and impaired neuro-hormonal functioning occur when environmental constraints and demands exceed BBY's resources for coping with them.[5]

Social and behavioral scientists, such as Margaret Spencer, Vonnie McLoyd, Cynthia Garcia Coll, and Velma McBride-Murry, explicitly or implicitly have documented the devastating effects of racial oppression and economic hardship but also the ameliorative impact of social and cultural resources. For example, Garcia Coll and colleagues have argued that minoritized children's development of competence varies with their social position (e.g., race, gender), their experience of racial discrimination and segregation (residential and psychological), their access to promoting vs inhibiting environments within school and health care, adaptive cultural traditions and legacies, and their family beliefs, values, and practices.[6] Accordingly, the likelihood of problematic development increases with exposure to racism and economic hardship. Conversely, positive development in the form of social competencies and emotional resilience is more likely with access to social and cultural assets, particularly from within family and community. Also important are critical periods, turning points, and the social assets that keep some BBY on a positive developmental path and diverts others from antisocial behavior onto a path toward prosocial development. The ideas we propose to account for the divergent paths of the two Wes Moores are presented in Figure I.1.

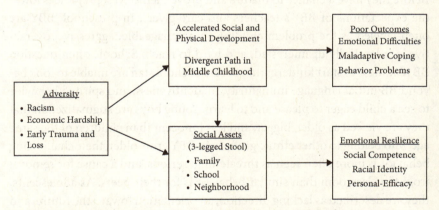

Figure I.1 Social Assets Foster Emotional Resilience and Buffer Against Poor Outcome Associated with Adversity

Note: **The Model:** The basic premise of this model is that adverse social environments significantly constrain developmental outcomes, such as socio-emotional functioning and social competence. However, this influence is moderated by social assets. In the case of BBY, social environments are dominated by racism, bias, discrimination, and economic privation. The social environment is seen as a significant form of stress that potentially disrupts BBY's normal functioning and development. It can impede the acquisition of developmental competencies in early and middle childhood, such as executive function and self-regulation. It can also influence and impair the formation of a positive view of the self and lead to internalizing of negative messages of self as deficient, ineffective, and incompetent. However, the impact of an adverse social environment can be moderated by social assets in the form of supportive relationships and social cognitive processes that make it possible to counteract negative influences and form positive representations of self, family, and the world.

Racism

The role of adversity linked to structural racism and discrimination is paramount. Racial bias and microaggressions dehumanize and marginalize Black Americans. Claims about White racial superiority are used to justify fear-based narratives that portray BBY as dishonest, lacking in self-control, and physically menacing. Some of these messages break through BBY's self-protective armor, to influence how they view themselves and limit their aspirations. Structural racism erects barriers which can make racist tropes and stereotypes a self-fulfilling prophesy by assigning BBY to failing schools, exposing them to neighborhood violence, and placing financial stability out of reach. By the time BBY become adults they learn to make do with little as life becomes an unending struggle for survival.

Implicit Bias and Development

Before they have a chance to mature and prove themselves, prejudices lower the expectations of BBY's teachers and care givers. In preschool, BBY are often labeled as the problem children—unmanageable, aggressive, overactive, academically disinterested, and hard to reach. Schools often question BB readiness to start kindergarten because school staff are unable to look beyond BB initial language immaturity, inattentiveness, and spirited behavior to see a child eager to please and to learn. Young boys are stigmatized in that they are viewed as older, bigger, and less innocent than children of the same age who belong to other ethnic groups. As BBY grow older, their challenging behavior is more often seen as threatening, serious, and a cause for removal from the classroom than similar behavior is for their peers. As adolescents, they are described as lacking direction, an orientation toward the future, and aspirations beyond the immediate gratification of hanging out and partying with friends.

Economic Status and Racial Inequality

The difficulties experienced by BB documented in the "My Brother's Keeper" report, undertaken by President Barak Obama's administration,[7] suggest that at least part of the troubled development of BBY can be attributed to adverse circumstances at home, at school, and in the community. At its core, low socio-economic status (SES) can best be indexed not by things owned, education completed, or occupational prestige but in terms of the household's ability to provide for basic needs, possession of the resources to manage unexpected crises or daily hassles, and provision of occasional extras that bring joy to life. Low SES that arises from the absence of these resources spawns a chronically disorienting state of worry and undermines adults' ability to function optimally as parents. Stress associated with economic deprivation can lead to substance abuse, mental health impairment, incarceration, and child abuse and neglect. The strains of economic hardship may also impact emotional availability, and work schedules may make it difficult for parents to invest time in monitoring, enriching, and supporting the development of their children. Economic hardship disproportionately affects Black lives because of the distress associated with constant worry about finances, food insecurity, losing one's home, attending failing schools, and experiencing neighborhood violence.[8]

Racism and material deprivation impede the acquisition of developmental competencies in early and middle childhood. The experience of adversity, poverty, and racism is highly distressing, disorienting, and constraining. Consequently, the stressful and harsh conditions BBY face undermine and impede their socio-emotional development. This leads to self-deprecation and internalizing external messages of self as deficient and incompetent. Nevertheless, the impact of adverse social environments can be moderated by social assets in the form of caring relationships and social cognitive processes that make it possible to refute negative messages and form positive representations of self, family, and the world. The effects of poverty are pervasive; nevertheless, many Black children who grow up in poor households develop into well-functioning adults.

Material Disadvantage and Adversity Are Linked

For a majority of BBY poverty is a consequence of racism. Poverty flows from a history of social inequalities, suppression or under-development of talents, structural impediments to economic advancement, diminished resources for education, and a whole host of other factors that have detrimental impacts on the lives of BBY and their families. The psychological, physical, and social consequences of poverty and racism can be traumatic and debilitating.

So, a central tenet in our understanding of the psychosocial development of BB is a causal chain connecting racism to poverty and poverty to trauma. These processes are invasive and central in their lives. Not all BB suffer economic insufficiency and material disadvantage, but they are all touched by anti-Black racism.

The combination of racism, poverty, trauma and gender place BBY on a unique developmental trajectory in which the promise and hopes arising at birth vanish for many as they lose the presumption of childhood innocence all too early, prematurely confront problems they do not have the resources to resolve, and take on adultlike roles they have not yet developed the capacity to perform. Adverse social environments present them with things no child should witness or experience (hostility, bias, marginalization, aggression, violence, sexual displays, etc.) and in the process create high levels of stress leading to strong emotional responses that overwhelm their abilities to cope. Because of low economic status, they are more likely to experience traumas: loss of loved ones, physical deprivation, family conflict and chaos, and ubiquitous threats of violence in their communities. Consequently, BB must grow up fast.

Protection Against Risks of Adversity

Resilience in the face of adversity is not only an individual achievement but also a consequence of propitious social conditions. Of special importance for the development of resilient BBY are (a) caring networks that provide empathy and support, (b) structures of control that provide clear guidance and firm direction for behavior, and (c) interpretive frameworks that convey meaning, provide a sense of purpose, and help BBY understand their place in the world. These elements—emotional support, behavioral guidance, and frameworks of meaning—are essential to positive development. They take the form of nurturing relations, behavioral expectations and consequences, cultural beliefs and practices, and religious or spiritual ways of looking at the world and the people in it. These social assets are especially important at inflection points in boys' development such as the transition from childhood to adolescence. When available, they prevent problems appearing in middle childhood from becoming entrenched, possibly extending into juvenile offending, and transitioning into adult criminal behavior, as it did for one Wes Moore. For most BBY these will come through relations within caring families, humane and inspiring schools, and engaging mentors at church, in their neighborhood, and in extended family.

Social Assets Create Auspicious Environments That Promote Resilience

A proclivity toward disruptive or problem behavior can be overcome with the help of social assets available in families, schools, and neighborhoods; reliance on cultural practices, oral traditions, and religiosity; and socialization into optimistic ways of thinking by trustworthy and caring adults that nurtures a positive identity and personal efficacy. These assets provide a foundation on which emotional resilience can be built. For BB, emotional resilience means the ability to bounce back from the strain of economic insufficiency and the personal degradation of racism. Emotional resilience flourishes in family environments characterized by secure relationships with primary caregivers. Emotionally resilient BB see things from others' points of view and find ways to compromise before differences upend relations with friends. This capacity for social awareness in turn encourages prosocial attitudes and caring about and for others as well as flexibility in solving life problems. When BBY have access to such social assets, there is reason for optimism that they will become resilient in spite of the adversity they face. Social assets are the principal reasons many BBY, like Governor Wes Moore, can attain rewarding lives, invest in their families, and become a positive force in their communities.

The Metaphor of the 3-Legged Stool

Families, schools, and neighborhoods function in tandem as parts of a 3-legged stool that makes possible a safe haven and nurturing environment in which BBY can thrive.[9] Together, the three legs of the stool support BBY's resilience in the face of adversity. They provide perspectives that counter the negative messages sent to BBY about who they are and what they can become. The 3-legged stool supports the development of social competencies by providing relational and cultural assets that tell BBY that they are worthy and that they matter. The legs of the stool offer an optimistic outlook, support a positive identity, and send powerful affirmations of BBY's abilities and potential. When the legs are sturdy and function as they should, they are the difference between negative and positive outcomes for BBY. In the case of the Wes Moore, who went on to become Governor of Maryland, his resilience was possible because of caring relationships with an actively engaged mother, extended family, and mentors. The people around him provided him with supportive relationships that enabled him to acquire important prosocial competencies, cope with racism, and attain personal agency in striving to achieve his goals. The grandfather with whom he lived was an Episcopal priest and likely helped to lay a foundation of spirituality to which the more mature Wes might return. Thus, protective factors within this environment of social contacts include family functioning characterized by warmth, effectively functioning schools with enlightened discipline, cultural and ethnic socialization, and psychological safety.

Wobbly Stools and Serious Behavior Problems

If the legs are not strong, the stool collapses, behavior problems fester, and serious emotional difficulty ensues. When only one leg of the 3-legged stool is a bit weak, wobbly, or unstable, the other two might compensate and still offer strong enough support to sustain positive development. If this metaphor reflects reality, BBY need at least two of the three legs to function well. However, if two of the legs are weak, the stool will be unstable and fail. It will be unable to provide sufficient support to make a difference for BBY. Unfortunately, this is the situation that troubled BBY face. Many BBY are raised in homes with chronic financial uncertainty, attend failing schools, and live in communities plagued by illicit substance use and neighborhood violence. Many experience some traumatic disruption of family life when they are very young such as homelessness or parental violence, substance abuse, or divorce. Juvenile offenders are an extreme case that highlights what happens when each of the stool's key supports fails to function. For the subset of BBY whose development veered seriously off course, dysfunctional families and schools together were unable to stem emergent behavioral difficulties appearing in early childhood. These behavioral challenges festered and consolidated in middle childhood and turned into serious offending by adolescence. BBY who become juvenile offenders represent a group growing up in a vortex of impoverished families, disorganized schools, and violent neighborhoods. In a series of predictable stages, BBY who engage in juvenile offending are socialized gradually into an antisocial way of life when they are left on their own without the effective support from family, school, and neighborhood.

Inflection Points

Fortunately, socio-emotional development is a flexible process that allows course reversals from negative to positive adaptation. In spite of the choices made at one point to veer off a positive, typical path, opportunities come along to redirect a boy's course toward prosocial ends. In time, some juvenile offenders reach turning points—events or relationships that caused them to pause and reflect on whether to persist in misconduct or to change the direction of their lives before they are trapped in a cycle of arrest, incarceration, and release that repeats itself for most of their adult lives. These are turning points in which BBY respond to the encouragement of family and mentors and allow traditional cultural values and religious practices to influence their choices and the direction their lives will take. At these turning points, access to social assets can make a difference in the choices BBY make. Thus, in spite of the restraints imposed by racism and economic deprivation, there is good reason for the hope that most BBY will develop socially competent skills such as friendliness, communication, and altruism that enable them to get along with others and cooperate and resolve conflicts peacefully. Moreover, social competence can be developed and displayed even if BB continue to be haunted by difficulties, problems, and past demons.

The Critical Period of Middle Childhood

Middle childhood, which encompasses roughly ages 6 through 12, is often viewed as a boringly stable period where little development occurs. For most children, middle childhood is a quiescent period of slower, subtle changes. Physical growth in middle childhood is less explosive and palpable than in early childhood. Cognitive changes in middle childhood as well are less dynamic and transformative than in adolescence. Instead, middle childhood is a period of restful consolidation and firming of the skills, cognitive capacities, and physical growth which developed so rapidly in early childhood. Because the changes taking place in middle childhood are subtle, they are often overlooked and regarded as unimportant. For BB, however, the picture can be entirely different in middle childhood. For these young boys, middle childhood can be a time of ferment and perturbation. In contrast to the typical and unremarkable emotional and behavioral development of BB up through early childhood, middle childhood is a time when the behavioral and emotional development of BB begins to diverge strikingly from what is observed in most other groups of children.

For many BB, middle childhood involves a puzzling divergence from the typical pattern. While other groups of children are displaying greater behavioral control and inhibiting disruptive behaviors, BB are not. Consequently, they are designated as having a higher prevalence of behavioral and emotional problems than most other groups of children. Specifically, BBY experience higher emotional distress, oppositional behavior, and increased rates of suicide in middle childhood. So, middle childhood is a time of turbulence and the beginning of the process by which individual BBY are defined and targeted as troubled and troubling. It is a starting point at which the developmental trajectories of BBY diverge from other groups of children. It is the period in BBY's life where the prevalence of behavioral and emotional problems is significantly higher than it is for other groups of children including Black girls. It is the point at which the disparities that are so striking in later life begin to appear. Thus, this period offers important clues about the direction the lives of BBY will take and identifies a time at which targeted preventive intervention could be helpful and change the trajectory of some BBY lives.

Focus of the Book

The socio-emotional development of BBY is somewhat unique in that serious behavioral and emotional difficulties of BBY are rarely evident before the age of five. Behavior problems appear gradually during middle childhood and can grow more troubling by adolescence if they are not addressed effectively. Accordingly, middle childhood is underscored as a key developmental period for many BBY because it offers strong signals about the direction of their future development. Many victim-blaming explanations have been advanced for the difficulties of BBY. Individual differences in abilities, temperament, learning styles, dispositions, and personality do play a role in BBY's behavioral and emotional functioning just as they do for other groups of children. However, this book concentrates on the risks of hardship associated with structural inequalities. It argues that external factors, such as racism and poverty, can impede BBY's social development, but that they are just half of the story. The nature and extent of those effects depend on BBY's access to and use of social assets and ways of thinking to strengthen personal efficacy and minimize trauma and self-blame.

This book positions racism and financial hardship as decisive environmental factors in BBY's emotional functioning and development. This is not a unique or novel assertion. Rather, it is about recalling age-old and self-evident truths that have been conveniently overlooked or forgotten in the case of BBY. Namely, poverty is bad, and extreme chronic poverty is debilitating. Racism is an evil that ultimately erodes the souls of those who harbor racial animus and can deprive its victims of the level playing field they need to achieve their goals and attain a satisfying life. At the same time, the book argues that many BBY are resilient and overcome the difficulties they face precisely because of the support they receive in their families, schools, and communities.

Principal Thesis

Racism and poverty are ubiquitous in the lives of BB and create high levels of stress and adversity. Early emotional development of BB seems largely unaffected, but their circumstances often require that they grow up fast. Adversity and stress contribute to accelerated development that is first evident for some in skipping past the golden age of middle childhood. Accelerated development occurs at multiple levels: social, physical, behavioral, and psychological. Socially, BB assume adultlike roles and responsibilities and are perceived by others as older than their same-age peers. Physically, accelerated development takes the form of early onset adrenarche, puberty, and shortened telomeres linked to aging. Psychologically accelerated development appears in the form of early independence, self-sufficiency, and disengagement from school. For some, the push to grow up fast leads to behavior problems and social maladjustment at levels higher than their peers. For others, access to social assets at home, at school, and in the community help them become resilient, cope effectively with stress, remain engaged in school, and develop social competencies that sustain well-being and adaptive functioning.

The thesis of this book will unfold in seven parts. Part I will explore the role of racism and material hardship and their consequences in the creation of adverse developmental environments for BBY. This section describes various forms of racism and their consequences for material and financial hardships. Part II lays the groundwork for understanding emotional functioning and presents information on the status of boys' emotional development early in life. Part III discusses how BBY's behavior diverges from typical patterns of behavioral development. Part IV explores the development of serious behavior problems and links the exacerbation of behavior and emotional difficulties to adversity at home, in schools, and in the neighborhood. In addition, it describes inflection points at which cessation of serious behavior problems can occur. Part V discusses messages given to boys about how to manage their emotions and reviews strategies that they use in coping with pain and adversity. This section addresses both effective and counterproductive ways of coping with distress. Part VI describes the concept of resilience and how social assets from family, school, and community overcome the effects of adversity on BBY through caring, control, and meaning. Finally, Part VII describes programs and interventions that have increased the effectiveness of families, schools, and neighborhoods as social assets that help BBY cope with racism and material hardship and become emotionally resilient.

Notes

1. Barbarin (2013). About two-thirds of BBY were rated by early childhood and primary school teachers as socially competent. Similarly, in a longitudinal study of youth from ages 10 through 21, Black youth had a relatively low risk for adverse behavior in that only 12.4% of boys were on a developmental course characterized by troubled or risky behavior (see Murry et al. (2013)).
2. Moore (2010).
3. Duncan (2021).
4. Wilkerson (2021).
5. Slaughter & Epps (1987).
6. See Garcia Coll et al. (1996); Gaylord-Harden et al. (2018); Spencer (2006).
7. https://obamawhitehouse.archives.gov/my-brothers-keeper
8. McLoyd (1998).
9. See Barbarin (2015) for a fuller discussion of the conditions at home, at school and in the community that constitute auspicious environments for the development of BBY. It describes how the three legs of the stool would look when they function optimally.

PART I
FACING ADVERSITY

1
Less Than Human

Black individuals are not really, fully human. So goes a basic tenet of anti-Black racism that affirms White superiority, genetic exceptionalism, and a predestination by God to dominate the rest of the world.[1] To maintain this racist fiction, it is necessary to portray Blacks as inferior, unworthy, degenerate, unclean, and dangerous.[2] Accordingly, Blacks are depicted in the White imagination as inept intellectually, unrefined socially, threatening physically, and lacking a moral compass and sensibility that distinguish humans from lower forms of life.[3] These beliefs are used to justify psychological degradation, social exclusion, and economic exploitation of Black people.[4] Encounters with anti-Black racism are ubiquitous and traumatizing. A majority of Black youth have reported racial discrimination, but Black boys report more frequent experiences of discrimination than Black girls.[5] The effects manifest subtly early in childhood but become glaringly obvious by the time of BBY transition to adolescence and adulthood. Racism is at work when Black workers are the last hired and first fired, when their rental applications or mortgage loans are rejected without explanation, when they are scapegoated at school, when they are insulted because of their physical appearance, or when they are ostracized and excluded from participation in activities by non-Black peers. Racism can be direct and interpersonal or it can be vicarious, institutional, historical, and transgenerational (See Box 1.1).[6]

Racism at a Distance

Vicarious Racism

The racial discrimination against BBY arises not only directly from personal experience but also indirectly through observations of discrimination against family members, friends, or Black people as a collective. For example, BBY can witness a friend being ridiculed for their appearance and feel the

> **Box 1.1 Sources of Racist Experiences of BBY**
>
> **Vicarious Discrimination.** An indirect experience of racism that occurs though witnessing directly or learning about racism directed at other African Americans and is especially poignant when racism affects a family member or acquaintance.
>
> **Transgenerational Racism.** Refers to the transmission of traumatic experience related to previous racist actions such as enslavement, segregation, lynchings, incarcerations, etc. It involves the long-term effects on health and well-being. It may result in trauma passed down through epigenetic transmission over time or through cautionary tales intended to control boys' behavior.
>
> **Institutional Racism.** Race-based disadvantages implemented by institutions and structures that support disparate biased treatment, sometimes subtle or indirect or laws and policies and practices that explicitly exclude Black individuals from a social benefit (e.g., income support, education, or health services).
>
> **Interpersonal Racism.** A direct in-vivo experience of racist encounters that occur in interactions with others at school and in the community; with acquaintances and strangers (e.g., negative stereotypes, discrimination, microaggression, implicit bias, social exclusion).
>
> **Online Racism.** Use of social media to slur individuals, disseminate racist stereotypes, inflame racial hatred, or stir racial resentment and conflict. Online racism can be interpersonal and direct, vicarious and indirect, or focused on advocating racist policies.

slight as though it was directed at them. They may witness threats, insults, or microaggressions against a family member and feel the pain themselves. They can be disturbed when they witness or learn about a parent or relative being demeaned, harmed, or treated disrespectfully because of their race, as when a salesclerk deliberately ignores a family member waiting patiently to be served. They may encounter racism vicariously when an arrogant civil servant demeans and chastises a parent for not completing a form correctly or understanding bureaucratic procedures, or when peers make fun of another BBY because of his complexion or home language. BBY might also experience threats, hassles, and harm online when they read about a Black person injured or killed by police officers.[7]

All of these forms of vicarious racism can have an effect even when BBY are not injured directly. Hearing or reading derogatory jokes about Black individuals online can be just as powerful and painful as if the pejorative remarks were targeted to them personally. For example, a peer might pass around a history book and poke fun at a photograph of enslaved Black individuals wearing sackcloth and picking cotton. Negative references take on an even more serious dimension when a child sees them made in person to another Black person. For example, someone might say mean things to or express contempt about another Black person's race/ethnicity, tell an offensive joke, or make an offensive comment when they think no Black individuals are around. Such joking, insults, and gossip can be especially hurtful when said unthinkingly and without recognition of the impact on Black peers who are supposed to be friends.[8]

Transgenerational Racism

BBY can also experience transgenerational racism that results from some historical trauma. For example, traumas of the enslavement and torture of African people, anti-Black riots in New York City, destruction of Black Wall Street in Oklahoma, lynchings of Black men, sharecropping and dispossession of Black farmers of their land, murder of civil rights workers, and so on are passed down to subsequent generations. Aspects of oppression-related historical events can be transmitted across generations perhaps epigenetically[9] or through discussion, storytelling, and lessons taught to children, as well as observation of long-term effects by the descendants of survivors.[10] In these ways, socialization of trauma-related behavior and beliefs about the world can replicate the effects of historical trauma across generations.

Institutional Racism

White individuals have marshalled institutional power and passed legislation that blocks social gains and deprives Black people of economic gains. This power is used to maintain structural inequalities that permeate the major structures of society: government, business, education, law, criminal justice, housing, health care, etc.

Black children's experience with institutional racism is manifest most clearly in the schools. There it takes the form of the hidden curriculum, which establishes expectations and rules that devalue and invalidate lessons taught to BB at home and clash with neighborhood norms. Meanwhile, White children's transition into school is seamless because there is less conflict between the cultures of school and home. Their behavioral and emotional adjustment to school life is smoother because school rules, procedures, and expectations are compatible with what they have encountered at home. Books used for reading instruction often depict narratives in which financial stability and access to adequate resources is a given. Very little of Black children's early exposure to literacy reflects their life experiences and challenges. The curriculum assigned by schools generally scaffolds and builds on White American contributions and assumes its exceptionalism. It reinforces an implicit view of patriotism in which Whiteness and Christianity are the standard. Whiteness embodies the essence of what it means to be American. In addition, school often reflects the interests and life experiences of the teaching corps which still draws mostly from the White middle class. For the Black student, the experience at school is often different and sometimes made difficult by the clash of culture and cultural expectations. Institutional racism can take the form of the "hidden curriculum" that privileges White middle-class values and lifestyles as the norm to be reinforced and an ideal to be emulated. Institutional racism begins with the miseducation of BBY, defining BBY as a problem, using harsh punishment to control them, criminalizing school discipline problems, placement of police officers on school grounds and referral for criminal prosecution.[11] Thus, the school-to-prison pipeline is a logical outcome of unwitting institutional racism.

Racism that BBY See and Feel

Early in life, BBY are stereotyped and marked as unruly, aggressive, and difficult to reach.[12] As they mature, stereotypes about them build on a foundation of fears, misinterpretations, and myths that represent them as cognitively inferior, impulsive, hostile, and defiant. Before BBY even have time to mature, they are viewed as irredeemable, angry Black men. As they grow older, additional stereotypes (lewd, treacherous, and dishonest are some of the most common) are applied to them.[13] Racial disparities in outcomes are attributed to poverty or BBY's own misbehavior, failures, and deficits.

School is the setting where BB are most likely to encounter racism directly for the first time because so much of their time is spent there. From peers, racism takes the form of teasing, social exclusion, and physical threats. Racism from adults is often subtle and often unintentional bias that can be just as destructive of BBY's emotional state and identity as what they encounter in interactions with peers. Racism from teachers occurs in the form of implicit biases, low expectations, and a tug-of-war over control, all of which shape how teachers view BBY and in turn how they teach and discipline them. Moreover, schools' disparate use of their institutional sanctioning powers to punish and exclude conveys unmistakably the belief that adults see BBY as more troublesome, incapable, and less likeable than their peers. School is where Black children report experiencing more discrimination, feeling less safe and connected with adults, and having fewer opportunities to participate.[14] School may very well be the place where the creativity, enthusiasm, and joy of BBY go to die.

Finally, today much of children's and youths' interactions occur online. Consequently, exposure to racism is happening increasingly online, as children spend more time on social media. Racism and hatred expressed online can also be more insidious and painful than face to face experiences because their expression can be explicit and anonymous, targeted against individuals, and spread widely with impunity.

Teasing About Physical Characteristics

Teasing and disparagement are common in school settings. The two terms refer to the tendency to belittle and to point out negative attributes. Teasing and ridicule hones in on potential weaknesses and exploits insecurities. Affirmation is rarely provided to disparaged populations. Instead, they are made to feel inadequate, unworthy, invisible, and unimportant.

Teasing is the intentional provocation targeting an important aspect of a BBY identity. Teasing is carried out under the guise of humor and playfulness, but its goal is to shame. It is demeaning, cruel, and stinging because it is intended to embarrass the victim. Although adolescents often characterize racial/ethnic teasing as innocuous and just fun, it has serious consequences. Being the target of racial teasing results in short-term increases in anxiety symptoms among adolescents of color.[15] Teasing is a common occurrence in school settings, and not surprisingly racist language becomes intertwined with this common social practice. Racist teasing makes use of stereotypes and slurs to elicit laughter at the expense of BBY. Racist teasing often targets a child's appearance, family, or cultural practices. It mirrors stereotypic beliefs. It can be the reenactment of slavery or imitation by White individuals of "black face" performers. Teasing is especially cutting and personal when it evokes stereotypes to poke fun at the physical features of BBY such as their lips, nose, hair texture, skin tone, or body shape and can sometimes escalate into bullying. To make matters worse, when White peers are called out for racism, they tend to downplay the harmful impact, excuse or justify behavior as harmless or unintended, and dismiss it as merely playful.

Social Exclusion

Although conventional wisdom advises us that teasing cannot hurt, teasing and social exclusion are the "sticks and stones" that break the spirit and undercut the morale of BBY at school. Peers and the opportunity to interact with them are highly sought after and constitute the highlight of most children's social lives. Acceptance and inclusion by peers are among the most affirming experiences of adolescent life. For this reason, rejection and exclusion are especially painful for BBY. Social exclusion may not always be direct and clear. It may simply be the standoffish behavior of White peers or a feeling in the pit of the stomach of feeling unwelcomed and out of place. This may occur when peers organize social events or study groups without informing BBY or giving them the chance to opt in. Another example is being discouraged or prevented from joining a club or clique of popular students. It may boil down to something as simple as being the last person chosen or not being allowed in a multiplayer game on the school playground or online. It can also come in the form of gossip or the spreading of rumors directly or—even worse—online, using popular social media apps such as Instagram, Meta, X (formerly Twitter), SnapChat, or TikTok.

Physical Threats

Social exclusion is painful, spirit-crushing, and destructive of self-esteem, but the stakes are even higher and the danger more ominous when racism takes the form of physical threats and injury. For example, White peers at school may push, shove, hit, intimidate, and mug Black students, especially in settings where BBY are a minority. Threats and acts of physical intimidation can also be perpetrated by peers and strangers online. Although most schools have developed programs and elaborate procedures to proactively create safe environments and respond to incidents once they occur, these efforts are rarely sufficient, and so much happens in the underworld of student interaction outside of the view and awareness of adults, that it is almost impossible to eliminate physical threats and injuries entirely. However schools must continue to try.

Implicit Bias

Racism in interactions with adults often comes in the form of implicit bias. Implicit bias refers to unconscious beliefs and attitudes that can unwittingly affect how adults or peers perceive and respond to BBY in the classroom. It includes teachers' internal representations of BBY that shape the ways teachers attribute motives, assess and interpret BBY's behavior, and decide about discipline. Implicit biases are evident in teachers' underestimation of BBY's competence and in their anticipation of BBY's misbehavior and disregard for learning in school. Teachers and school counselors exhibit implicit biases when they discourage and block BBY from pursuing a challenging goal or assume BBY are interested only in Black issues or topics. For example, they can refuse to recommend that BBY take an advanced course, participate in an honors program, or enter some academic competition. In addition, they may show surprise or disbelief when BBY perform competently and are successful in completing a difficult task.

Stereotypes and Unfair Discipline

Racial stereotypes also lead to unfair disciplinary practices for Black students. As a consequence of stereotypes and implicit bias, BB are more likely to be punished harshly. The biases against BBY have a number of detrimental outcomes including scapegoating, disparate discipline, and strains in the relationships of boys with their teachers. BBY are blamed for problems and conflicts in the classroom, even when they are the victims or bystanders, and are chastised for behaviors that are overlooked in their classmates.[16]

A consequence of this stigma and implicit bias is that BBY are subjected to unfair and harsh discipline, especially in the form of suspension and expulsion from preschool.[17] They are placed in timeout, have privileges withdrawn, and are excluded from the classroom and school at disproportionate rates beginning already in preschool and extending into high school.[18] Bias and stigma also feed into strained and conflict-filled relationships with teachers. Prejudgments about BBY's behavior, attitudes, and abilities, especially on the part of persons responsible for teaching and caring for them, can end up becoming self-fulfilling prophesies as early as preschool. In turn, this harsh discipline often has the opposite and unintended effect on BBY of worsening behavior, frustration, and emotional disengagement at school.

Okonofua and Eberhardt explored how racial bias might influence the intensity of a teacher's response to the misbehavior of BBY.[19] Specifically they asked if teachers would respond more harshly to repeated misbehavior by BB than they would to that by White boys. In their study, teachers described BB as having more negative and ominous, sulking demeanors, perceived them as having endemic difficulties as troublemakers, and judged them to be less competent academically than White boys. In online experiments, Okonofua and Eberhardt showed teachers records of two students, one with a stereotypical Black name and one with a stereotypical White name, both of whom were involved first in being insubordinate and, at a later time, in disrupting the class. The researchers assessed teachers' responses separately for the first infraction and the later or second infraction. Teachers reported how upset they felt after each infraction and how severely they would discipline the student. Teachers were more upset when the Black student committed two infractions than when the White student misbehaved twice. Moreover, teachers thought that BB but not White boys should be punished more severely after a second infraction than after the first infraction. For Black boys the second infraction confirmed in the mind of the teacher that the BB was a chronic problem and deserved to be punished more severely than the White boy who exhibited a similarly egregious pattern of behavior. In a second study using a similar procedure, teachers reported whether they would suspend the student. Teachers viewed the misbehavior of the BB as a pattern of misbehavior that merited suspension more often than the misbehavior of the White student. These experimental data cannot be treated as conclusive proof that every teacher is inclined to prejudge the behavior problems of BBY as part of a pattern and to conclude that strict punishment is warranted. However it does suggest that subtle unintended biases may not be uncommon in teachers. Moreover, if these biases are not surfaced and raised into consciousness, they are likely to lead teachers to behave toward BBY in ways that are counterproductive to having a caring and effective relation and achieving the academic goals that teachers have for BBY.

Implicit Bias Justifies Violence and Harsh Punishment of BBY

Implicit bias and stereotypes about Black individuals were harmful in the past because they were used to rationalize and excuse the cruelty of enslavement. They continue to cause harm today because they are still used to condone harsh punishment and violence against Black individuals. One of the most harmful biases is the idea that Blacks are regarded as animals and thus are less than human. Goff and colleagues demonstrated the relationship between these biases and the inclination to justify severe punishment of Black individuals.[20] The researchers subliminally primed research participants with words associated with apes or big cats. Participants then viewed a video of a group of police officers beating a suspect whom some participants were led to believe was a Black man, while others were led to believe that the suspect was a White man. When the suspect was thought to be White, participants who had been primed with words related to apes or cats were not more likely to justify a beating of the suspect. But when the suspect was thought to be Black, the priming with words related to apes and cats did increase the likelihood of participants concluding that beating the Black suspect was justified. Specifically, respondents were more likely to condone violence if they were primed with words relating to apes but only if they thought the suspect was Black. This suggests that such stereotypes are harmful to BBY because viewing them as less than fully human may mean they are seen as deserving physical punishment.

In addition, Goff and colleagues found that the association of Black individuals with apes was bidirectional or worked both ways in that being first primed to think about Black people they were more likely to identify the picture of an ape.[21] Using a method similar to that used in the study discussed above, they found that when subliminally presented beforehand with blurred Black male faces, respondents were able to identify the cloudy, out of focus picture of an ape more quickly and accurately than respondents presented with neutral pictures.[22] Experimental subjects subliminally exposed to pictures of apes also completed a task that involved visual attention in the presence of Black faces more quickly than in the presence of White faces. Moreover, the participants in this study were not consciously aware of the connection they were making between Black people and apes. Thus, they had the potential of acting on biases against Blacks all the while claiming with sincerity that they harbored no racial prejudice or bias.

Racism and Racial Disparities in Discipline at School

Sometimes racist effects can occur that are unintended but clearly evident to all. Such is the case with the use of exclusionary punishment by schools. The adverse impacts of racial disparagement and stigma are evident but often unintended in school discipline. While suspensions and expulsions of preschool children occur for all groups of children, Black children, especially boys, are disciplined in this way more often than their peers.[23] One out of every 10 teachers in a national sample of state supported pre-K programs reported expelling at least one child in the previous year. About two percent expelled more than one child. Black children are over-represented among the children who were suspended and expelled.[24] Black students represent 16% of enrollment, but they account for 48% of preschoolers receiving more than one out-of-school suspension.[25] By comparison, White students account for 43% of enrollment but only 26% of suspensions. Although males account for 51% of preschool enrollment, BB account for 72% of multiple out-of-school suspensions, and 74% of expulsions. Though these findings might not be surprising, it is shocking that BB in pre-K were suspended or expelled at rates that exceed those for older boys in K-12 education.[26]

Black boys are also suspended from K-12 grades at rates that exceed those of other ethnic groups. The disparate rates of suspension are greater for BB than Black girls. For both Black boys and girls in grades pre-K to 12th grade, the percentage of children suspended from school increased between 1980 and 2006. The disparities are specially marked for Black boys. Their suspensions rose from slightly above 15% to almost 25% in 2006. It is astounding and worrisome that almost one in four Black boys in public school were suspended in the year 2006.[27] Data for the 2017–18 school year from the US Department of Education's Office for Civil Rights are not much better. Black boys were suspended at the highest rate of any gender and race group, with 15.3% of all Black boys receiving at least one out-of-school suspension.

Rates of suspensions and expulsion are also higher in programs serving high need, impoverished, and ethnic-minority communities. In these programs, Black students are suspended and expelled at a rate that is three times higher than White students.

Scapegoating in Preschool

Implicit biases can lead to the stigma and scapegoating of BBY already in preschool.[28] Stigma refers to negative attitudes toward characteristics of individuals or groups that mark them as deficient, different, and inferior and are used as the basis for discriminating and denying social acceptance. Scapegoating is the identification of an innocent victim to whom blame is attributed for misbehavior or misdemeanors more broadly performed by an entire group. Barbarin and Crawford have documented multiple instances of stigmatizing practices and disparate treatment of BBY in early childhood classrooms.[29] In high-quality early childhood classrooms, children usually share a table and are encouraged to work with other children. A teacher may encourage students to go to one another for help before they reach out to her by instructing them to: "Try three before me." Children considered difficult and disruptive are sometimes excluded from these interactions and isolated from the rest of the children at a separate desk close by the teacher as a way of controlling them and keeping them on track. In one national observational study of pre-K classrooms, the children singled out for this treatment were almost always BB.[30] This effectively designated BB as bad in everyone's eyes.

One research observer was approached on her first visit to such a classroom by a little girl who wanted to make sure the observer knew who the designated bad child was. She pointed to a boy, one of the few Black children in the class, who was working quietly and alone at his table. The little girl proclaimed with an air of authority, "That's Marcus, he's bad," leaving no doubt about his role as the classroom scapegoat. Another observer watched how Theron, who impressed her as a bright, sweet, and good-natured boy, was assigned to and eventually accepted the bad boy role. He was singled out and separated at a desk isolated from the other children. "He was treated as though he were a bad child, and not surprisingly he started to act that way" the observer noted.[31]

Observers were most disturbed, however, by a flagrantly discriminatory teacher they observed at work. The teacher was like Dr. Jekyll—kind, decent, and loving—with White students, and Mr. Hyde—cruel and harsh—with Black students. With the White students, she was warm, positive, and tolerant of rule violations, but she was irritated, inflexible, and punitive toward similar behavioral offenses committed by Black children. Black children, particularly boys, were always in trouble with her, always having privileges taken away, and always in timeout. Moreover, the teacher was less likely to recognize and affirm the positive behavior and competence of BB or offer them access to the most desirable activity spaces. Black children were less likely to be called on when they raised their hands, less likely to be invited to share during circle time, and less likely to be allowed to have the first choice of a learning center to play in. There were gross disparities in discipline; Black children were reprimanded for behaviors that White children got away with.

Microaggressions against BBY

Microaggressions represent another form of racism that BBY encounter in their lives. Microaggression is a term coined by psychiatrist Chester Pierce.[32] It refers to "subtle, innocuous, or unconscious degradations and putdowns," slights, exclusions, and humiliations that may be preconscious and passive-aggressive. They can take the form, for example, of being ignored or overlooked by a restaurant seating host, being singled out for an intensive check before being allowed entry to a secure area; being mistaken for the waiter, stocking clerk, delivery man, maid, or bellboy instead of a patron or resident, and being followed by store security or viewed suspiciously in a predominantly White neighborhood.[33]

Microaggressions can be experienced in the form of differential treatment. Take, for example, seven-year-old Elijah at the supermarket with his mother. They were next in line at the fresh seafood and meat counter behind a White mother and her son. Elijah watched as a White boy boosted himself up onto the display case pressed his face up against the glass and left smudges on the glass as he surveyed the diverse fish in the case. When it was Elijah's mother's turn, Elijah pressed up against the display case similarly to get a closer look at the different fish just as he saw the White boy do. The butcher turned around and yelled sternly at Elijah to get off his display case. Elijah's mother was embarrassed about this reprimand and quickly pulled him back. On the surface, this was an insignificant event, but Elijah's mother recognized that her son was being chastised for doing the same thing that the little White boy in front of them did without any hostile reaction or reprimands from the butcher. The painful lesson for Elijah is that he was different and that he could not presume to engage in behaviors like other boys. His mother realized she had to teach him about the more serious dangers that he would face in public settings. He had to learn the painful lesson early on that there might be consequences for saying or doing things that boys who were not Black could do with impunity.

Microaggression may also take the form of a seemingly innocuous act of showing BBY racist images or hateful propaganda online. It could be the experience of constantly being mistaken for and being called by the name of another BBY who bore little or no resemblance. Although he would stand out in a mostly White crowd, apparently all BBY looked the same to them and could not be distinguished from one another. For BBY it is not uncommon for teachers to assume that he is an expert on all things to do with Black affairs and history and to turn to him to represent the concerns of the Black community as a spokesperson. A less obvious microaggression for a young BB is being misdiagnosed and moved from a regular to a special education classroom due to behavioral or emotional difficulties. White individuals do not admit and often question the validity of classifying microaggressions as racist. They may see them as mistakes that are so minor, they are considered inconsequential and should be overlooked. For BBY, however, these experiences can feel demoralizing, dehumanizing, disrespectful, or objectifying (i.e., being treated as a stereotype) and should not be discounted because of their enduring effects on BBY's emotional life. They accumulate and do great harm. No matter what form racism takes, its consequences for health and well-being are dire.

Notes

1. Wilkerson (2020).
2. Racism is a system of attitudes, behaviors, and policies organized to oppress and dominate a group that is identifiable by nationality, ethnicity, or phenotypic markers of social difference. Racism confers and maintains societal privilege for the dominant group and appropriates social resources preferentially for the benefit of the dominant group at the cost of the subordinate group. It relies on laws, policies, and institutional practices that are often masqueraded as impartial and color-blind in order to maintain the fiction that its selective conferral of privileges is based on merit alone.
3. The Smithsonian National Museum of African American History and Culture (2018). Black males are depicted as threatening, ignorant, lazy, incompetent, and irresponsible. Black women also experience negative stereotypes, misrepresenting them as the mammy (dependent, contented, self-sacrificing caregiver), Sapphire (aggressive, loud, angry, sassy, emasculating, and domineering), or as a hypersexualized vixen. A particularly vicious racist trope portrays Black mothers as "welfare queens," as the shiftless and undeserving poor gaming the system, while

28 FACING ADVERSITY

> having multiple babies and squandering money intended for children on drugs, fancy hairdos, and manicures.

4. Harrell (2000); Wilkerson (2020).
5. Seaton et al. (2008).
6. Coker et al. (2009); Lanier et al. (2017)
7. The early and unexpected death of a family member or acquaintance due to random violence is a common experience among BBY and contributes to hopelessness and fatalism. Expecting death at an early age by homicide is realistic for many Black males. Young Black men die at a rate that is at least 1.5 times the rate of young White and Hispanic men, and almost three times the rate of young Asian men. While the death rate drops for men ages 25 to 29 for most groups, it continues to rise among Black Americans. According to the Centers for Disease Control and Prevention, the top three causes of death for Black males, aged 18 to 24 in 2004, were homicide (2,140 deaths), unintentional injury (948 deaths), and suicide (332 deaths). Deaths from HIV AIDS ranked sixth (67 deaths).
8. Hearing about and witnessing racial discrimination against family members has a detrimental effect on children's well-being. Hearing about racial discrimination toward family is related to poor socio-emotional outcomes and negative emotionality. See Rosenthal et al. (2018).
9. Epigenetic transmission refers to changes in gene expression or cellular phenotype that occur without changes to the underlying DNA sequence and that are passed down from one generation to the next. These changes may occur through a variety of mechanisms such as: DNA methylation, histone modification, and non-coding RNA molecules. Additionally, epigenetic modifications can occur during early embryonic development and can influence gene expression patterns in different cell types. We speculate that epigenetic changes may be triggered, for example, by the stress of slavery, trauma, severe deprivation, or environmental toxins that are a sequelae of racial discrimination. These modifications can affect gene expression and be passed down from one generation to the next with adverse effects on the health and development of offspring.
10. Greene (1990).
11. Barbarin (2002a).
12. Todd, Simpson et al. (2016); Todd, Thiem et al. (2016).
13. Stereotypes, prejudice, bias, and stigma are the building blocks of racism at the individual level. They are beliefs and attitudes based on a cognitive shorthand in which traits are assigned to BBY simply on the basis of their race and gender while individual differences are ignored. They can be explicit and conscious or implicit and unconscious. Discrimination is prejudice, bias, stigma, and stereotypes in action. Discrimination can be intended or unintended.
14. See Voight et al. (2015).
15. English et al. (2020).
16. Barbarin & Crawford (2006).
17. Barbarin (2002a)
18. Barbarin (2002b); Calabrese & Barton (1995); Gregory & Weinstein (2008); Skiba et al. (2011); Zimmerman et al. (1995).
19. Okonofua & Eberhardt (2015).
20. Goff et al. (2008).
21. Goff et al. (2008).
22. Goff et al. (2008).
23. Skiba et al. (1997).
24. Fenning & Rose (2007).
25. U.S. Department of Education Office for Civil Rights (2016).
26. U.S. Department of Education Office for Civil Rights (2016).
27. Wallace et al. (2008).
28. Nyborg & Curry (2003).
29. Barbarin & Crawford (2006).
30. Barbarin & Crawford (2006).
31. Barbarin & Crawford (2006)
32. Pierce (1995).
33. Harrell (1997).

2
Barely Making It

Dear God, you made many, many poor people. I realize, of course, that it's no shame to be poor. But it's no great honor either!
(lyrics from "If I Were a Rich Man" by Sheldon Harnick, 1964)

Poverty has many facets. It means not having enough to feed and clothe a family, not having a school or clinic to go to, not having the land on which to grow one's food or a job to earn one's living, not having access to credit. It means insecurity, powerlessness, and exclusion of individuals, households, and communities. It often implies living in marginal or fragile environments, without access to clean water or sanitation. The essence of poverty is "a denial of choices and opportunities, a violation of human dignity,"[1] according to the United Nations. As the song lyrics quoted above suggest, living in poverty rarely earns respect and reverence from others. The poor are often scorned, and their opportunities to participate effectively in society are restricted. Overcoming poverty is not just about accessing material resources but is also about re-claiming human dignity and honor. For the Black poor, the struggle against poverty is also a struggle against racial denigration.

Socio-Economic Status of Black Families

Each year approximately a quarter of a million BBY are born into families without sufficient incomes to meet their needs. Economic hardship and material deprivation are a constant source of stress as their families' lives are consumed by a continuous and often losing battle to secure food, shelter, and other necessities. Although Black Americans constitute only 13.2% of the US population, they make up 23.8% of those that struggle to survive on incomes at or below the government designated poverty level.[2] BBY are overrepresented among children from low-income families at about twice the rate of White boys.[3]

Racial disparity in income has long been a fixture of American economic life. Between 1990 and 2020, the median income of Black households was $45,870 compared to $76,057 for Whites and $98,170 for Asian Americans. For every dollar earned by Whites, Blacks earned 61 cents. Even with declines in the US government's official poverty rate from a high of 40% in 1965 to 19.5% in 2020, Black individuals as a group still fell disproportionately among the lowest income groups in America.[4] Moreover, they have comparatively little or no material wealth to speak of. On average, Black individuals had a net worth of $24,000 in 2020 versus $188,000 for White individuals.

It may come as a surprise to many that racial disparities in income are not the inevitable consequences of lower educational achievement by Black individuals compared to White individuals.[5] White earners received higher wages than Black earners with equivalent education. In fact, White high school graduates on average earned as much as Black college graduates.[6] In addition, racial disparities in home ownership mirror the disparities income (45.3% of Black households own their homes vs 74.6% of White households).[7]

Material Hardship and Family Life

Although Black families can be found at every income level, the majority cluster toward the lower end of the economic scale due to low incomes and under-employment. Life in households at lower end of the scale is marked by uncertainty and worry, as families struggle to afford food, find shelter, and provide for other necessities. Their economic situations are so precarious, even minor unexpected expenses are catastrophic and can turn their lives upside down. Economic hardship means putting off car repairs, ignoring worn shoes and clothes, and having to choose whether to purchase food and medicine or pay overdue rent, heat, light, and other bills. It means desperation when a car, essential for transportation to work, suddenly breaks down, or the electricity is cut off. It means shame and helplessness over having to scramble to salvage a few possessions when sheriff's deputies evict them and place everything they own on the street. For poor families, economic hardship means that life is unpredictable and filled with stressful events over which they have little control.

Disruptions in Family Life

The stress of material hardship takes a toll on parents and their ability to function.[8] It lends to disorganization of family routines and discord in family relations. Economic worries increase anxiety, depression and conflicts among adults, and disengagement from children. Parents' emotional availability to their young children may be diminished by long workdays and unpredictable work schedules and made worse by financial worries. When parents are not available and supervision or monitoring is lax, children may be subjected to physical abuse by others and even exploitation by sexual predators. Random and extended work schedules may mean that there is no set time for eating, sleeping, self-care, and being together as a family. Family routines become random and catch-as-catch-can. For BBY, the combination of adverse events and a lack of parental availability is toxic.

Economic disadvantage operates in tandem with racism to affect physical and psychological development. Together they alter the typical course of brain development and functioning. They stunt physical growth and limit opportunities for prosocial development. They are associated with increased exposure to family violence and parental substance abuse and incarceration. Together they erect barriers that ultimately disconnect Black men from family, work, and community, and life becomes just about their own survival. Children from low-income households show an increasing lifetime prevalence of depression. This means that, compared to higher income families, BBY in low-income families are more likely to experience depression at some point in their lifetimes than BBY from higher income families.[9]

Adverse Child Events

In addition to increased stress related to the inability to meet basic needs, low income is associated with a high prevalence of adverse childhood events, such as direct or vicarious exposure to violence, parental incarceration, alcohol or substance abuse, and severe depression or other mental illnesses.[10] About 10% of BBY in families with below-poverty level household income experience at least one of these adverse events; most of these BBY in fact experience multiple adversities. These sources of adversity disrupt family relationships and can produce lasting emotional scars.[11] Substance abuse, economic difficulties, divorce, and incarceration are often given as reasons for father absence and the consequent fraying of a BBY's relationship to his father. Exposure to violence is common and has been linked to depression, anxiety, aggression and posttraumatic stress disorder, substance use, and suicide attempts among youth. Maternal depression is associated with adolescent depression and is a direct cause of difficulties in peer relations in early and middle childhood. For boys, paternal depression is also accompanied by an increased risk of behavioral problems, poor academic performance, and risk of psychiatric disorders.

Food Insecurity

A family's low income often means cutting the size of meals to stretch food until the next payday. It may mean skipping meals entirely with uncertainty about where the next meal is coming from. Many low-income families must rely on family and friends, food banks, or public bureaucracies to provide for the nutritional needs of their children. This means finding food pantries that give out food or figuring out which relatives a family can visit for a meal when there is no food in the house. This is an added source of stress for families.

Residential Insecurity: Owning, Renting, or Staying

Food insecurity is not the only problem facing low-income families. Securing stable housing becomes another source of worry and stress.[12] It is expensive to be poor. Low-income families pay more but get less. Few low-income families have the opportunity to purchase a home in which to live permanently. Instead, their options are to rent or to move in with someone else. Renting is the most common choice. When incomes are unstable, families move frequently to find rentals they can afford and often face evictions because they lack the money to cover their rent. In addition to depending on others for food, low-income families often have to depend on others for shelter. Avoiding homelessness means staying somewhere with others willing to take them in.

Some boys come to know firsthand insecurity and dislocation when family are evicted from their homes or have to move in with one relative and then another because the family is months behind in paying rent. BBY learn to say "I *stay* at my grandmother's" when asked where they live because they don't have a home, and they do not live anywhere on a regular basis. Instead, they move from place to place as relatives' generosity is exhausted.

Poor Schools and Communities

The household is not the only locus contributing to the emotional distress of poor children. The impact of poverty on children flows not only from parenting and a child's home environment but also from the accumulated disadvantages to which they are exposed at school and in their communities. Poor children live not only in poor households but also live in resource-deprived communities with a high density of poor families. Household poverty brings its own challenges, but living in communities with high concentrations of poverty is associated with an additional set of risks. Poor communities are likely to be ethnically segregated and deprived of many of the resources that contribute to a high quality of life. For example, poor children often attend failing schools with high concentrations of other poor children. Communities with high poverty rates are plagued by a host of social ills; these include high unemployment, housing instability, homelessness, crime and violence, and crippling economic stagnation.[13]

Fewer opportunities for upward mobility at work, high rates of violent crime, limited access to quality healthcare, declining quality of housing stock, and living in what many call a food desert due to the lack of access to fresh and healthy foods can weaken parents' capacity to cope and contribute to their demoralization. These conditions diminish both parental well-being and the capacity of parents to provide the resources needed to invest in their children's development. Thus, the social and economic consequences for poor children extend beyond family life to include disadvantages in community life as well. These effects trickle down to children and undermine the ability to adapt at school. Consequently, poverty-related risks can be understood as flowing from multiple sources. They arise not only from growing up in poor families but also from residing in economically struggling communities and attending racially segregated schools.

Neighborhood Deprivation and Volatility

Low-income neighborhoods can be lively and bustling or the opposite—desolate and barren with most children restricted to home by their parent out of justified concerns for their safety. Neighborhoods are often as problematic as schools and are not much better at offering BBY auspicious and safe environments in which to develop. BBY who are low-income often reside in unsafe and under-resourced neighborhoods.[14]

> Sometimes was bad ... we had some people downstairs they used to fight all the time. The man used to beat on his wife downstairs or whatever that used to make me scared, you know I used to didn't like that. Some of the things like people had broke into our house and taken our TV and video games and then that made me feel bad because you know my mother being a single mother had to strive to get them things you know."
>
> (Justin, 16)

On other occasions, BBY treat neighborhood violence in a matter of fact way. Because it is so common, their adaptation and accommodations to this violence accept it as a typical aspect of life that is a given for the neighborhood. Take for example the remarks of Aiden, an eighth-grade boy in a counseling group who was sharing a story and was setting it up by telling the rest of the group, "you know how when you are asleep and your mama comes in and tells you to get on the floor because of the gun shots, and then she comes back and tells you it is safe to get back in bed?"[15] His example was a common aspect of their experience that they could relate to. The rest of the boys nodded knowingly and said, "Uh-huh." They knew from personal experience exactly what he was referring to. Gunfire was an all too common occurrence, a part of ordinary life in their neighborhood.

Struggling Schools

Household poverty creates distress for BBY not only in family life and in their neighborhoods but also by increasing the likelihood that they will attend under-resourced, struggling schools. Many of the nation's public schools serving low-income children themselves fail to secure the resources they need to educate their students effectively. For low-income BBY this means that access to quality education is elusive. Their schools are not only under-resourced but have concentrations of other high-need, high-poverty students. Also, unstable housing means that regular and punctual attendance is more difficult for BBY because it requires very early rising to be dropped off before a parent must get to work or the use of public transportation when the temporary home is too far from the school to walk.

Casey Parks provides a compelling and insightful account of how schools fail BBY and the role of poverty combined with institutionalized racism in this failure.[16] At the center of this account is Harvey Ellington, a BY with high academic aspirations who is nevertheless struggling to get a high school education against overwhelming odds rooted in neglect by a society that treats him as expendable. He is the collateral damage of an inadequately resourced school district housed in crumbling structures with malfunctioning sewers and drainage and without the support of HVAC to protect students from bitter cold and sweltering heat. He lives in a rural county with a population that is majority Black and only 15% White. All but a few white students attend private schools. Rural schools like his are chronically underfunded by the state, an example of institutional racism. Wealthier suburban districts access local property taxes, but the tax base of his rural county consists mostly of struggling farms with few businesses. Public schools offer no extracurricular activities, no respite from Mississippi's stifling heat, and not even a home playing field for the successful high school football program. Many classes are taught by a revolving set of substitute teachers. Science, math, and language arts use outdated textbooks if they have any at all. Moreover, conditions such as low salaries, few books, and no supplies have driven the district's best and most dedicated teachers out to the more hospitable conditions of suburban schools. Chronically inoperable drainage has allowed toilets to overflow and sewage to spill onto the kitchen floors posing a health hazard to all. "While wealthier districts were buying interactive whiteboards and sophisticated science equipment, this county was spending its budget on plumbers, roofers, and temporary fixes to make the schools habitable."[17] The state has threatened to end local control if average achievement levels are not raised. At the same time, state lawmakers have refused to help pay for new facilities. Given the school district's outdated textbooks, its underpaid, unfilled teacher positions, and decaying buildings, this has amounted to a sisyphean challenge of pushing a huge boulder up a hill only to have it come sliding back, erasing progress and hope along with it.

These institutional difficulties have significantly impaired the life of Harvey Ellington, a 17-year-old BY, and dashed his hopes for a good education and a better life. He recognizes the importance of believing in himself as evidenced by the affirming sign on the dresser reminding him "you are worth more than gold." He is a go-getter. He has worked hard to improve life at school for himself and others. He volunteered for the student advisory group in his first year at the high school and was class president in his second year. He was a highly motivated, ambitious, and visionary student. He dreamed of restoring currently defunct academic clubs and organizations to improve writing and scores on standardized tests. He pushed to develop a local Boys and Girls Club for recreation and social events. In more auspicious settings, he would have been the young man described as a natural leader and that everyone voted "most likely to succeed." He had the highest ACT score at his school, but it was still below the state average. He instinctively knew that he had to do better.

"He dreamed of attending college. However, his science class offered no lab experience. He wrote to the superintendent complaining that his algebra class didn't have textbooks. The class wasted half the instructional time copying equations onto loose sheets of paper."[18] The teacher assigned homework provided online by Khan Academy, a nonprofit source of tutorials, but Ellington didn't have a computer or internet access at home, and he couldn't figure out how to complete the lessons on his phone. He was embarrassed when chastised publicly for not finishing them and was sent to the office when he became indignant and argued with the teacher.

During the lockdowns associated with the Covid epidemic, the district provided students with Chromebooks and internet hotspots for online instruction. Six weeks passed before his arrived and before he could begin his work. Because his mother worked an hour away, he was responsible for feeding and monitoring the virtual instruction for his 5 and 6-year-old siblings. His assigned English teacher did not show up for virtual classes. He learned later that she had died of Covid. It took months to find a replacement English teacher, and no one sent instructions for signing in for the replacement English class to which he was assigned. Consequently, he was given a failing grade on his 9-week report card for not showing up. He devoted nights and weekends to make up the work, but he still received a final grade of D. He worried that he would be rejected by colleges as a science major when they learned that he had attended a failing school with no science lab.

Even worse, if he were accepted, he feared he would be too far behind other students to catch up. So, he gave up on his dream. Harvey truly was a victim of institutional racism in the form of underfunded schools in this case. This virulent racism traumatizes, humiliates, confuses, demoralizes, and enrages its victims. It has direct and indirect negative effects on the emotional and academic functioning of BBY, as it did for Harvey.[19]

Low Salience of Race for Poor BBY

An argument can be made that the pressures of economic hardship and absolute segregation may consign awareness of race deep into the farthest subconscious recesses of the minds of Blacks struggling with economic survival. Low-income BBY may have less contact with Whites and may not see the connection between their material disadvantages and racism. Overt acts of racism may be less apparent and relevant to low-income BBY than their daily experience of material disadvantage. As young children, financial difficulties color their lives so completely and so immediately that the impact of race and racism seem secondary and distant. In many ways, the role of race may seem irrelevant to the trials they face day to day. Their poverty means that they are isolated from and have little contact with White individuals or with others who are better off financially. Most remain in the comfort zone of their neighborhoods, the areas in which they feel safest. Only the most adventurous roam beyond their own neighborhood to take advantage of the array of recreational facilities and venues available elsewhere, to enjoy nature in public parks, zoos, or nature trails; to attend music performances, state fairs, or festivals; or engage in informal learning activities in museums and libraries. To a great extent, their lives are circumscribed due to invisible boundaries that separate them from more affluent and often predominantly White parts of the community. Being low-income means BBY are often disregarded and ignored. And when they cannot be ignored, they are regarded with a patronizing noblesse oblige or with a combination of ambivalence, fear, and contempt. At the same time, although race may not be as salient as their impoverished conditions, most BBY will ultimately make the connection between the color of their skin and the conditions of their housing, schools, and neighbors. Families and others in their lives will be critical in helping them to recognize and face that connection.

Growing up with Economic Advantages Does Not Immunize against Racism

Like all groups, Black families and their children vary by socio-economic status (SES). Consequently, not all Black families are poor or suffer from the adverse sequelae of poverty. They vary in income and differ in educational attainment. Affluence does not immunize or protect against racism, however. Black–White achievement gaps occur for boys in middle-class homes just as they do for BB from poor households. Racism trumps SES. Middle-class boys have challenges that are unique to their economic status. Because of racism they often don't entirely receive the benefits and privileges that typically accompany higher parental education and income, that is, social status. Many BBY whose parents often represent the first generation to attain some degree of affluence sometimes still live in segregated neighborhoods and attend under-resourced schools. They are susceptible to many of the same risks faced by peers from household with less financial means. Some parents send their sons to private schools to secure a better education for them. Often, they are the only or one of the few Black students in the school. Their solo status often brings social isolation and difficult questions about how to fit in. In these settings they are likely to experience racial microaggression and implicit biases of staff who may not be accustomed to working with Black students. For Black families who choose to live in integrated and more affluent neighborhoods, their sons are likely to be challenged about whether they belong there as has been the case in several well-publicized attacks on Black males in predominantly White neighborhoods. Whether at school, on the street, or in stores, BBY are subject to discrimination, suspicion, and possibly harm. This constitutes a continuing source of worry for their parents who must elevate discussions of racism so that their sons are aware of the risks they may face and how they are unable to do things that their peers may get away with doing. These boys may have all the things money can buy and all the skills that come with educational attainment, but their money and their skills are not enough to protect them. In effect, they face threats to their emotional and physical well-being similar to those of BBY from economically disadvantaged households.

Although the issues facing BBY from affluent household are serious and deserve attention, the difficulties of living with economic hardship and the challenges they present for BBY development cannot be overstated. These adverse conditions do not occur by accident. As noted in the previous chapter on racism, they are connected to Black individuals' low wealth accumulation and their concentration in low-wage, low-mobility jobs which are the products of policies and institutions designed to subordinate Black individuals. The next chapter reviews what happens to BBY as a consequence of their encounters with racism and living with economic hardship.

Notes

1. United Nations Human Development Report (UNDP 1996).
2. Census Bureau (2020).
3. BBY whose parents are married and living together are much less likely to be in an impoverished household than those (roughly 2/3) who live with a single parent (6% vs 28% poverty rate).
4. According to the US Census of 2020, 18% of Black households earn less than $15,000 per year, and 11.7% earn between 15,000 to 24,999 per year. This suggests that, give or take $5,000, almost 30% of Black households would likely be near or below the poverty threshold. In the United States, poverty is conceptualized as the ratio of household income to the cost of providing basic needs for food, shelter, clothing, etc. As many as 20% of Black households live on annual incomes below the US government standard for poverty.
5. Inequality of educational opportunities effectively blocks access to many well-paying careers and advancement up career ladders leading to executive suites. See McGhee (2021). High school graduation is lower among Black students than White students (69% vs 86%). A host of factors are involved in this disparity, but chief among them are inequalities in the funding and quality of public education available to many Black children. Similar disparities exist in higher education; 44% of White youth have earned a bachelor's or master's degree compared to 25% of Black youth. Increasing costs and reductions in financial assistance for the needy have made college and graduate education unaffordable and out of reach for many Black Americans.
6. Income disparities are most likely linked to educational differences and to higher White than Black participation in well-compensated blue-collar trade occupations.
7. Tim Henderson (2022).
8. Conger et al. (2010).
9. Yoshikawa, Aber, & Beardslee (2012).
10. Shonkoff et al. (2012).
11. Barbarin et al. (2022).
12. The financial status of a household determines whether the family owns or rents their home and even whether they have a home or a place to stay. African Americans are renters on average. As a group, only 44% of Black households own the homes in which they live as opposed to 75% of White households. Home ownership is virtually unattainable for low wealth households unless ownership comes as a legacy from a prior generation. Less than 18% of low-income families and less than 10% of extremely low-income families own the homes in which they live. Moreover, families whose incomes place them among the low-income or financially fragile need to allocate a higher proportion of their total income for housing. In one study of Black renters in Milwaukee, families spent as much as 60% of their total income on housing, leaving precious little for other essentials. They live in substandard housing marred by infestations and mechanical systems that do not operate properly. Moreover, the quality of the housing of low-income residents is often substandard with multiple housing code violations including peeling lead-based paint, inoperable elevators, mold from leaky pipes that have not been repaired, toilets that don't flush, the absence of hot or potable water, and heat in the winter. Sleeping arrangements are shared with multiple siblings and relatives on sofas, chairs, or porches. Air conditioning in the summer is an unattainable luxury.
13. Allard (2008).
14. Sampson (2019).
15. Oyserman & Yoon (2009).
16. Chavous et al. (2003).
17. Parks (2021).
18. Parks (2021).
19. Parks (2021).

3
Racism and Poverty Matter

Together racism and poverty strain and destabilize Black family life in ways that have negative consequences for Black boys and youth (BBY) health and well-being. This chapter considers how racism and poverty foster instability in family life that undermines family relations and stunts BBY's development—especially their emotional and physical health. It offers examples of how adverse events associated with racism and poverty give rise to BBY emotional distress, distrust of others, and concerns about their lives and their futures.

Poverty and Family Instability Spawn Behavior Problems

Poverty introduces instability into the lives of low-income BBY. Accidents, unanticipated reductions in wages or financial support, rising costs, sudden illness, or other uncontrollable events become catastrophic and disruptive even when they are minor. BBY's worries about family financial troubles often render them anxious, sad, and helpless.[1] Low socioeconomic status (SES) and family disruptions—such as homelessness, parental discord, divorce, or separation—are related to adolescent depression by age 14. In addition, economic hardship and adversity can have devastating consequences for BBY's self-regulation of behavior and emotions. For example, when family life is destabilized by adverse and uncontrollable events, even minor provocations, such as racist slights or microaggressions, may lead to frustrations that spill over into explosive anger, lashing out, uncontrolled crying, or impulsive self-destructive behavior.[2]

Health and Psychological Consequences of Racism in All Its Forms

Often implicit biases are so subtle their existence can be questioned or denied. Microaggressions may seem so harmless that BBY reactions to

Building Emotional Resilience in Black Boys. Oscar A. Barbarin, Oxford University Press.
© Oxford University Press 2025. DOI: 10.1093/oso/9780197747490.003.0004

them may be dismissed as hypersensitivity. However, a growing body of evidence leaves little room for doubt all these forms of racism do harm to and interfere with BBY's optimal development and psychological health.[3,4] The effects of racial discrimination accumulate and compound over time.[5] Distress stemming from racism is associated with elevated levels of depression.[6] Moreover, disobedience and other conduct problems, for which BBY are frequently censured, can also be seen as a form of resentment against structures and rules perceived as racist and resistance to adults viewed as treating them unfairly.[7] BBY's reactions to racism last long after their immediate emotional arousal and behavioral responses. Racism alters the course of lives across multiple domains including long-term psychological and financial health.[8] Box 3.1 lists the many ways in which racism is evident in health disparities and emotional difficulties Black males encounter over the life course.

Box 3.1 Racial Disparities in Physical and Psychological Health of BBY

Physical Health
- Prematurity, very low birthweight, low weight for gestational age
- Pediatric illnesses
- Metabolic diseases, insulin resistance
- High blood pressure, feeling unhealthy
- Increased inflammation, cancer
- Obesity and heart disease
- Victimization due to violence; poor quality of life

Psychological Health
- Emotional problems, somatic symptoms, distress, post-traumatic stress, anxiety, depression, hopelessness, loneliness, suicide
- Behavioral problems, aggression, peer conflict, delinquency
- Drug use, alcohol, smoking
- ADHD, cognitive problems
- Low self-esteem

Strained Relations with Teachers and Adults as a Result of Implicit Bias

Schools in the United States have taken on a number of functions that, in the past, were relegated to families—providing meals, childcare, moral guidance, and instilling values. In so many ways schools function *in loco parentis*. Many BBY experience loving care from teachers and other school staff who dedicate their lives to teach and prepare BBY for life. The discussion that follows is not an inditement of schools staff, as a whole, who do all they can to promote BBY wellbeing. This is not always the case. For some BBY, adults at school who can be indifferent to BBY trauma and are often the impatient and sometimes rejecting parent who harbors implicit biases that augur against a positive relation with BBY. Instead of comity and mutual liking, these relations are strained and marked by conflict, withdrawal of affection, and scapegoating. The unfortunate position of BBY in school can be gleaned from their answers to several questions. How does it feel when you realize that school staff do not really like or value you or think much of your abilities and promise? Do adults make you feel safe, supported, and encouraged to do and be your best? Do adults at school often seem afraid, punitive, or irritated in dealing with you? What is it like when you recognize that the adults treat other children with greater love and concern? BBY answers to these questions reveal their perspective on authenticity of adults who are responsible, presumably, to care for them. BBY can sense when implicit biases infuse teachers' perceptions and behavior toward them even when teachers appear on the surface to be solicitous or concerned. BBT are sensitive to assumptions that they cannot handle demanding academic work, they will fail to stick with it when tasks become difficult, or they will perform more poorly than their peers when challenged intellectually. They recognize when people act superior, patronize, talk down to, ignore, or treat them as though they were stupid. These realizations are painful and require much psychic energy to cope with once they become aware of them. Moreover, the consequences of bias are daunting because of their impact on BBY's self-perceptions. With enough exposure, these biases can break through BBY defenses and lead them to resign themselves to identities such as incorrigible, irredeemable, and expendable. They may come to accept that they are inherently unlovable and problematic. The churning of this self-deprecation produces emotional strain and irritability that may be expressed in disobedience and conflict with peers. As a consequence, they may withdraw from school, at first psychologically and in time physically. Cooke and colleagues found that microaggressions and social exclusion were emotionally debilitating and associated with high levels of distress among BBY in middle childhood.[9] Thus, BBY may not find psychological safety and emotional security at school that they need to support prosocial development. The material deprivation they encounter at home is matched in socio-emotional deprivation at school. The internalization of negative social messaging contributes to chronic stress responses that in turn alter neuroendocrine functioning and contribute to divergent development by the time BBY reach middle childhood.

Distrust, Anger, and Emotional Distress

The experience of racism in childhood can have deep and lasting consequences for mental health. Just like political despots, racist institutions apply their power to dominate, frighten, and elicit despair. In some cases, though, instead of helplessness they activate defiance; instead of fear, they instill distrust and anger; instead of cowering, resistance. To take a single example, such was the outcome in the case of Ethan who experienced racism and prejudice in school as a small boy with an emotional impact that endured throughout his adult life. Even with his intelligence, self-awareness, and career success, he was so tormented by a signal experience of racism in middle childhood that much of his adult life was consumed with distrust of the intentions of Whites, rage against injustice, and a struggle to temper his emotional pain with uncontrolled alcohol consumption.

At the age of 10, Ethan experienced a blatant case of racism. He was the first Black boy to attend his school. It was a time in life when he was most vulnerable, attempting to establish social connections, form an identity, and define his place in the all-White world. On his way home from school one day, he was confronted by five White boys, some of whom were older and from another class at school—but one was a boy he had trusted as a friend. They taunted him with racial slurs, punched him in the chest and knocked him to the ground. They encouraged one another to kick and laugh at him while he was down. The physical pain was palpable but he seethed with shame and feelings of betrayal. Once he got home, he could not bring himself to tell his parents about what had happened especially about the one boy they thought of as his friend. The betrayal by this boy was painful and confusing. However, an even greater insult and betrayal occurred the next day at school. It was shockingly carried out by his teacher whom he had liked. She called him to the front of the class and excoriated him for fighting the day before. In front of the class he was accused of starting the fight when in truth he had been viciously attacked by schoolmates who did not like that he was Black. He could not believe that the teacher did not see him as the victim but assumed that he was the instigator apparently because he was Black. He was presented to the class as a bully when in fact he was the victim. He could not talk and was not allowed to tell his side of the story. He felt helpless and overwhelmed by the teacher's unjust accusation and misuse of her authority to sanction. It would be years before he could deal with the pain of this injustice.

This experience left a deep emotional scar on Ethan's psyche that lasted into his adulthood. His anger at this mystifying miscarriage of justice was one he would never forget and could not let go of. He had panic attacks and post-traumatic rage over even minor instances of unfairness because it was like reliving that unresolved incident from his childhood. He was emotionally intense, hypervigilant, and sensitive to racial slights in interactions with White individuals because they brought back memories of that original racial trauma. He often seethed with anger over microaggressions and injustices with an intensity that his family and friends considered disproportionate to the provocation. He became deeply introspective and a loner. His rage was always just below the surface, although it was well disguised by a usually peaceful and intellectual demeanor. Unfortunately, he found relief from his emotional demons in alcoholic binges. Though the relief was always short-lived, it disrupted family relationships and destroyed his marriage. He finally attained sobriety and relief from his mental anguish with the aid of a psychologist who helped to reframe this experience. She helped him to overcome the shame and sense of helplessness by understanding that as a child he was let down by the people who should have supported him, people who were guided by stereotypes of who he was but who did not take the time to know that he was a gentle soul who avoided violence. With help, he was able to resolve his anger by re-enacting the episode in his mind and imagining what Ethan the adult might say to the teacher. He was able to go back in his mind and provide the injured boy with the defense, solace, comfort, and protection he deserved as a child.

Beliefs about Personal Efficacy

One of the most insidious impacts of racism and poverty is the effect they have in general on how BBY see themselves and their families, and in particular on BBY's beliefs about their ability to shape their futures. This can affect the amount of control BBY believe they have over their lives. As BB progress toward adolescence, these beliefs become stronger as they and their families experience success or failure in overcoming impediments to their goals. These experiences may take the form of interpretive frameworks, which are used to explain the degree of personal efficacy or helplessness BBY generally feel in their lives and the importance specifically of their own efforts to shape the outcomes. These frameworks are part of a meaning-making process through which individuals come to understand themselves, the world around them, and their place in the world. They influence how BBY cope with difficulties, life disruptions, and disappointments. They also impact BBY's levels of motivation in pursuing their goals. These frameworks or worldviews color BBY's understandings of racial hierarchies and affect the conclusions they reach about how much control they have over what happens to them and how successful they will be in pursuing their goals.[10] They help to determine whether BBY see themselves as victims controlled by structural inequalities or as masters of their own fates able to overcome the impediments imposed by racism through their own efforts.

As BBY encounter racism, they either internalize or reject disparaging views of Black individuals. In the absence of affirming messages about Black people, they may come to feel defeated, adopt the role of victim, give up hope, and become suspended in inertia. Alternatively, the experience of racism and material inequalities can motivate, give rise to energy, grit and determination to overcome the odds despite impediments and difficulties.

In school settings, BBY face a barrage of stereotypes about themselves and low expectations regarding their abilities. These experiences are disappointing enough when they come from peers but are even more damaging when they reflect the behavior of adults who are responsible for protecting, nurturing, and guiding their development. What are the cumulative effects of knowing that your teacher thinks little of you, of being reprimanded and labeled as bad and oppositional for the same things other children do without repercussions or recrimination? What are the emotional consequences of knowing that peers perceive you as bad before they get to know you just because of what you look like? BB's answers to these questions are clear.

- It means not fitting in no matter how much you try.
- It means being invisible, overlooked, and suspect.
- It means being excluded from playgroups at school by White boys.
- It means getting into trouble for behavior that other boys get away with.
- It means people assume that you are better at sports than at math.
- It means people acting as if you are not smart and you pretending not to care.
- It means people treating you as older than you are.
- It means being treated as a spokesperson or expert on any issue affecting Black people.
- It means that teachers have given up on you and that a paycheck is what motivates them.
- It means having to scatter when the police appear even though you have done nothing wrong.

Consequences of Poverty

Poverty, as well as racism, has a substantial impact on child and adolescent well-being. Yoshikawa and colleagues point to strong evidence of a relationship between poverty and mental health problems in children growing up in households experiencing economic deprivation.[11] Similarly, Brown and colleagues studied the effect of economic disadvantage and maternal distress on a nationally representative sample of BBY.[12] Emotional distress in mothers was associated with emotional difficulties of BBY during middle childhood. Specifically, their study found that maternal worry was correlated with internalizing problems of BB from early to middle childhood.[13] The impact is greater for cognitive and academic outcomes than for emotional functioning.[14] Chronic or long-term poverty is also associated with antisocial behavior.[15] Moreover, poverty and material hardship are associated with anxiety and depression.[16] Clearly, BBY born into poverty face enormous headwinds. While systemic racism can induce fear, hopelessness, shame, a sense of futility, and self-hatred in BBY, severe economic disadvantage and poverty, in addition, give rise to increased emotional dysregulation in the form of pronounced anxiety, loneliness, anger, and desperation.

Cortisol Stress Response

Advances in the life sciences, particularly neuroscience, have yielded helpful insights into the ways poverty and its stressors are related to hormonal functioning and brain development. Relevant to understanding BBY's socio-emotional development are findings about the relationship of poverty to cortisol response and executive function. Poverty and the chronic adversity associated with it affect the biology of BBY by repeated activation of the stress response network (i.e., the hypothalamic-pituitary-adrenal (HPA) axis). Poverty is also associated with higher levels of cortisol in the brain. Cortisol, a hormone that is secreted in response to stress, occurs normally in the blood; cortisol levels typically decrease over the day from morning until night. *The Family Life Study*, a longitudinal study of the development of low-income Black and White children found that cortisol responses in children from highly stressed and materially deprived homes deviated from the typical diurnal pattern. Children growing up in poverty had high overall levels of cortisol that did not attenuate or decrease, as is normal, but remained elevated throughout the day.[17] This pattern of non-attenuation was significant because high levels of cortisol at 7, 15, and 24 months of age were predictive of low executive functioning (EF) at age 3.[18] EF is in turn an indicator of high-level cognitive processes required for self-regulation of attention, behavior, and emotions.[19] Accordingly, high levels of cortisol lead to anomalies in concentration and regulation of attention, impulse control, and regulation of emotions.

Adverse Childhood Events

Poverty is also associated with an increased prevalence of exposure to adverse childhood events (ACEs), and such events are ubiquitous in the lives of many BBY. ACEs have been defined by researchers as experiences such as (a) insults, humiliations, or physical threats; (b) severe physical punishment (e.g., slapping, being hit hard); (c) sexual abuse; (d) low affection and family support; (e) food and social insecurity (e.g., wearing dirty clothes and having no one to protect and care for you); (f) disruptions of family life (e.g., parental separation or divorce); (g) mother hit, kicked, or threatened with a weapon; (h) living with an alcoholic, drug-abusing, depressed, mentally ill or suicidal family member; and (i) arrest and incarceration of a household member.[20] As a consequence, life in poor households is associated with a range of adverse experiences, including emotional trauma, material deprivation, poor nutrition and health, as well as exposure to violence. When these events occur, they have a devastating effect on boys' socio-emotional development. In addition to socio-emotional impact, poverty-related adversity has been linked to aberrations in brain structures and functions, physical growth, and cognitive and language development as well the compromised neuroendocrine functioning described above.[21]

Brain Development

Research on brain development provides additional insights into the origins of executive function deficits observed in low-income children's such as attention, planning and decision-making, as well as their regulation of emotions. Longitudinal studies of children's brains demonstrate palpable differences between low-income and affluent children's brain development particularly involving the process of pruning unused neuronal connections that occur as children mature. Material deprivation and adversity related to poverty are linked to slower growth and smaller volumes in sections of the brain responsible for controlling impulses and regulating attention, and for emotional and behavioral responses to threats and provocations. Poverty's impacts are observed in functional anomalies in areas of the brain including the amygdala (responsible for processing fear) and pre-frontal cortex (judgment and decision-making). These anomalies may be due to the effects of chronic stress, exposure to environmental toxins, and poor nutrition in low-income children. Specifically, comparisons of low-income and affluent children's brain development reveal that children growing up in low-income families have lower volumes of gray matter in the frontal and parietal lobe, the temporal cortex, and the hippocampus than children growing up in financially secure families. Poverty is associated with smaller white and cortical gray matter and hippocampal and amygdala volumes. These brain structures are important for stress processing, emotional functioning, and mental health. The amygdala is activated when BBY perceive danger or threats or are exposed to fear-inducing situations. The hippocampus located within the temporal lobe is activated by tasks involving learning and the creation of new memories, the recall of emotions, and emotion regulation. It is centrally involved in processing emotions, and is responsible for facilitating memory and responding to stressful situations. There is little doubt that BBY growing up in impoverished households are vulnerable to anomalies in brain growth, size or amount of white and gray matter, and connections and function. Notably though, the negative effects of poverty on hippocampal volume were less intense for low-income children raised with warm, supportive caregivers. These findings are significant for understanding the anomalies or puzzles sometimes, like those noted in the case of the two Wes Moores' socio-emotional development wherein BBY growing up in similar conditions develop along different lines. This is an issue we will return to later in this book.

Poverty is a risk factor not only for difficulty in processing emotions and regulating behavior; it is also linked to differences in social cognition concerning the intentions and motivations of others. By middle childhood, children from lower SES backgrounds are more likely than higher SES peers to attribute hostile intentions and motivations to the behavior of others. When children are distrustful and suspicious of others and expect that others will act aggressively toward them, they may be inclined to interpret otherwise innocuous behavior as hostile aggression. This quick judgment and erroneous interpretation of someone else's behavior may lead a child to act preemptively and respond with aggression even in situations where intent is unclear and where hostility is not present. In addition to overt aggression, children from low-income households also have higher rates of covert aggression (e.g., lying/cheating, stealing) than peers from higher economic status households.

Poverty and Traumatic Experiences

The stress and instability wrought by poverty exacts an emotional cost on BBY. For BBY, low SES and related adversity have immediate and long-term consequences on their emotional and physical health. There is emotional pain in watching parents struggle to make ends meet. Rates of stress and trauma exposure—which covers chronic poverty, loss of family members, violence, sexual abuse, and bullying—among BBY are high. BBY are affected emotionally when they see family members arrested, are threatened by neighborhood bullies, or harassed by abusive collection agencies. Chronic trauma in boys may take the form of unfulfilled longing or reactive anger over abandonment by a biological father who is only peripherally involved in his life, if at all. Boys are saddened and confused by their depressed mothers who vacillate between catatonic indifference and anxious, concerned involvement, or lashing out with caustic irritability. At an early age, they may imbibe the futility and hopelessness of adults looking in vain for work and the futility and desperation of not being able to provide for the family. Trauma comes to them from being attuned to the heartache on the faces and in the behavior of family members who at times vainly attempt to drown their sorrows in alcohol or to soothe their psychic pain with drugs.

Emotional Problems

Trauma exposure can lead to emotional and behavioral problems and traumatic grief reactions that interfere with academic achievement and social functioning. In fact, children exposed to trauma have almost twice the rates of affective, anxiety, and disruptive behavior disorders as those who are not exposed. The likelihood of developing a psychiatric disorder is directly related to the number of traumatic events experienced by children.[22] The traumatic impact of adversity and the consequent emotional difficulty increase to the extent that the BBY is cognizant of the hardship and understands its impact on parent and family functioning. The myriad of traumatizing experiences associated with poverty exacts a heavy toll on BBY's psychological, physical, cognitive, and social development and on relationships with family.

The Meaning of Financial Hardship

So, what then does living with financial hardship and poverty mean for BBY? Anecdotal comments collected from a variety of sources point to a range of impacts that are poignant and informative:[23]

- It means Anxiety: Worrying with your parents about bills they can't pay.
- It means Desperation: Having to steal food just to have something to eat.
- It means Loneliness: Eating alone each night because your mother has to work several jobs.

- It means Fear: Recognizing that in the neighborhood you are on your own, and your parents can't protect you.
- It means Embarrassment: As Wilkerson wrote, "not finding words to answer teachers' questions about why your work is not done, why you are late for school, why you wore the torn shirt to school."
- It means Anger and Shame: Seething inside at the disrespect and condescension from the landlord, the principal, and the store cashier when they criticize, threaten, or patronize your mom.

Poverty and economic insecurity are hardships that are associated with a high prevalence of mental health difficulties, such as depression and drug addictions. These disorders in turn affect the relationship of caregivers to children. In particular, they affect parental accessibility, dependability, recognition of and responsiveness to children's needs, and they can impact the emotional functioning of parents. As we will see in the next chapter, this significantly affects early emotional development because it impairs the development of attachment. Another study by Dodge et al. (2008) suggests that in low-income families serious behavior problems are more likely as a consequence of harsh parental discipline, exposure to violence, and maternal values that support and sanction aggression.[24] It appears that the stress related to marginal SES and material disadvantage is the critical driver of mental health disparities.[25]

Possibility of Resilience

Families with adequate incomes have less stress, engage in more positive parenting, and have fewer child behavior and emotional problems. Conversely, families experiencing material hardship face a number of stressors that impact the quality of parenting, schooling, and neighborhood life and contribute to a host of behavior and emotional problems. Together racism and poverty create a welter of adversity for BBY. Because of a legacy of racism and structural inequalities, most BBY are born into families that are not affluent or even economically stable. For those who are low-income, life can be a web of hardships that exposes them to toxic traumas and increases their risk of developing externalizing problems (i.e., fighting, disobedience, disruptive behavior, hyperactivity, inattention).

At the same time, environmental adversity does not have to be the entire story of BBY development. Poverty and racism do not predetermine poor outcomes. Encountering racism or living in economically stressful conditions does not mean that BBY will gravitate toward mal-adjusted behavior at home and in school or in the community. The impact of racism and material hardship can be moderated by an auspicious family life. Many BBY benefit from strategies and perspectives on race, identity, and self-worth shared by parents, mentors, and churches that mitigate the effects of material hardship, reduce emotional distress from racism, and motivate them to remain on a prosocial trajectory. The contributions of positive relations with family and mentors should not be underestimated and overlooked in considerations of BBY emotional development.

Notes

1. Conger et al. (2010).
2. Evans & Kim (2013).
3. Cooke et al. (2014).
4. Brody et al. (2015); Yoshikawa et al. (2012).
5. Brody et al. (2014).
6. Woody et al. (2022).
7. Brody et al. (2006).
8. Mortality rates for young Black males are three times higher than among White males with a 50% rate of dying by age 20, most often from homicide, drug abuse, and suicide. BBY also have high rates of unemployment, up to three times the rate of White males. The wealth they accumulate is less than 10% of that possessed by White males. See Blake & Darling (1994).
9. Cooke et al. (2014).
10. Bandura (1986).
11. Yoshikawa et al. (2012).
12. Brown et al. (2013).
13. Brown et al. (2013).
14. Brooks-Gunn & Duncan (1997).
15. Strohschein & Gauthier (2018).
16. Racial differences have been observed in rates of depression, but the higher rates of depression in Black individuals can largely be accounted for by difference in income and social status. See McLeod & Shanahan (1996).
17. Blair et al.(2013); Blair & Raver (2012).
18. Berry et al. (2016).
19. Blair (2010).
20. Roberts et al. (2014).
21. Shonkoff et al. (2009).
22. Copeland et al. (2018).
23. Some were BBY I met in volunteer work with schools, others boys in my family with whom I have had informal conversations and one in a newspaper account by Isabel Wilkerson (2020).
24. Dodge et al. (2008).
25. Adkins et al. (2009).

PART II
FOUNDATIONS OF EMOTIONAL RESILIENCE

4
Emotional Development

Emotional development refers broadly to the maturation of capacities to understand and label emotions accurately, express them appropriately, manage them effectively, and to continue normal functioning in spite of emotional arousal, disappointment and distressing setbacks. This chapter discusses what we know about Black boys and youth (BBY's) early emotional development. It is organized around two concepts that are fundamental to how psychologists conceptualize the socio-emotional functioning of infants and toddlers: temperament and attachment security. In previous chapters, I have argued that racism and financial hardship are likely to have adverse consequences for the emotional development of BBY. However, as this chapter will discuss, the evidence shows that their impact seems minimal in the early years of BBY's lives.

Infant Emotions

Like other infants, Black boys have a rich emotional life that matures with time. In the first few weeks of life, their emotions are reflected in smiling, crying, and gazing with intent interest,[1] but these simple responses grow in complexity over time. Like other infants, at 8–10 weeks Black boys smile predictably at the sight of a human face. Between 2 and 3 months, they enchant their caregivers with spontaneous "social smiles." Between 2 and 6 months, they display sadness, surprise, and fear. By 3 months of age, their emotional lives are expansive and differentiated enough to include frustration, empathy, shame, and pride.[2] At 4 months, infants entertain caregivers with spontaneous gurgles and smiles, greeting them with joy and excitement upon their arrival and displaying sadness when they withdraw. Between 4 and 6 months, they can exhibit anger and frustration when prevented from moving, achieving a goal such as reaching for and grasping some shiny object, and from inserting into their mouths everything they can get their hands on to explore. At about 5 months, they begin to differentiate among people and smile more often to familiar caregivers than to others. Sometime around 5 or 6 months, a dark cloud emerges as they begin to display fear of unfamiliar persons. This fear can be thought of as a protective response to threat. By about 6 months, infants experience the pain of teething and can cry inconsolably for long periods at a time. By month 7, the dark clouds of distress over the arrival of strangers become a storm as they start to express unmistakable reactions, such as fear and discomfort, when strangers approach. However, there are compensating developments at this time, as they charm parents with grinning, and they signal the desire for close contact by stretching out their arms to be picked up and comforted when distressed. Beginning around 8–11 months, they react visibly to the approval or disapproval of others. They beam when praised for some new accomplishments or pout and cry when reprimanded.

Separation Anxiety

Distress over separation from a primary caretaker is likely to peak at around 6 or 7 months of age and then diminishes with time. Later, this fear and a resulting desire to be near a caregiver may increase again in the presence of strangers or in unfamiliar places. At 12 months, babies form a distinctive and predictable pattern in which they signal distress by crying, reaching up, and crawling or walking to be near the caregiver to seek safety and comfort. Over time, the way the caregiver responds in this situation teaches a child, by example, what he can expect of others when he needs comfort and assurance. This fear and the proximity-seeking have a biological and ethological underpinning: they drive toddlers to move closer to familiar caretakers whom they believe will comfort them when distressed, protect them when threatened, and keep them safe from harm.

Individuation

Between 18 and 24 months, toddlers become aware of themselves as separate individuals interacting with other individuals. At this stage, they exhibit a range of emotions that include embarrassment, envy, empathy, pride, shame, and guilt. By the time they are toddlers, BB, like other children, become aware of the behavior and feelings of others, something which is expressed in the form of contagious crying when hearing others cry or in emotional distress at the sight of others' pain. Although individual differences exist in the timing and intensity of each of these phases, there is a remarkable similarity across cultures and social contexts that suggests that Black infants and toddlers will progress emotionally in pretty much the same sequence as other children.

Temperament Styles

At birth, some infants are very active, often fussy, and frequently irritated. Others are relaxed and have a more placid demeanor with a happy, calm disposition from birth. Few things seem to disturb them; they roll with the punches and seem to adapt well in most circumstances. Some infants accommodate to change easily, and others are upset even by minor disruptions of their routines. Some are easily comforted, and others take a long time to calm when upset. Some are curious, friendly, and happy in contrast to others who are fearful, reserved, and shy. These characteristic patterns of behavior and emotional responses have been observed from birth and are often referred to as a child's temperament.[3]

Temperaments are conceived of as biologically based individual differences in behavioral and emotional functioning. Accordingly, emotions arise from genetic predispositions and are biologically based. Different temperaments reflect variations in reactivity and sensitivity to the environment, are evident from the start of life, and are relatively stable over time. Temperament is often described in terms of (a) infant activity levels; (b) frequency of negative emotions, such as fear, anger, irritability (e.g., crying and fussing); (c) frequency of positive affect, such as joy or displaying eager anticipation of a pleasant event; (d) quickness to be startled; and (e) soothability (when afraid or distressed) and adaptability to change.[4] These traits or dispositions are used to categorize infants and toddlers into one of three temperament types: easy-going, active, or cautious.

- *Easy-going*, or flexible, children are characterized by a calm, pleasant, even disposition with predictable eating and sleep and wake cycles.
- *Active*, or feisty, children are characterized as difficult, irritable, avoidant, and fearful of unfamiliar people and environments; easily

overstimulated; intense in their reactions; and with unpredictable feeding and sleeping patterns.
- *Cautious*, or slow to warm, children are less active, tend to be fussy, and may withdraw or react negatively to new situations. They take time and repeated exposure to acclimate to unfamiliar persons, objects, or situations.

Almost two-thirds of children can be categorized emotionally with one of these styles: 40% as easy-going and flexible, 15% as cautious and slow-to-warm, and 10% as active or feisty.[5]

Understanding infant temperament is useful, *in se*, because temperament offers a glimpse into the inner lives of infants and toddlers but also because it signals how they are likely to respond emotionally to the stressful situations they encounter later in life. As such, temperament tells us a great deal about how toddlers will interact socially with others and the possible challenges they will face in accommodating to their social environments over time. For example, the challenges of regulating emotions will be different and arguably more difficult for a child with an active temperament—who is feisty, chronically irritable, and prone to intense anger or one with a cautious temperament who is slow-to-warm and responds with fear—than a child with an easy-going temperament, who possesses a more flexible disposition and who is outgoing, adventurous, and not easily aroused or disturbed in the first place.

Temperament of Black Boys in the Early Childhood Learning Study-Birth Cohort

Published data on temperament of Black boys are limited but suggest that BB are remarkably typical on indicators of temperament, including regularity of sleep and wake cycles, crying, fussiness, and regulation of attention. For example, the Early Childhood Longitudinal Study-Birth Cohort (ECLS-B) collected infant temperament information on a nationally representative sample of children, including a large sample of Black boys born in the United States, in 2001 when the children were approximately 9 months and again at age 2.[6] The study interviewed mothers in their homes and observed children in activities designed to elicit socio-emotional skills and reveal the quality of parent–child attachment. The distribution of BB temperamental styles was typical of the frequencies found among other racial and ethnic groups. Like other groups of children, BB jabbered expressively and, with very few exceptions, demonstrated early communication and problem-solving skills.[7] BB were similar to Latino, Asian, and Native American boys in the display of negative affect (i.e., crying and fussing), interest in play materials, attention to tasks, and social engagement.[8] If anything, Black toddlers seemed to be happier and more adaptive babies. They displayed higher rates of positive affect, such as smiling and laughing, higher activity levels, and were less distressed when they were explicitly prevented from moving as freely as they wished. The ECLS-B data suggest that, as a group, Black infants compared to their peers are just as happy, active, and adaptive.

Sleep, Irritability, Adaptability, and Reactivity to Others

The 2019 Child Health Supplement of the National Health Interview Survey (NHIS) commissioned by the Center for Disease Control offers another source of information on early emotional development of BB.[9] As part of a broader health survey, interviewers gathered information on temperament indicators and social competence of toddlers from a representative sample of American households.[10]

Like the ECLS-B, this study found that the distribution of temperament type indicator and emotional functioning for BB corresponds to the distributions observed in other groups of boys. For example, the NHIS data confirm the similarity in the proportion of easy and difficult temperaments across racial groups. No differences were found with respect to temperament indicators such as crying, irritability, or the ability to control themselves. There were minor differences on a few aspects of temperament, however. Compared to White toddlers, BB were described as having less difficulty getting to sleep but were more likely to have trouble remaining asleep. BB were less likely to have difficulty being around or being helped by unfamiliar persons and more likely to accept comforting and respond positively to the efforts of others to soothe them. BB were also rated as more adaptive in the face of change than White boys. With respect to social competence, as a group, they were more often described as making new friends and engaging others readily; but at the same time, Black toddlers were rated as aggressive (hitting, biting, or kicking others) slightly more often (less than 5% of total). These findings suggest that as a group compared to White toddlers, BB are easy, flexible, and sociable. Kicking and biting is noted in early childcare settings as unfortunately normative at this early age, and with proper socialization, they usually resolve without becoming a chronic problem.[11] On the basis of the data on temperament, it is reasonable to conclude that Black infants and toddlers are relatively well-adjusted and that racial and ethnic differences in temperament are minimal and perhaps inconsequential; but there are a few behavioral issues that are normative and may blossom into difficulties at a later stage of development if not addressed by caregivers.

Attachment

Temperament offers a useful lexicon for describing relatively stable dispositions that appear in children from birth. Attachment offers a different but complementary perspective on emotional development not arising from fixed and predetermined attributes of the child but evolving over time as a consequence of transactions between toddlers and their primary caregivers.[12] Attachment is characterized as seeking comfort and safety when distressed or threatened through proximity to a primary caregiver. A major premise of attachment theory is that, as infants develop, they become adept at reading emotional cues about danger and forming expectations about the likelihood of receiving help based on the past behavior of caregivers. They rely on those cues—especially from familiar figures—to discern, for example, whether fear is more appropriate than excitement in novel situations or unfamiliar circumstances. They also develop expectations about caregiver response when they are distressed and adopt coping responses to match those expectations. Accordingly, attachment is a way to characterize the relationship that forms over time between a child and his primary caregivers that serves as a protective mechanism helping children deal with stress, novelty, and ambiguous situations.[13]

Attachment Styles and Strategies

Four attachment styles have been identified as resulting from early interactions with caregivers: secure, anxious, avoidant, and disorganized.[14] All attachment styles or patterns are strategies, designed to help the child stay safe, and are strongly linked to experiences they have with their primary caregiver.[15]

Secure attachment exists when a child views a caregiver as a secure base who is reliable, trustworthy, and who responds to the child's need for comfort and soothing when distressed; who is encouraging when the child seeks to explore; and who jointly celebrates with the child over mastery of developmental tasks or skills. Securely attached toddlers use their caregiver as a source of comfort. They are confident and able to regulate their emotions with help if needed.

Insecure-Ambivalent attachment describes children who desire closeness but, because of caretaker inconsistency, do not trust that their needs will be recognized or responded to. They seem overly dependent and clingy but at the same time reject or are unable to benefit from caregiver attempts to soothe them when distressed. This style results when caregivers are inconsistently available; sometimes attentive, sometimes not; or are intrusive, overprotective, and prevent the child from exploring the environment. The critical point is that their caregiver is really inconsistent. As a result, they learn that they need to be the squeaky wheel and take responsibility for getting the care they need by heightening their bids for care.

Insecure-Avoidant attachment is used to describe children who do not seek connection when distressed. Over time they come to expect that caregivers will not respond to their need for help and comfort. Avoidant attachment styles are likely to occur when the primary caregiver is emotionally unavailable or rejecting; when they are overbearing and overstimulate the child; or when they respond harshly to the child's distress signals. These kids have faced pretty consistent refection when they want care, so their avoidance is a way of protecting themselves from the negative emotions that typically emerge when they seek care.

Disorganized attachment occurs when the child shows no consistent pattern of attachment. They often demonstrate features of both ambivalent and avoidant patterns.

Fundamentally, attachment styles describe the extent to which a child believes that he matters to others and the extent to which he has expectations that others will rise to help when needed.

How Secure Attachment Develops

Infants and toddlers rely on relations with caregivers to regulate arousal by signaling their distress and seeking closeness. They signal to their primary caregiver their need for proximity by crawling, reaching up, smiling, or crying. When these signals elicit concern and a propensity to provide care, a secure attachment may form. This happens specifically when caregivers recognize the toddler's need for reassurance and respond to this need by welcoming closeness and comforting the toddler. At the same time, when the toddler is ready to relinquish closeness and return to exploring his environment, the caretaker responds appropriately by encouraging the toddler's moving away.

Based on their experiences of caregiver responses, children develop expectations about their caregiver's attunement and their likelihood of receiving help when needed independent of temperament (i.e., whether or not the child is excitable or phlegmatic, easy to arouse or nonresponsive, active or lethargic). Distressed toddlers are primed biologically to seek safety through closeness to their caretaker, and when upset or threatened, they seek closeness to the caregiver as a way to reduce distress.[16] Through repeated cycles of distress signaling by the child and distress reduction by the caregiver, toddlers develop the capacity for self-regulation. This capacity is protective and reflects a growing trust of primary caregivers and promotes positive internalized working models or representations of self and others. Caregivers are viewed as a secure base from which to acquire a sense of self-confidence about one's ability to explore the world, master potentially difficult skills, and handle the challenges that arise in life. How well caretakers recognize toddlers' distress signals and take steps to bring their children closer and comfort them are key in reducing the child's distress and in facilitating their development of strategies for managing emotional arousal by themselves. Accordingly, emotional expression and coping evolve over time as a function of the dynamics within the caregiver–toddler relationship.

Attachment quality is foundational to development of a child's sense of security, self-confidence, and ability to regulate emotions. However, it is not a one-way street. Infants and toddlers are not only passive recipients of caregiver actions but also influence what caregivers do.[17] Attachment between a child and their caregivers is, at its best, like a dance. It involves moving and feeling in synchrony with the partners. The dance involves children responding to caretakers as well as caretakers responding to them. The movement of one is followed by a complementary move by the other. As the child moves closer, the caregiver embraces; as the child moves away, the caregiver lets go approvingly; as the caregiver directs, the child complies. Attachment is a mutually fashioned and accepted compact.

Secure Attachment

The categorization, secure attachment, indicates that a toddler exudes confidence and trust that his caregiver will protect him and keep him safe. This sense of safety arises from the predictable experience of a "Goldilocks" level of response from a caregiver to match a child's needs for support—not too much, not too little, but just right.[18] A secure attachment signals trust that a caregiver will reliably provide comfort when a child is distressed and safety when threatened. It also indicates that a child knows that a caregiver will offer encouragement and affirmation, and take delight in the toddler's efforts and successes in mastering new skills and exploring the world around him. As a result, securely attached children are able to explore their environment while periodically looking to their caregiver for reassurance or using their caregiver as a secure base. Secure attachment also facilitates learning, presumably because it enables children to explore actively and learn from experiences in their environments.[19]

Secure Attachment in Black Boys

Across a number of studies, about half of BB have been rated as securely attached using the strange situation paradigm.[20] This is generally the same proportion of securely attached children as in other ethnic and racial groups. The ECLS-B utilized the Toddler Attachment Sort-45 (TAS-45) to rate children's attachment security, dependency, and sociability on the basis of observations made in the home. Within this representative sample of American boys, slightly over half of Black boys and about two-thirds of White boys were rated as securely attached in that they actively sought out and enjoyed physical affection with the primary caregiver, whether or not they were distressed.[21] They complied and cooperated with parental requests and suggestions. They were sociable and enjoyed the company of others. They rarely, if ever, became angry when a parent did not respond immediately.

They never hit the primary caregiver, went limp when held by the mother, or rapidly changed moods (e.g., from calm to rage for no apparent reason).

The National Center for Early Development and Learning (NCEDL) also provided data on attachment among BB and their primary caregivers.[22] Following the theory of attachment, BB who rated as secure had caregivers who recognized their need for comforting when distressed. But data from this study went beyond categorizing boys based on the type of attachment to provide details about specific aspects of the mother–son relationship. Indicators of the quality of the parent–child attachment were assessed using ratings of positive and negative affect, mutuality of the emotional connection, and engagement of parent and child in a prescribed task.

Caregiver positivity: Positivity refers to positive regard, emotions, and support, on the part of the caregiver during the learning and free play tasks. Positive regard is evident when the caregiver listens, watches attentively, looks into the child's face when talking to him, has affectionate physical contact, and is playful. Over two-thirds of the Black, White, and Latino caretaker–toddler dyads were high in positivity. In these dyads, positive emotions were expressed frequently and spontaneously. Positivity was reflected in caregivers who spoke in a warm tone of voice and often showed signs of physical affection. As well, they praised their sons' efforts—smiled, laughed, and displayed general enjoyment in being with them.

Child negativity: This refers to boys' expressions of anger, hostility, dislike, non-compliance, irritability, or resistance to completing the task. Boys high in negativity were repeatedly and overtly angry at the caregiver, pouting, or being unreasonably demanding or critical of the caregiver. Negativity was rare among all toddlers and seen in 5% of Black toddlers and 2% of White and Latino toddlers.

Dyadic mutuality: The dyadic mutuality of emotions refers to a combination of intimacy, closeness, palpable comfort and ease in the relationship, a sense of security in expressing feelings and a shared pleasure over working together. This reflects how secure the child feels with the caregiver. The child appears free to express positive or negative emotions or feelings. Mutuality of affect is also marked by the caregiver's tone of voice in communicating warmth and regard for the child. They almost always have a moment of shared emotion that is pleasurable. Among these dyads, there is a sense that experiences (both positive and negative) are shared, that the caregiver responds to the child's emotion and vice versa. Smiling back and forth takes place. Eye contact occurs when the child or caregiver seeks it, and there may also be physical proximity-seeking behaviors, help seeking, or some reflection on an experience with toys (e.g., "this is hard" or "this is silly"). Whereas 30% of Black caregiver–child dyads were rated high on this scale, 49.5% of White and 55.6% of Latino dyads were. The racial/ethnic differences were attributable to differences in family SES.

Overall, there is little basis for asserting racial/ethnic differences independent of socio-economic status in the strength and quality of parent–child relationships and child attachment style. Moreover, the available data point to a comparatively positive environment and high-quality relationships between BBY and their parents when they are young. Given BB similarities to other groups of children in temperament and attachment styles, it is reasonable to conclude that the emotional development of BB follows the same ontogenetic blueprint as other groups of children. Finally, it is important to emphasize that attachment styles are not fixed after early childhood but continue to develop and are subject to change depending on the boy's subsequent experiences.

Impact of Past and Current Experience of Support on Resilience

The early years of a child's life merit special attention because their initial adaptations are a starting place for subsequent transactions, framing how new experiences and interactions with others will be interpreted and acted upon. Early experiences with responsive adults who offer protection when needed lead to secure attachment, which promotes strengths, while the opposite leads to insecure attachment, which imposes costs and strains that then influence how a boy might react to later experiences. Early traumatic experiences can play a critical role in pushing boys toward antisocial behavior. However, early experiences are not determinative. Much depends upon subsequent experiences and the availability of social resources. A boy's beliefs and expectations of how he will be treated are based on his interactions in the past but they can be changed by future interactions. Consequently, as important as the early childhood period is for laying a foundation for emotional functioning, BBY's emotional development is not determined solely by their early experiences with caregivers. Attachment styles are working models of the world: beliefs that are constantly put to the test. Emotional development is a dynamic process that is continually shaped by new experiences over time. When life disruptions are few and social supports are adequate, BB have a similar prospect to children of other races and ethnicities for establishing a solid foundation on which to build effective socio-emotional skills and resilience.

Notes

1. Lewis (2000).
2. Lewis (2000).
3. Chess & Thomas (1996).
4. Lieberman (1993).
5. Chess & Thomas (1996).
6. National Center for Education Statistics (2023).
7. Mulligan & Flanagan (2006).
8. Halle et al. (2009).
9. National Center for Health Statistics (2020).
10. The Early Childhood Longitudinal Study-Birth Cohort (ECLS-B) gathers longitudinal data on a single cohort at 9 months and 2 years of age, while the NHIS survey provides cross-sectional data on randomly selected cohorts of Black boys at ages 1, 2, 3, and 4. It is especially helpful because it provides data on the prevalence of infant/toddler difficulties and strengths.
11. For example, Trembley et al. (2005) found that moderate and high levels of aggression increased among 86% of a community sample of children between 17 and 42 months old.
12. Bowlby (1969, 1973, 1982).
13. Cassidy & Shaver (2016).
14. Ainsworth (1978); Main & Solomon (1990).
15. See Cassidy (1994) and Cassidy & Berlin (1994).
16. Ainsworth (1978).
17. Goldsmith & Campos (1982).
18. Parents learned this through experience. For newborns, signs of pleasure and distress were non-contingent. Positive reactions, such as gazing and smiling, did not distinguish familiar from unfamiliar persons. Although most caregivers recognize that infants will gaze intently at people and objects and display fussiness or irritability, in the beginning this may be difficult to interpret. Over time displays of positive affect, such as smiling, occur specifically in response to social interactions initiated by primary caregivers more than others. In turn parents become more adept at reading infant emotional signals accurately.
19. Bretherton (1992).
20. In a meta-analysis of studies using the Strange Situation paradigm to assess attachment security, Madigan et al. (2023) reported that 52% of children overall are rated as securely attached and 48% insecurely attached (36% of these are anxious organized, 11.5% are disorganized).
21. Several studies examining the prevalence of secure attachments show differences in the rate of attachment. For example, data from the ECLS-B show 65% of White, 58% of Latino, and only 53% of Black infants as securely attached. However, the differences are likely to be due to income. For Black boys, primary caregivers most often include mothers, fathers, grandparents, siblings, other relatives, and even non-familial caregivers. Toddlers may have a secure system consisting of more than one person from whom they seek comfort and security when distressed.
22. The NCEDL family study (Barbarin, 2006) observed children ages 3 and 4 in their homes. Participants included boys enrolled in public-sponsored pre-K in four states. Trained observers video-recorded parents interacting with their children as they engaged in two structured teaching tasks (Etch-a-Sketch, block building) and unstructured free play with puppets and toys. About half of the sample were from households with incomes below 150% of the federal poverty threshold. About 60% of the Black and Latino families were poor, but only 26% of the White families were poor.

5
Development of Social Competence

Attachment security and temperament are widely accepted ways to characterize socio-emotional functioning in infants and toddlers. However, the concept of social competence is widely used to describe the socio-emotional functioning of older children. *Social competencies* refer to an array of interpersonal, behavioral, reasoning, and emotional skills through which children demonstrate mastery of developmental tasks, respond to performance demands, and cultivate favorable social ties with peers and adults.[1] Social competencies include the ability to manage feelings, to moderate arousal, to direct behavior in socially acceptable directions, to cultivate and maintain friendships, and to accommodate the diverse demands of social environments. Social competence is a useful addendum to attachment security and temperament because it underscores the influence of children's maturing cognitive abilities on their emotional and behavioral responses to the demands they encounter across multiple social settings outside of the family.

Cognitive Capacities Underlying Social Competence

Maturation of thinking and reasoning skills adds complexity to social and emotional functioning. The earliest signs of social competence are found in toddlers and preschoolers who control their impulses for immediate gratification, sustain their attention on required tasks, and are flexible problem solvers. These competencies enable children to understand and follow rules in play and in instructional settings. Socially competent children use words to label their feelings accurately and trust caring adults to protect and support them. In middle childhood, socially competent children might be described as affable, even-tempered, agreeable, and fun to be with. They are not impulsive or easily angered. When agitated or upset they calm down quicky and easily. They are relatively easy-going and attract others to themselves. High levels of socio-emotional competence builds on a foundation of self-awareness, social awareness, and self-regulation. These skills rely heavily on brain development and the maturation of thinking processes that this development enables.

Self-Awareness

Self-awareness originates in a consciousness of one's physical and psychological attributes. It is a recognition not only of physical appearance, such as size, shape, skin color, and hair, but also of enduring social attributes, for example, personality, congeniality, altruism. Self-awareness expands with the child's growing capacity to observe self, analyze motivations, and evaluate personal thoughts and feelings. It includes a recognition of an inner state of personal thoughts and feelings unknown to others. Self-aware children realize when they are frustrated, overwhelmed or scared, or lonely and when they are in need of support from others. By middle childhood, they have the capacity to evaluate self and observe that they possess both desirable and undesirable attributes. They have preferences and dislikes and can formulate reasons why they prefer some things and dislike others, why they are drawn to some peers and not attracted to others. Even when these preferences are unspoken, their behavior reveals their inner states. By preadolescence, self-aware children recognize complex layers of their identity that include strengths and talents as well as limitations. By adolescence they may define an identity and burnish the image they want to project to the world. In doing so they may recognize, painfully, the gap between the self they embrace and the one they wish the world to see. In adolescence, this growing self-awareness can have both positive and negative consequences. Self-awareness may be reflected for example either in encouraging self-talk, praise, and affirmation or negative messages, guilt-inducing injunctions, and self-criticism. In the extreme it can make Black youth awkwardly self-conscious and motivate them to protect themselves from criticism or rejection by withdrawing from social contact, concealing weaknesses and aspects of themselves that they deem undesirable.

Social Awareness

Social awareness, which has also been called social perspective taking, refers to an understanding of others' motives, preferences, or desires and an understanding of rules, sanctions, and rewards that govern how the social world works. It describes the capacity to see and understand that other people have emotions and perceptions that determine how they will act and respond to situations. Social awareness involves a recognition of differences in the ways people express feelings and behave. It is an ability to step outside of oneself and recognize that other people can think, feel, and react differently. The capacity for social awareness makes it possible to understand that another person's affect and reactions change over time and in response to the demands of the social situation. By middle childhood, social awareness can be reflected in evaluations of the behavior of others and predictions of how they will react. Social awareness can lead to expressions of concern and the inclination to respond to others' distress with direct help. Social awareness is particularly important because it involves the ability to see things from the perspective of others, understanding their intentions, motivations, and needs, and predicting their behavior. For example, a child may understand and predict that a peer will get angry or sad when not chosen to play on a team. Boys in middle childhood know they will be teased if they cry, or worse, if they talk to or play with a girl. Social awareness is the foundation of empathy, altruism, positive peer relationships, and the ability to negotiate, compromise, and resolve conflicts without resorting to aggression.

Self-Regulation

Self-regulation refers to the capacity to manage attention, behavior, and emotions to facilitate adaptation to environmental demands. It involves the ability to control the expression of feelings and inhibit impulses so as to avoid personal harm and to behave in a way that is appropriate for the situation. In school settings this might mean speaking in a low tone or with an "inside voice." It can mean resisting the temptation to rush into a busy street to retrieve a lost ball before looking each way or to throw food at another child who has teased and antagonized you. Self-regulation benefits from the cognitive ability to understand what is expected and anticipate the consequences when behavior standards are not met. Self-regulation is aided by improvements in executive function, namely, working memory (i.e., the capacity to hold and process multiple ideas simultaneously such as several steps in directions from a teacher), inhibitory control of behavior and thoughts, and cognitive flexibility. Executive function enables planning and flexible problem solving. Regulation of emotions involves the ability to accept and cope with disappointments, uncontrollable life events, and frustrations.

It enables BB, for example, to display positive affect, cooperate, and interact productively with peers and adults. Social awareness can influence and facilitate self-regulation to the extent that knowledge of the thoughts, feelings, and motivations of others is considered when responding in social situations.

Importance of Social Competence for BBY

As BBY mature, their increasing capacity for thinking and reasoning enables them to understand and regulate their own emotions and behavior, form social identities and bonds, and recognize others' views, motivations, and emotions. Development of these skills enables them to adapt emotionally to an ever-widening array of social demands.[2] These social demands require recognizing and managing personal feelings, getting along, and responding appropriately to the feelings of others. Being able to do so makes possible the socio-emotional competencies described above that lay a foundation for psychological well-being, achievement, and self-control.[3] Self-awareness is important for Black boys and youth (BBY's) self-concept, racial and gender identity, self-acceptance, and personal efficacy. Social awareness engenders a recognition of the needs and dispositions of others. As such it is critical for displays of empathy, altruism, tolerance, and interpersonal skills at home, in school, and in the community. Self-regulation is essential for a BBY's adjustment to school and academic skill development, attention and impulse control, as well as their development of close relationships and avoidance of danger and harm. When fully matured, these socio-emotional skills become important personal assets that BBY can leverage to cope effectively by managing emotional arousal, adversity, and stress in their lives.[4]

Social competence is a key contributor to psychological health. Table 5.1 describes the prosocial outcomes of high levels of social competence that include self-control, effective coping and communication skills, and positive relations with others.

Description of Socially Competent BBY

BBY who are high in social skills are often outgoing, affable, and popular. Positive relationships with peers, defined as a child's ability to form strong social bonds with others and to work and play constructively with others,[5]

Table 5.1 Prosocial Outcomes Related to Social Competence

Effective coping	Ability to moderate emotional reactions to frustrations, limits, disappointments, failure, and teasing.
Self-control	Ability to moderate impulses, comply with rules and use of non-aggressive tactics to resolve conflicts, and get along with others.
Communication skills	Ability to express self, discuss thoughts, defend own ideas, question unfairness, and influence others.
Positive social relations	Ability to behave in an affable and friendly way that results in being popular and well-liked by peers, perspective taking, empathy, development of intimacy, and friendships.

are facilitated by the same qualities of agreeableness, flexibility, support, and an ability to resolve conflicts that are required for positive relationships with adults. In interactions, such boys come across as friendly and sensitive, and others respond well to them, as reflected in their popularity and influence over others. BBY who are flexible, empathic, and caring—and who are not argumentative or aggressive—tend to do better at forming and sustaining positive peer relationships.[6] Socially competent boys exhibit a range of skills in their interactions with peers that facilitate the development of close ties and friendships. These include flexibility, smiling, and a sense of humor; acceptance and respect of differences; an ability to compromise; recognition of needs; and the offering of unsolicited help. At the opposite end of the spectrum, Rubin and colleagues have noted that children with poor peer relations are more often characterized as exhibiting friendship-destabilizing behaviors that discourage or subvert social ties.[7] These destabilizing behaviors include having difficulty initiating social contact or entering a peer group that has already formed, as well as maintaining social connections over time. Poor relations with peers are also reflected in deficits in emotional self-regulation, such as when children are easily angered, are impulsive, lack empathy, and are uncaring and dishonest in dealings with others. Difficulty in peer relationships is often characterized by aggression, avoidance, retribution, and rejection by peers. Difficulties in relations with peers augur poorly for BBY health and well-being in the long run. Without socio-emotional competencies, children may be more susceptible to anxiety, guilt, aggression, impulsiveness, delinquency, substance abuse, and hopelessness.

Research on the Social Competence of BBY

Evidence of social competence among BBY is available from several studies: the Family Life Study,[8] the Early Childhood Longitudinal Study-Kindergarten (ECLS-K),[9] the National Center for Early Development and Learning (NCEDL) study,[10] and Promoting Academic Success of Boys of Color (PAS) study.[11] These studies support the view that young BB evidence generally high levels of social competence in the early years of school. For example, young BB are rated highly on self-regulation[12] and effortful control[13] on an absolute basis by teachers. A more nuanced and complex longitudinal story about BB social competence emerges from a study conducted by the NCEDL.[14] Barbarin et al. explored boys' development of social competences, examining whether social assets in the form of propitious environments (i.e., adequate family resources, a positive emotional climate, and teacher responsiveness) are related to this development in an economically diverse sample of BB. Participating BB who were enrolled in randomly selected public pre-K programs in 11 states were assessed over a two-year period. In the fall of pre-K, about a third of boys included in the study were judged competent in regulating emotions and half were competent with respect to peer relationships. Boys' competencies in both behavior self-regulation and peer relations improved over the pre-K year, but they declined by the end of the year in kindergarten to the levels seen at the beginning of pre-K. Black and Latino boys were rated by teachers as having lower levels of competence than White boys and all boys were rated consistently lower than girls. In general, girls are more often rated as more socially competent than boys, and racial differences between boys are usually small in early childhood, though they grow larger as boys progress through school. Although there are significant differences between girls and boys in social skills during early childhood, racial differences among the boys were not meaningful. BB were more socially competent when their mothers attained education beyond high school, when the classroom to which they were assigned were emotionally warm, and when their teachers were more understanding of and responsive to their needs.

On emotion regulation, the percentage of Black, Latino, and White boys rated as competent was 33%, 41%, and 40%, respectively. Girls were more often rated as socially competent than boys. Only 66% of Black, Latino, and White boys were rated as competent with respect to peer relations compared to 75% of each group of girls. For self-regulation of behavior, about 60% of BB and 70% of Latino and White boys were competent compared to over 80% of girls. In all, teachers viewed BB positively on self-regulation but held less favorable views about the quality of their relations with peers.

Difficulties in peer relations is the principal domain in which BB social development lagged behind boys of other ethnic and racial groups. These difficulties were apparent in early childhood programs, in that pre-K teachers rated BB as more likely to bite, kick, or hit and have conflicts with peers. Caution is required before attributing this outcome to race or culture alone, however. In the NCEDL study that did control for family poverty, ethnic/racial differences in behavior problems such as peer conflict were not found among 3- and 4-year-olds.[15] The differences are likely attributable to low family socioeconomic status and exposure to violence as a norm for dealing with conflicts.[16] In other words, the causes are complex, more likely resulting from differences in economic disparities and qualities of social environments than in race *per se*. As shown in Chapters 3 and 4, economic and material hardships disproportionately affect Black families. Food insecurity, parental under-employment, financial worries, housing instability, and inadequate health care are defining features of many BB's social environments. These sources of distress strain and distort emotional functioning most likely through their impact on parental health and well-being and through the quality of school and neighborhood environments. For BBY, this means dealing with scarcity, chronic stress, physical threats, and diminished access to adult support. Although the prevalence of emotional difficulties was very low, often less than 5% overall, boys from low-income households were more often rated as shy, withdrawn, worried, frightened, and sad than their economically advantaged peers. Moreover, they were less able to cope effectively and maintain equanimity in the face of teasing from peers or failure at a task.[17] They may conclude that they are on their own and instead must learn to comfort and protect their mothers. Early on, BB whose parents are distressed by a combination of life circumstances—financial inadequacy, single parenting, and housing instability, for example—may learn that parents are not able to protect them from harm or offer a secure base from which to explore. Consequently, economic hardship is associated with a decrease in frustration tolerance, mood, and conduct problems, as well as lower social competence, particularly in peer relations.[18]

What can we take away from this research on social competence in BB? The findings are summarized in the following five points.

1. *As a group, BB demonstrated high levels of social competence although they were viewed by teachers as less socially competent than girls.* Each of the studies noted competent levels of behavior regulation, but some noted boys' inability to get along with peers. The Family Life Study found generally high levels of social competence among BB early in life. BB in the PAS study received average scores above 4 on a 5-point rating scale study of multiple aspects of self-regulation. These social competence ratings are associated with better achievement in math and reading.
2. There were no racial differences in behavior problems or peer conflict among 3- and 4-year-olds. Teachers interviewed in the PAS project viewed BB as having strengths with respect to behavior self-regulation but held less favorable views about their ability to get along with peers. In contrast, a majority of BB in publicly supported pre-K programs (NCEDL study) were rated as competent on both self-regulation and peer relations. The difference on peer relations may occur because the PAS teachers were rating BB who were older than the BB rated in the NCEDL study of early childhood.[19]
3. *Attendance at pre-K programs improved social competence.* BB who attended pre-K programs showed improvement in social competence after a year in the program. Specifically, the NCEDL study found that behavior self-regulation and peer relations improved over the pre-K year.
4. *The behavior of BB seems to have gotten worse between the end of pre-K and the end of the kindergarten year.* The data document a well-known "kindergarten transition effect" in which progress in the development of social competence halted and, in some cases, reversed when BB experienced the more structured and less developmentally appropriate approaches common in primary schools. This kindergarten effect has been noted for most children but is particularly striking for BB. Although the NCEDL and PAS studies found that BB improved in peer relations over the time spent in pre-K programs, this progress did not continue once they entered primary school. The quality of peer relations actually reversed with a loss of the progress made in pre-K. In essence all of the gains made in the quality of peer relationships and getting along with others during pre-K were lost or disappeared during the year in kindergarten. Similarly, in the PAS study, although emotional self-regulation was stable across cohorts, BB in higher grades

were lower in self-regulation of attention, quality of peer relations, teacher-rated closeness, and satisfaction with life at school than BB in pre-K and kindergarten.
5. *The older the BB and the higher the grade in elementary school, the more BB social competence levels* lagged behind other groups. BB in pre-K and kindergarten received comparatively high ratings from teachers on self-regulation of emotions and attention and the quality of the teacher–child relations. However, among cohorts that spent more time in school, teacher ratings of BB social competence declined. BB in grades 1–3 received lower ratings on self-regulation of attention, and on peer relationships as well as on self-rating of satisfaction with their lives at school.
6. *BB declines in self-regulation of emotions continued through the fifth grade.* Data from the ECLS-K show that BB had increasing difficulty regulating their emotions starting in kindergarten and continuing through fifth grade. A typical pattern for BB development of social competence is that they improve somewhat in pre-K only to lag behind other groups as they progress through school.

What this body of research substantiates is that racial/ethnic differences in early emotional development are minimal and primarily due to the effects of economic hardship. The early emotion development of BB is typical of children generally but is sometimes made more difficult due to the disruptive effects of poverty and material hardship. Differences between BB and other boys are most often attributable to differences in their socioeconomic situations in which BB come from lower income households. Data on BB emotional functioning mostly present a pattern of development that is fairly similar across racial groups once economic status is taken into account. For example, few differences are found on indicators of emotional functioning such as temperament, attachment security, and social competence. Like most children, Black toddlers receive high ratings on both emotion-regulation and effortful control.[20]

Differences between BB and other boys are most often attributable to differences in their socioeconomic situations in which BB come from lower income households. To the extent that there are racial differences in the prevalence of secure attachment and social competence in the early years of life, the differences are most likely attributable to parental education, family economic status, and other indicators of socioeconomic status.[21] The destructive pressures of racism and material hardship on development emerge slowly in early childhood. They may not be evident immediately but may manifest themselves slowly over time. The constraints imposed by poverty and racism grow in power over the course of the child's life. Their influence is probably weakest early in life but gain strength as BB moves through middle childhood into adolescence and adulthood. Much of what happens during the preschool period sets the stage for later success or difficulties. Two concerns about the socio-emotional development of BB that call for deeper analysis and understanding emerge from this research. The first relates to the difficulties BB have in getting along with peers. This is true even in the pre-K years. The second is the difference between BB and other children in the mastery of self-regulation of behavior. Here the concern that needs further interrogation is why differences which are miniscule at the end of pre-K grow wider from kindergarten to fifth grade. Why does the trajectory of BB behavior development deviate from what is typical for other groups of children?

Notes

1. Rubin et al. (2006).
2. Saarni (1990).
3. Mendez et al. (2002).
4. Kraag et al. (2006).
5. Thompson & Twibell (2009).
6. Hintsanen et al. (2010).
7. Rubin et al. (2006).
8. Clincy & Mills-Koonce (2013).
9. U.S. Department of Education (2015).
10. Early et al. (2005) collected direct child assessments and reports from teachers on 920 four-year-old children from 238 randomly selected sites in six states: California, Georgia, Illinois, Kentucky, New York, and Ohio. Assessments were gathered in the fall and spring of the children's pre-K and kindergarten years. Assessments included cognitive, language, and socio-emotional measures.
11. PAS, Barbarin (2013). The Promoting Academic Success of Boys of Color (PAS) study explored the development of psychosocial competence in boys of color (BOC; 226 Black boys and 109 Latinos). Changes in competence were assessed over 2 years in cohorts of low-income BOC beginning in pre-K, kindergarten, or first grade. Psychosocial competence was assessed in terms of self-regulation, interpersonal skills, and positive relationships with peers and teachers in pre-KK through second grade using teacher reports, child reports, and normed measures. One-year follow-up data were available on measures of psychosocial competence.
12. Barbarin et al. (2013).
13. Clincy & Mills-Koonce (2013).
14. Barbarin (2013). Black boys attending pre-K in public schools serving an overwhelmingly poor student population in five different states were rated by their teachers on the social competence they displayed in the classroom. On a 5-point scale, teachers rated boys' self-regulation of emotions and relationships with peers. On the whole, the ratings of these young boys were relatively high, averaging 4 on a 5-point scale for self-regulation. However, ratings for their relationships with peers were slightly lower and averaged about 3.4 out of 5 points.

15. Barbarin (2013). Pre-K teachers rated a majority of Black boys proficient on self-regulation and peer relations. Black boys did not differ from White boys on competence ratings at any of the four time-points at which data were collected from pre-K to kindergarten. In general, boys as a group were rated as less competent than girls.
16. Sroufe (2021). BBY may fight more as a consequence of socialization and a mutual understanding with parents that the adults in their lives cannot protect them when they are outside of the family. As part of that understanding, parents often admonish their sons never to start a fight. However, they are told they had better fight back and finish off any fight that is started, or they will be bullied until they do.
17. Early et al. (2005).
18. Early et al. (2005).
19. Early et al. (2005).
20. Barbarin et al. (2013); Clincy & Mills-Koonce (2013).
21. Halle et al. (2009).

PART III
DIVERGENT BEHAVIORAL DEVELOPMENT

6
The Golden Age of Childhood

If the period of life from birth to age four is correctly characterized as turbulent and challenging, life in the succeeding period from about age six to eleven is just the opposite. For children whose lives are unaffected by extreme adversities and material deprivation, this period is typically placid and free of life-threatening diseases. It roughly coincides with the period that developmental scientists refer to as middle childhood and the primary grades in school. It is a period for acquiring mature behaviors, for example, through play-acting of adult roles. It is also a time of remarkable physical change, rapid brain growth, and the development of cognitive, social, and motor skills. Because of the maturation of social competencies, robust health, and the relative absence of problems, it is often considered the Golden Age of childhood.

Del Guidice highlights several domains where substantial growth is evident in this Golden Age, including acquisition of social norms and moral reasoning and the establishing of status hierarchies among peers.[1] Colarusso has noted that children at this age are reasonably self-sufficient in that they are more able to feed, dress, and go to the bathroom themselves, and more importantly, it is a time when they seem to genuinely like and admire caregivers and teachers.[2] The Golden Age is also characterized by a decreasing prevalence of aggression; the onset of romantic attraction and sexual play, a solidifying of gender identity, and a peak of sex-differentiated social play and conduct problems. An even more remarkable feature of this Golden Age is a display by boys of cooperation and cheerfulness. This is a welcomed departure from the whining, tantrums, and opposition that are commonplace among toddlers. Gone are the embarrassing instances when, as toddlers, boys push, kick, or bite other children.[3] More common in this stage are teacher reports of cooperation, caring, and helpfulness with peers. In the Golden Age, most boys, both Black boys (BBs) and others, seem more content, cooperative, and eager to please.

Growing Social Competence in Middle Childhood

The Golden Age marks a time when children expand their worlds beyond the confines of family to engage with a broader world at school and in their communities. For children entering middle childhood, social situations and demands become more complex, as responsibility for their care and socialization is shared with schools. It is a time of a growing capacity for prosocial behavior where they show that they care about and attempt to accommodate the feelings and wishes of others. Their social world extends to same-age peers with whom they develop close bonds and have mutually rewarding interactions at school. Children broaden and intensify their friendship networks. These sometimes blossom into best friendships with other children whom they invite to play dates and birthday parties. They learn to engage and respond to other children with positive affect; leading and following the lead of others; co-creating rules for games. Their social worlds expand to include adult caregivers, teachers, religious leaders, and coaches. In the Golden Age, the first shoots of social competence emerge. These shoots form the basis of altruism and affability: behaviors, such as caring about others, and social skills that support positive relations with peers and adults. Children acquire the skills needed for healthy adult relationships such as caring about others, providing help without being asked, and resolving conflict through compromise.

Thus, for most children, the path through middle childhood is smoother and less problematic than that of early childhood. The trajectories of externalizing behavior decline for most, reflecting increasing adaptability and behavioral and emotional regulation. As a consequence, the Golden Age of childhood is a less onerous time for parents and caregivers and relieves them of the need for constant vigilance, rule enforcement, and correction of misbehavior. The reasons for this period of behavioral quiescence in the Golden Age of childhood center around boys' brain maturation and a responsive socialization that improves boys' ability to manage their behavior and emotions, focus on goals, accept the direction of adults, and get along well with peers.[4]

For many boys, the capacity for controlling behavior and emotional expressions are preceded by a gradual growth in cognitive abilities that enable operational thinking and understanding of cause-and-effect relationships. These are stronger in middle childhood than they were earlier in life. These skills enable boys' peaceful accommodation to the demands of the external world, their acceptance of adult authority, appreciation of the support and security provided by these same adults, and a growing satisfaction in the mastery of valued skills that eluded and challenged them in the past. They find satisfaction in pleasing adults and find comfort in routines. They can be occupied for extended periods catching bugs, playing with dirt, throwing rocks, and watching work at construction sites. They accept gummy bear candies with the same joy adults reserve for gourmet chocolate. They possess rich imaginations that enable them to find pleasure in small things: a wood block transformed into a formula one race car, a forked twig that becomes a fighter jet, or a turtle rescued from the side of the road that becomes an object of fascination and a treasured pet. Unlike the solo play of toddlers and the simple cooperative play of early childhood, by middle childhood, play is built around elaborate games with sequential interactions and complex rules. Children's pretend play becomes more complex with multiple layers, defined roles, and rules with a purpose and an end in mind. In this stage they graduate from ad hoc scripts for games, created and revised as they go, to planning and setting strictly governed roles ahead of time. They are attracted to group activities such as sports teams. They compete intensely, are indignant when others break the rules, and personally offended when others do not play fairly.

Residential camps offer an ideal venue in which to observe the unfolding of these skills in middle childhood. To give a single example, the strengths of young boys at this age were evident to staff in a summer camp in upstate New York. The camp provided two weeks of experiences in a wooded rural setting and was attended by boys from New York City, who were mostly Black and Puerto Rican. The campers ranged in ages from 4 to 15. For programming purposes, they were grouped by age, with boys ages 4–6 forming the Junior group, and the 6- to 11-year-olds the Intermediate one. The Juniors were not quite prepared with the skills that would make camping fun. They were frequently clueless and homesick. Many wet the bed at night, and in general, they required a lot of attention and care. They needed help with the most basic tasks: tying shoelaces, selecting clothing to match the weather, airing out urine-saturated bedsheets, making beds, finishing meals within the allotted time, keeping up with the group as they moved from one activity to another, and working and playing as a team. The Juniors were a collection of needy individuals who were clueless about how to work together and were rarely motivated to do so.

By contrast, the Intermediates in middle childhood learned to work together to accomplish a common goal. They did not require coaxing to try new activities: canoeing in the river, hiking deep into the woods, singing camp songs, or creating arts and crafts. They took pride in winning the prize for the best-cleaned cabin after daily inspections. They loved organized sports, especially when they had opportunities to compete against their adult counselors. The Intermediate boys were in the Golden Age of childhood. They were independent, malleable, and charmingly gullible. They were completely taken in and enthralled by night-time stories of ghosts roaming the campgrounds. At the same time, they were smart and organized enough to pull off mischievous pranks on their counselors. They were clever and planful enough to conceal contraband frogs on the return bus trip to home, much to the surprise of camp counselors and the consternation of parents dismayed by the prospect of another pet in the household.

Building Blocks of Positive Emotional Development

Plainly, as BB transition to and through the Golden Age of childhood, they undergo a remarkable maturation in terms of the self- and social-awareness and self-regulation that form the foundation of their social competencies and abilities to cope with life challenges. Together these attributes, dispositions, and skills are the basis of BB's emotional functioning. In the Golden Age, a foundation of self- and social-awareness sets the stage for high level social functioning later in life. Although social competencies do not fully mature until much later, middle childhood marks an important start of a process that continues through adulthood.

Antwon, a typical ten-year-old BB growing up in a small city in North Carolina, illustrates what emergent social competence looks like in middle childhood. He exemplifies how these socio-emotional competences emerge, however imperfectly, during the Golden Age of childhood. Antwon is outgoing and often lights up the room with a broad, disarming smile. He is well-liked by peers and adults alike because he is friendly, funny, helpful, and kind to others. He tries not to react to teasing and resists opportunities to make fun of others. He enjoys participating in many team sports. He cheers for Black quarterbacks no matter what football team they play for. He admires their style and wants to emulate them. Antwon spends most of the time with his "boys" on the school playground or playing online games with them using his cell phone. He has little use for most girls who he thinks are not much fun because they spend so much of their time gossiping or discussing fashion. With his "boys" he is competitive and confident of his athletic abilities, but he practices a lot to get better at dribbling a ball behind his back and completing free throws. He realizes that he sometimes loses his temper and that he needs to control the urge to argue or push back on a player who flagrantly fouls him on the basketball court. He is something of a leader and can be bossy. He is helpful to and protective of his little brother and his brother's playmates, though they are sometime irritating. He makes sure that bigger kids do not pick on them. With adults he is sociable, and he can turn on the charm with teachers. He worries when his mother is upset. He goes out of his way to help out when he notices she is angry, sad, or worried. At the same time, he is not perfect and can be stubborn. In an argument, he often has to have the last word even with his mother and teachers. Antwon is beginning to manifest some of the qualities that emerge in middle childhood. These include awareness of self and others and its by-products of empathy, emotion regulation, adaptability, and conflict resolution.

Self-Awareness

For Antwon, self-awareness involves a deepening recognition and understanding of his inner life, his fears, sadness, and joys. He turns inward when he is feeling sad or mad, identifies the feelings, and uses his inner voice or meta-communication to soothe or calm himself down. In addition, he possesses an increasing ability to label his emotional states and manage them. Like other boys in middle childhood, his personal identity often comes from comparing himself to others. He often contrasts himself to others in regard to physical dimensions and other features: how tall or strong they are, how good they are at computer games, how fast they can run, how high they can jump, how far they can spit and, to the embarrassment of their families, how loudly they can fart or burp. Growing up in a predominantly Black middle-class neighborhood, he does not think much about race explicitly, though it always lurks beneath the surface. For him, middle childhood is a period when a sense of his gender and race solidify. It is clear that Antwon identifies himself as a Black boy and is so identified by others.

Another adolescent, different from Antwon in many ways, described the slow emergence of his self-awareness and his understanding of racial differences and his identity as a Black boy that began in preschool but did not crystallize until middle childhood.

> Since I was in kindergarten, no, probably preschool. I always knew there was a racial difference but, I didn't really start thinking on it, and realizing what the difference was until, let me see, maybe the third or fourth grade probably, around then.[5]

Black identity is not always positive. One BB made a distinction between African American and Black identity.

> African American is, in my eyes, I feel, are people that's making steps to do SOMETHING, like keep their jobs, owning their own homes and business and stuff like that. But, Black people, or when they call us Black, or we call each other Black, in my eyes, it's like, the people that's out there running the streets. So African Americans are the educated ones, living in the suburbs, and the Black people are the ones running in the streets, doing nothing but getting into trouble.

Gender identity was palpable and fixed in a group of five middle-school BB observed during their lunch at school. When asked what it was like to be a boy and how boys were different than girls they made the usual references to physical differences—hair, dress, genitalia—but they also talked about social behaviors that fixed the gender boundaries and set different expectations for boys and girls. In doing so they articulated an emerging sense of their own masculine identity that differentiated them from girls. "Girls talk too much." "Their feelings get hurt for no reason." "They can't stand pain." "They cry too easily." They are "goody two-shoes," "tattle tales," and try to be the "teacher's pet." "Boys have muscles; girls don't." "Boys play football and wrestle with each other."[6] Each boy in the group vied to prove he was the strongest and had the biggest muscles. They strained to flex and show off their biceps. Their self-esteem and identity were clearly tied to how well they met the social expectation of masculine strength. When told that each one of them was really big and strong, they seem satisfied for the moment with this affirmation of their masculinity.

Social Awareness

During middle childhood, BB slowly develop the capacity for social awareness, that is, the realization that family members, teachers, or friends don't always see things the way they do but have contrary thoughts, feelings, and reactions.[7] They learn that others have emotions and an inner life that is different from their own. They consider things from the perspective of others and do not assume that everyone views and interprets things in the same way. BB sense of justice and fairness evolves beyond self-centered considerations to awareness of the feelings of others and the social tendency to respond to those feelings. Antwon's growing awareness of others resulted in empathy and respect. He was able to identify when his parents were upset and would try to do or say something to make them feel better. He recognized that his friends did not always feel like playing the games he wanted to play, so he would compromise and play something they liked. He also acquired nascent skills with respect to understanding the fairness and social justice that undergird fair treatment of others.

Self-Regulation

One of the most remarkable changes that takes place in the Golden Age is a boy's growing capacity for self-control. For Antwon, signs of disappointment and frustration over not getting his way disappear more quickly. Gone are the temper tantrums and the resistance to being told "no" when he asks his mother to buy some newly popular toy that all his friends are talking about. He seems more patient and less annoyed by the antics of his younger sibling. He volunteers to help around the house and stops watching cartoons to set the table for dinner. He does not need constant reminders to clean his room, take out the garbage, and collect his dirty clothes to be washed. Although he displayed a difficult temperament as an infant, and as a toddler was irritable and easily upset, he seems less moody, easier to soothe, and is more content in middle childhood. He has a good friend with whom he gets along well. He can get animated and excited, but he seems to have better control in how he reacts to frustrations when learning does not come easy and disappointments when he is not able to get his way. In all, the Golden Age of childhood of BB is a boon to parents, a time when being together is more easily joyful and when emotional bonds grow strong.

Typical Decline of Misbehavior

For most children, the transition into middle childhood is accompanied by significant decreases in the frequency of misbehavior and its related problems.[8] For example, by age 6, rates of misconduct decline and continue to do so through about age 12. This reflects the development of social competencies in middle childhood.[9] Thus, a typical developmental course is characterized by growth in self-regulation and correspondingly low levels of behavior problems after early childhood up through preadolescence. At that point BB, like other children who pass through middle childhood as a golden age, are cooperative, congenial with teachers and peers, and are usually able to avoid getting into trouble or smart enough not to get caught. They are viewed as well-mannered by schools and considered to be adapting well.

BB Who Pass the Golden Age

While the lives of many BB are characterized by the quiet tranquility of the Golden Age of childhood, some BB undergo changes that are not as favorable. Juwan, age 7, is typical of these young BB, whose behavioral trajectory ushers them past the Golden Age without stopping. He ignores rules and rarely completes his work in class. He often seems bored, distracted, and disinterested in his work. He moves about the class talking to his buddies when he is supposed to be working at his table. He is forgetful and seems not to listen to instructions. For Juwan, reading is labored and rarely a source of pleasure. Given the shift in middle childhood from learning to read to reading to learn, Juwan's avoidance of reading and growing disinterest in things academic augurs poorly for his future at school.[10] Teachers worry that he seems not to care about school and about doing well. He is bossy, though not mean, to others. Oddly, he is very popular and a natural leader whom the other boys tend to follow.

For BB like Juwan the deceleration of behavior problems expected in middle childhood does not materialize, and evidence of the improvements in self-regulation expected during middle childhood are not as evident in group-level data for BB. Unlike other groups of children, the frequency of BB behavior problems rises again as they enter primary school.[11] Thus the rates of problem behaviors for BB continue to climb while the rates for other children decline. From about age 4 to age 9, BB rates of externalizing problems rise as the rates for other groups remain stable or decline. This implies that some BB experience a comparative stagnation in the development of self-regulation at about the time they enter kindergarten and that this stalling continues throughout middle childhood until age 11.[12] Rates of teacher-rated opposition and defiance behavior among BB continue to rise from ages nine to 11 years, but aggression and emotion dysregulation remained stable for these BB, though higher than their White peers.[13] Thus the downward trajectory for behavioral self-regulation and social competence and, conversely, the increase of behavior problems appear in early primary school and are fully evident by the end of middle school. Similar differences are found on measures of social-cognitive processes associated with aggressive behaviors, such as hostile attribution bias and aggressive interpersonal negotiation skills.[14] *Hostile attribution bias* refers to the tendency to distrust the motives of others and to view their behavior as hostile, in the absence of confirming information, and interpret their intentions as malign even when they are neutral or ambiguous.

For many BB, middle childhood is marked by a continuing and rising frequency of conduct problems and emotional difficulties at school and sometimes in the community. While disruptive and non-compliant behavior is on the decline among their peers, these BB persist in rule breaking and conflict with peers. Thus, they veer off from the typical developmental course and bypass the Golden Age of childhood entirely. The contrast in behavioral adjustment is jarring. BB's difficulties are judged to be more serious than they would be without such comparison. School teachers and leaders are left scratching their heads, wondering, "Why can't BB behave like the other children?" BB are tagged with the label of "bad boys" and sometimes embrace this status. Schools respond with the few tools they have available: restriction of play time and removal from desirable activities, timeout, suspensions, and expulsions.

Just prior to the beginning of adolescence, changes occur in the comparative rates of problem behaviors that often go unnoticed and are rarely reflected in school discipline data. While the rates of behavior problems among BB are finally leveling off, the rates for other groups of children begin to rise and catch up to BB. See Figure 6.1 for an illustration of these trends.[15]

90   DIVERGENT BEHAVIORAL DEVELOPMENT

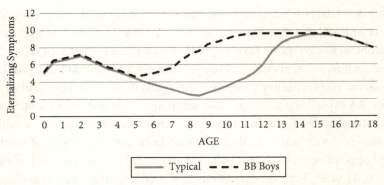

Figure 6.1 Comparison of BB and Typical Trajectories of Externalizing Systems

Note: Problems in middle childhood. Figure 6.1 illustrates these divergent trajectories. This illustration is a derivative integration of data trends reported by Aber et al. (2003); Olson et al. (2013); and Petersen et al. (2015).

Black–White disparities in behavior problems begin to narrow after age 10, and the prevalence of problems among White children catches up to BB by age 15.

A Framework for Understanding BBY Development as Juvenile Offenders

The lines in the graph in Figure 6.1 represent the prevalence of behavior problems for BBY compared to the prevalence of problems for other groups. The graph, which represents what is a typical pattern in the development of conduct problems, shows that for most groups of children the peak prevalence, or the highest proportion of children exhibiting behavior problems, occurs at about age 15; but for BB, it occurs earlier at about age 10 or 11. BBY's ascent to high levels of behavior problems begins earlier, in middle childhood, rather than adolescence as it does for other groups.[16]

By adolescence racial differences in problem rates are minimal. Nevertheless, BBY still stand out in the minds of peers as being more often involved in fighting, social aggression, and rule-breaking than other demographic groups. Similarly, BBY are more often categorized as victims of aggression than White children by both Black girls and peers from other racial/ethnic groups. The pattern for BB diverges from that of other children in a way that might be interpreted and described as an accelerated rate of behavioral development. These data suggest that BB are growing up too fast.

Heightened Emotional Distress in Middle Childhood

Behavior is not the only domain in which BB diverges during middle childhood. In addition to the higher prevalence of behavioral problems in middle childhood, many young BB also experience increases in emotional distress and have more frequent and serious emotional difficulties in middle childhood than their peers. In a comparative study of children of different ethnicities, Black children were high on teacher ratings of internalizing problems in the third through seventh grades.[17] In a nationally representative sample of BBY reviewed by Barbarin and Soler, researchers found that the frequency of depressive symptoms peaks in boys between the ages of nine and 10, then falls to levels typical of other children. For girls, depressive symptoms are only moderately elevated up through age 10, but rises and peaks around ages 15–16. Black boys in middle childhood (grades three through five) report more depressive symptoms than White boys.[18] In a follow-up, the same study found that BB reported more depressive symptoms than Black girls and White children.[19] Black boys were twice as likely as Black girls to score in the clinical range. They reported more feelings of diminished pleasure, increased anger, aggression, and irritability, all symptoms associated with depression. Moreover, their depressive symptoms increased over time, in contrast to the stability of symptoms for White children and Black girls. Elevated depression scores of BB appeared to be a middle childhood phenomenon, as these same higher levels of depression among BB in middle childhood are not found among BY.[20] However, Black adolescents living within predominantly White neighborhoods exhibited a notably high risk for frequent depressive symptoms.[21] Black individuals tended to report more somatic symptoms than other groups, such as appetite and sleep problems. Steele and colleagues found that in a sample of preadolescent and adolescent children, BBY had small but slightly higher rates of clinical level depression than White boys (7.3% vs 4.9%).[22] Similarly, another school-based study found that Black boys in the third through fifth grades reported higher levels of depression, as measured by the CDI, compared to Black girls.[23] Moreover, data on suicide rates among BB in middle childhood revealed an alarming increase from 1993 to 2017. During this period, the suicide rates among BB in middle childhood doubled even as the rates of suicides among White boys decreased.[24]

Similarly, treatment-seeking BBY reported fear more often than White children, controlling for SES and age.[25] Black school children, ages 7–13, self-reported more worries about war, personal harm, and family than White and Latino youth.[26] In addition, they reported more health and performance worries than the other groups.

Labeling Boys in Middle Childhood

For those BBY who bypass the Golden Age, problems appear in middle childhood and worsen progressively until adolescence. During middle childhood, an important shift occurs in how BB are seen and treated. In early childhood the focus is on behavior itself. Boys' difficulties with restlessness, temper tantrums, disobedience, rule-breaking, inattention, and conflicts with peers are labeled as challenging and interpreted as troubling but may not yet be seen as inherent and immutable. By middle childhood the labeling shifts from labeling the behavior to labeling BBY themselves. They are viewed and treated as the problem.

In 1903, W.E.B. DuBois, in his landmark book *The Souls of Black Folk*, made a similar observation when he noted that White society viewed Black people as a problem. This observation is as true now as it was then, particularly for BBY. This suggests that their difficulties and troubles are seen as inherent qualities and are tied to their identity as young, Black, and male. In other words, racism is in play here. BBY capture in their own words what this means for them:[27]

> It means being nothing more than a problem.
> It means you do not matter.
> It means being invisible.
> It means that life is cheap, and death will come early.
> It means the only choices you have are bad choices.
> It means pretending not to care.

What makes the development of Black boys as a group remarkable is that the trajectory they follow with respect to conduct and emotional problems is atypical. Usually, conduct problems, oppositional behavior, and aggression decrease from a high at age two to much lower levels by the time children are four, due to their improved capacity for self-regulation. This pattern of improved self-regulation is evident in all groups of children as they accommodate to the demands of family life and the regimes of early childcare. The capacity for behavioral self-regulation grows as the prevalence of problem behaviors decreases, stabilizing at age four or five.[28] At age four (usually the preschool year) the trajectories of Black boys diverge from those of other groups. While the behavioral trajectories of other groups of children show stable or decreasing levels of aggression and conduct problems, the prevalence of these problems among BB continues to rise. Studies using both cross-sectional[29] and longitudinal designs support this observation of increases in externalizing problems during this critical period from ages four to 10 or approximately pre-K through grade four.[30]

It appears that the routines, demands, and expectations of pre-K and formal schooling elicit higher levels of conduct problems among BB; whereas other groups of children seem to accommodate more often to these demands and are therefore less frequently rated by teachers and parents as having difficulties with opposition, fighting, and attention dysregulation. Data from a study of multiple school districts participating in a Kellogg Foundation-sponsored project to promote academic success of boys of color (PAS) reveal a decline in peer relations due to fighting and poor conflict management across cohorts of boys in pre-K through second grade. These teacher-reported data, which compare Latino and Black boys between pre-K and second grades, show that contrary to the expectations that self-regulation would lead to more harmonious relations with peers, the quality of peer relations decreased for Black boys. Black boys also follow a divergent path of emotional development.

For many children, emotional difficulties, such as anxiety and specific fear, decrease as they enter middle childhood. Moreover, the prevalence of emotional difficulties such as depressive symptoms is relatively low in middle childhood. The onset of serious and chronic emotional difficulties, especially for girls, typically occurs in adolescence. The emotional development of BB diverges from this typical pattern. Compared to their peers, BB have elevated levels of depressive symptoms during middle childhood. Consequently, middle childhood and the transition to adolescence is a troubled time for BBY. To cite one example of this, suicide attempts, injuries from attempts, and deaths by suicide increase significantly for BBY and have risen to a level that is greater than the rates for other ethnic groups although they had historically been comparatively low. Young BB are twice as likely to commit suicide as other groups of children and accordingly suicide has become the second leading cause of death for young people.[31]

Notes

1. Del Guidice (2014).
2. Colarusso (2011).
3. Aber et al. (2003); Olson et al. (2013).
4. Bub et al.(2007); Owens & Shaw (2003); Spieker et al. (1999); Vernon-Feagans & Cox (2013).
5. This quote is from respondents participating in an unpublished qualitative study of Black youth conducted by Barbarin (1995).
6. This quote is from respondents participating in an unpublished qualitative study of Black youth conducted by Barbarin (1995).
7. Selman (2003).
8. For example, see Campbell (1995).
9. Bub et al. (2007); Owens & Shaw (2003); Spieker et al. (1999); Vernon-Feagans & Cox (2013).
10. A review of longitudinal studies examining children's externalizing behaviors (i.e., aggression, oppositional/defiant, impulsivity/inattention, emotional dysregulation, conduct problems) shows that in their early years of development (two to six years) children demonstrate decreasing trajectories of externalizing behaviors. However, these trajectories vary as a function of children's gender (Spieker et al., 1999), maternal risk factors (Owens & Shaw, 2003; Vernon-Feagans & Cox, 2013), parent–child relationships, income (Vernon-Feagans & Cox, 2013), and temperament (Owens & Shaw, 2003). This research shows that boys tend to have higher levels of externalizing behaviors than girls and that decreases in negative behaviors are slowed or halted by negative parenting, low income, maternal risk, and difficult temperament (Owens & Shaw, 2003). Upon entry into formal schooling this decreasing trend, however, has been shown to turn into an increasing trajectory from first to third grade (ages six to eight) in some studies (Aber et al., 2003; Olson et al., 2013) or has shown stability and slight decreases in other studies (Miner & Clarke-Stewart, 2008; Vernon-Feagans & Cox, 2013). While research is mixed on how externalizing behaviors manifest in the early years of elementary school (first to third grade), studies that followed children to the end of elementary school (ages 10–11) do eventually show decreasing or stable trajectories (Aber et al., 2003; Olson et al., 2013). These findings were based on teacher reports (Achenbach, 1991; Dodge & Coie, 1987) and vary by the child's socio-economic background, ethnicity or race, and gender. In addition, the trajectories for externalizing behaviors differed, for example, for overt versus covert aggression. In Olson et al. (2013), subscales of externalizing behaviors such as covert aggression, oppositional/defiant behavior, impulsivity/inattention, and emotional dysregulation showed steady growth from kindergarten to second grade (ages five to eight), which were followed by a period of stability from third to fifth grade (ages nine to 11), with the exception of emotional dysregulation which continued to increase during middle childhood. On the other hand, overt aggression showed stability from kindergarten to fifth grade. In addition, findings provided evidence of increased initial status of many domains of externalizing behaviors for boys and children from low SES backgrounds compared to girls and their higher SES peers, respectively. Low SES children showed higher rates of growth in covert aggression (e.g., lying/cheating, stealing) than their higher SES counterparts. Meanwhile, Black children compared to their White peers showed early growth (first to second grade) in overt aggression, oppositional/defiant behavior, and emotional dysregulation. Oppositional defiant behaviors in Black children continued to increase from third to fifth grade while other behaviors stabilized; but in later school years, they also showed an increase in impulsivity and inattention which were originally stable from first to second grade (Bub et al., 2007; Owens & Shaw, 2003; Spieker et al., 1999; Vernon-Feagans & Cox, 2013).
11. Aber et al. (2003).
12. Barbarin (2013); Barbarin et al. (2019); Barbarin (2019); Aber et al. (2003); Olson et al. (2013).
13. Dodge (1986) also found differences on measures of social-cognitive processes associated with aggressive behaviors, such as hostile attribution bias and aggressive interpersonal negotiation skills. Black children had higher levels of hostile attribution bias than White children across

the entire range from ages six to 12. As a group, they had higher rates of growth in aggressive fantasies compared to their White counterparts In addition, Black children had higher levels of aggressive interpersonal negotiation skills than their White counterparts.
14. Dodge (1986).
15. An analysis of BB individual developmental trajectories reveals a less dire view than the one rendered by group-level comparison. For example, latent group analyses of individual behavioral trajectories of BB from kindergarten to fifth grade and from age 10 through to early adulthood found that about 85% of boys fell into the group that had minimal difficulty with behavior regulation. See Brown et al. (2013); Murry et al. (2014).
16. Behavioral trajectories converge in early adolescence. In effect behavior problems are just as common among other groups, although it takes them longer to converge and reach the same levels as BB. As Figure 6.1 shows, BB reach the peak prevalence of behavior problems sooner than other groups. The peak prevalence of problems is about the same for all groups including girls. By early adolescence in seventh or eighth grade, the prevalence of behavior problems tends to increase in frequency sufficiently so that they merge and become indistinguishable. However, the nature of the problems differs, particularly by gender. For example, girls tend to engage in relational aggression such as spreading false rumors, social ostracism, online bullying, and status offenses; whereas boys tend at this age toward physical aggression, substance abuse, and delinquency. Girls are also more likely to have issues related to emotional and eating disorders. Beliefs that other people's behavior are motivated by hostility are more common among boys than girls (Dodge, 1986).
17. Cole et al. (1998).
18. Kistner et al. (2003).
19. Kistner et al. (2007).
20. Angold et al. (2002).
21. Wight et al. (2005).
22. Steele et al. (2006).
23. Kistner et al. (2003).
24. Bridge et al. (2015, 2018); Lindsey et al. (2019).
25. Last & Perrin (1993).
26. Silverman et al. (1995).
27. Barbarin (1995).
28. Bub et al. (2007).
29. Barbarin & Soler (1993).
30. Aber et al. (2003); Broidy et al. (2003); Fontaine et al. (2009); Olson et al. (2013).
31. According to the Congressional Black Caucus Emergency Task Force on Black Youth Suicide and Mental Health (2019) the suicide death rate for Black Youth increased from 2.55 to 4.82 (per 100,000) in the 10-year period between 2007 and 2017. Suicide attempts increased by 73% between 1991 and 2017, and injuries from suicide attempts increased by 122%.

7
Growing Up Fast

Behavioral development unfolds
 . . . in response to the quality of the environment, including the level of danger and unpredictability (embodied in the experience of early stress) and the availability of adequate nutritional resources. In a nutshell, dangerous and unpredictable environments tend to favor strategies characterized by . . . impulsivity, risk taking, aggression, whereas safe and predictable environments tend to entrain slow strategies characterized by high self-control, aversion to risk, and prosociality.[1]

Economic disadvantages, racism, and other forms of adversity profoundly shape the lives of Black boys and youth (BBY). They require adaptations that accelerate development at multiple levels: neuroendocrine, psychological, behavioral, and social. At the neuro-endocrine level, danger and chronic stress stimulate the release of hormones such as cortisol, which over time can activate the adrenal cortex. This in turn increases blood levels of neurohormones which can trigger early physical maturation and are associated with increased levels of socio-emotional difficulties and behavioral problems. On a social and psychological level, material hardship and trauma can also result in BB taking on adultlike responsibilities within their families and place them in situations outside of the family in which they are treated as older and more mature than their chronological age. Under these conditions, BB may prematurely seek independence and gravitate toward settings in which they are able to engage in exciting but risky behaviors away from adult supervision and control. Behaviorally, a complex interaction of hormonal, psychological, familial, and social factors contribute to levels of opposition and aggression that in most children are more common in early adolescence than in middle childhood. Academically, prematurity may be expressed in

BBYs' disinvestment in education long before they are legally permitted to leave school, live independently, or support themselves financially.

Evidence that many BBY grow up faster than their peers is found in BBY early loss of innocence, their premature self-reliance, assumption of responsibility for themselves and others, and seeking independence far from the monitoring and supervision by responsible adults. (See Figure 7.1.) Explanations for why BB grow up fast, bypassing the Golden Age of middle childhood and exhibiting higher levels of behavior and emotional difficulties, reside somewhere in the complex interactions of biological vulnerabilities related to male gender and material deprivation as well as the social risks of adversity related to racism and financial hardship. Racism, material hardship, and the stress associated with them diminish physical and emotional well-being early in life and disrupt the acquisition of self-regulation and social competencies. Moreover, family responses to financial hardship often involve BBY assuming adult roles and responsibilities. Together they set off a chain of events that can account for why BBY grow up fast, suffer a loss of innocence, and gain independence before they are truly self-sufficient and ready for that responsibility. The process originates in the stressful sequelae of racism and financial hardship, which increase the likelihood of adverse events. High rates of adversity in turn continuously activate the stress response system and elevate levels of cortisol in the blood. Sustained elevations of cortisol stimulate premature adrenarche and early pubertal timing. Early

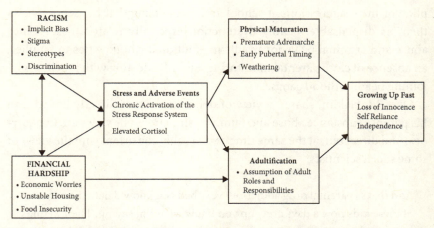

Figure 7.1 How Racism and Financial Adversity Affect BBY Development

pubertal timing may lead to engaging in associations and behaviors that are best left until they mature.

For some BBY, the outcome of growing up fast is not always negative. They respond to the challenges of growing up fast by behaving responsibly, doubling down on their academic pursuits, developing prosocial competencies, and caring for others. Others do not have such a positive resolution to this process. The stressors causing them to grow up fast lead them in a different direction toward irresponsible choices, diminished aspirations, school disengagement, and sometimes juvenile offending. For this group, the sequelae of racism, material hardship, and adversity are the catalysts for their skipping past the Golden Age of childhood onto a divergent path marked by behavioral and emotional difficulties.

Adversity in Family Life

The adverse effects of racism and financial hardship on boys' development are often amplified by family disorganization, dangerous and inefficacious communities, and attendance at failing schools.[2] These aspects of the social environment in turn are linked to chronic trauma, involving the frequent exposure to loss and other threats to well-being. Loss can come in the form of a family member, neighbor, or peer who is a victim—sometimes fatally—of random violence. It can occur when BB see family members arrested, threatened by neighborhood bullies, or harassed and disrespected by abusive collection agencies. It can come from BB experiencing disparate discipline or microaggressions at school and recognizing that the school views them as dispensable. Family dysfunction especially related to substance abuse and criminal behavior results in emotionally hollow ties to families, an absence of close parental monitoring, and BB's dealing with loneliness by joining neighborhood gangs.[3]

One BB, Hakim, shared a view of delinquency that directly linked it to his parent's substance abuse and family dysfunction. His views are unequivocal and direct but, at the same time, remarkably consistent with the views of some social scientists:

And that's [parental drug addiction] very bad you know. That's the way a lot of these kids now a days grew up you know what I'm saying. Their mama's been on drugs and stuff, and that's another reason why there's a lot of bad kids today, 'cause they see how their parents, their family is, your mom and your daddy on drugs, you ain't gonna, it's hard for you to, survive, 'cause they ain't gonna feed you. They too busy trying to get high. (Hakim, 17)[4]

Adversity, Trauma, and Stress

As seen in Chapter 3, chronic trauma is deleterious for BBY. As a consequence of it, some boys feel perpetually insecure and vulnerable with no one to protect them. Adverse environments do not always divert BB onto divergent behavioral pathways in middle childhood, but they force many to adapt to chronic threats by reflexively scanning their environment for possible signs of danger.[5] This results in a continual state of hypervigilance and arousal. Because they are hypersensitive to threat and danger, BB may become irritated and overreact to minor provocations from others. These dysregulated emotional responses are sometimes manifested in anger, aggression, and intermittent explosiveness. The effect of such responses on peer relations and relations with adults is chilling and predictable. Peers pull away and avoid boys. Adults at home and at school may not be sympathetic and may punish harshly.[6]

Because of the effects of adversity in their lives, not all BB experience middle childhood as a calm and predictable Golden Age. As noted in the Chapter 6, middle childhood for many BB is disturbed by rising rates of behavioral and emotional difficulties that might be characterized as "growing up too fast." Growing up fast means that BB actively seek out or are placed by their circumstances in situations that call for skills and psychosocial competencies that they have not yet fully mastered. It means that they cannot rely on anyone but themselves for protection and the acquisition of what they need and want. As a result of accelerated development, many BB skip right over this golden age of childhood. Instead, the BB developmental path is marked by a growth of social competencies during the preschool years (from birth to around age five), but this growth is stunted and declines relative to that of their peers in early elementary school (middle childhood, that is, the years from about six to 11).[7] At the same time, it bears repeating that the majority of BB do not develop serious behavior problems that meet the diagnostic criteria for conduct or oppositional defiance disorder.

In his book, *There Are No Children Here*, Alex Kotlowitz describes how stress and adversity in the lives of two BB living in an inner city Chicago neighborhood required them to grow up before their time.[8] The boys encountered an urgent imperative to grow up quickly because they saw so much violence and faced so much uncertainty about their very survival. For them, discussions of the future began with "*If* I grow up" rather than "*When* I grow up" because so many of their peers were killed, and life as adults was not a given. Clinging to childlike innocence was naïve and could prove deadly. To survive in their world, they had to remain alert to signals of danger and be ready to flee or fight at a moment's notice. Worry and fear were constant. They had to recognize the cues that a gun fight was imminent and avoid areas where danger was omnipresent. The pressure for survival meant growing up fast. There was also the pressure to give in to the illusory promise of safety and camaraderie by aligning with a neighborhood gang. Growing up fast was evident in the social, psychological, and physical indicators of the boys' development. These indicators included premature physical development (early onset adrenarche, pubertal timing, and cellular aging), social indicators (assumption of adultlike roles and responsibilities), and perceptions by others that BB were older than they were.

Shonkoff has proposed a conceptual framework that can help explain the atypical developmental trajectory of BBY.[9] He considers, in particular, how adversity creates the conditions for that development. Typically, genes provide a template for physical development. When an environment is auspicious, development follows a typical sequence, and it is usually a positive course. However, the inauspicious quality of BBY's environment shapes and redirects the path of that development. Material hardship, unsupportive social relations, and high levels of stress influence how the neural circuitry within the brain will form. In this way, genetic predispositions and early environments interact with one another to influence the adequacy of the foundation on which physical and emotional well-being depend. Shonkoff goes on to argue that gene environment interactions are coded and embedded in the body as "biological memories." These biological memories affect self-regulation of behavior and emotions, and result from epigenetic modifications, manifested within brain circuitry and physiological systems responsible for stress management, immunological responsiveness, metabolic and neuroendocrine regulation, and cardiovascular integrity.

Adversity-related stress can come from multiple sources: familial and social environments that are harsh or neglectful, unsafe or toxic physical environments, and inadequate nutrition. These sources of adversity interact with genetic predispositions to impact BBY's physiological and psychological functioning. Physiological functioning includes metabolic, neuroendocrine, cardiovascular, immune, and brain systems. Deficits in these systems in turn adversely affect physical health, making diabetes, cardiovascular disease, and poorer emotional functioning more likely.[10]

Elevated Cortisol in Response to Chronic Stress

As we have already noted in Chapter 3, cortisol is a key player in the body's response to stress. When BB experience stress, the body's "fight or flight" response is activated, which triggers the release of cortisol from the adrenal glands and thus increases glucose levels in the blood. It is these increased glucose levels which give the body the burst of energy it needs to react to the stressor.[11] The chronic adversity BB often experience can lead to sustained high levels of cortisol in the body, which can have negative effects on physical and mental health. For example, sustained high levels of cortisol have been linked to elevated blood pressure, impaired immune function, and decreased bone density. Cortisol can also affect mood and cognitive function, contributing to symptoms of anxiety and depression. High cortisol levels may also lead to changes in the tempo of physical development with respect to puberty.

Elevated Cortisol and Early Onset of Adrenarche

Chronically high levels of cortisol, generated in response to stress, can stimulate the production of androgens, a class of hormones that includes testosterone, DHEA, and DHEA-S which can trigger the onset of adrenarche prematurely.[12] These hormones are associated in particular with the growth of pubic hair, oily skin and hair, and an adultlike body odor. Secretions of these adrenal androgens typically occur within a wide window between ages six and 11. For some children, this process occurs early in life and increases quickly, while for others it takes place later and unfolds more slowly over time. Compared to other groups of boys of the same age, BB five to 12 years old had lower testosterone levels overall but higher testosterone reactivity to stress.[13]

Early onset adrenarche is a risk factor for high rates and increased intensity of conduct and emotional problems in boys.[14] For example, high levels of testosterone and DHEA-S in eight- and nine-year-old boys are associated with emotional and behavioral problems. Higher than normal levels of testosterone are also associated with more conduct, emotional, and social problems, particularly in young boys and adolescents.[15] These can take the form of aggression and other externalizing behaviors in male adolescents;[16] moodiness in males nine to 12 years old; and low sociability and poor peer relations in boys three- to eight years old.[17] Higher concentrations of testosterone in the umbilical cord are also related to attention problems in boys ages five to 10, indicating a sex-specific effect and a long-term effect of early testosterone exposure.[18] These hormones had a different effect for girls. For girls, higher DHEA-S was associated with problems in peer relations.[19]

Although the evidential base has yet to be establish, we speculate here about a link among adversity, cortisol reactivity and early onset adrenarche as a possible contributor to the fast development observed among a subset of BB. How is this possible? The exact mechanisms linking stress to premature adrenarche and to behavior problems are not fully understood. DelGuidice speculates that adrenarche acts like a developmental switch in which the resulting behaviors differ depending on environmental conditions.[20] For example, when environments are stable and safe, adrenarche is associated with low aggression. When the environment is threatening or violent, however, environmental adaptation during adrenarche leans toward higher levels of aggression.[21] Thus, accumulated stressors of environmental risks associated with poverty may explain BB's shift from a rather typical early development to a high prevalence of socio-emotional difficulties that arise in middle childhood and place boys at risk for behavioral and emotional maladjustment.

Early Pubertal Timing

The evidence about the early timing of puberty in BBY offers some basis for speculation about the role of early onset adrenarche which can affect pubertal timing. The evidence regarding the relation of pubertal timing, hormone secretion and behavior is stronger. The timing of puberty can vary widely between individuals and is influenced by a range of factors such as social environment, nutrition, and physical activity. Boys as a group are growing and maturing faster than in the past.[22] Although the data are not entirely consistent in that not all studies report evidence of racial difference in the onset of puberty,[23] there is considerable evidence to suggest that Black boys may experience a form of accelerated development that results in their maturing physically more quickly than White boys. For example, Borges and colleagues found that BB entered puberty earlier than White boys.[24] Similarly, Mendez and Hillman report evidence of the early onset of puberty in BB.[25] By fifth grade 81% of BB had begun or were far along in pubertal change as reflected in body and facial hair, skin changes, and growth spurts.[26] Almost one-third of BB ages 13–17 years old perceived themselves as looking older than their same-age peers. Argabright and colleagues report evidence of accelerated pubertal development in BB (mean age 10.9).[27] Compared to other groups, more than twice as many BB under 11 were in late puberty though the numbers in both cases were small (3.6% of BB vs 1.5% of non-Black boys). Similar results were reported by Rice and colleagues.[28]

There is strong evidence that early puberty has consequences for behavior and emotional functioning. The onset of puberty involves the maturation of the adrenal gland and the production of androgens, or male hormones. These are associated with increases in emotional difficulties, antisocial behavior, and social competence. Early pubertal changes have been associated with depressive symptoms among BB in fifth grade. Among boys with early onset puberty, social competence increased when they had access to positive parenting. Conversely, problem behaviors were more likely to occur in the presence of deviant peers, negative school experiences, harsh parenting, and neighborhood disorganization.[29] As well, early pubertal timing of Black males is associated with the experience of racial discrimination.[30]

Weathering: Premature Aging of Telomeres

Accelerated development in BB has also been suggested by research on telomeres. Telomeres are repetitive DNA sequences at the ends of chromosomes that protect the genetic information within a cell. They act like the plastic tips at the end of shoelaces, preventing the chromosome ends from fraying and sticking to each other. Telomeres naturally shorten as we age to the point where they are no longer effective in protecting the chromosomes. Telomere length is considered a useful biomarker of both aging and health, as it reflects the cumulative effects of various biological and lifestyle factors on our bodies over time. Shorter telomeres are related to cellular aging, poorer immune function, a risk for age-related diseases (such as cancer and cardiovascular diseases), and shorter life spans. Conversely, longer telomeres have been associated with better health outcomes, including increased lifespan and improved cognitive function.

Emotional distress associated with adversity and economic disadvantage may contribute to this accelerated cellular aging in children.[31] For example, studies have found that children from low-income families had shorter telomeres compared to those from higher-income families. Shorter telomeres have also been used as an indicator of the effects of chronic disadvantage and stress. Several studies have shown that Black males who experience more racial discrimination and material deprivation related to a low socio-economic status have shorter telomeres compared to others of the same age.[32] Similarly, Black children who grew up in poverty had shorter telomeres compared to other children who did not.[33]

Assumption of Adultlike Roles and Responsibilities

Adrenarche occurs at a time when children in many societies are expected to take on greater responsibility for self-care, caretaking of others, and contributing to work in the household. For the 75% of BB who reside in households led by a single mother, these responsibilities may come early. Mothers' work schedules require many to leave their sons at home with the responsibility to feed, care for, and accompany younger siblings to and from school.[34] When fathers are not present, BBY often assume the role of "man of the house" and provide reassurance and emotional support to their mothers as best they can. Boys may shield mothers from berating by landlords and browbeating of collection agencies over unpaid bills. Take for example a passage from *The Other Wes Moore*, in which the author is distressed at the sight of Mary, his mother, sobbing over having to quit college and surrender her dreams of a better life due to elimination of her need-based financial aid.

> When Mary saw Wes standing there, one hand flew to her face to wipe her eyes. The other slid a sheet of paper under her leg. [He knew] something was wrong... He wanted to ask what was wrong but decided against pressing his mother... The letter Mary was hiding explained that the federal budget for... Pell Grants was being slashed and her grant was being terminated... Mary realized the letter effectively closed the door on her college aspirations... Wes went to check on his mother again. He felt he had to take care of her: his father had been a ghost since his birth... Wes

was the man of the house. As Mary wiped her still-damp face ... She just had to quickly recalibrate her ambitions."[35]

Wes was sensitive to the pain and life-changing disappointment his mother felt in the moment. His empathy for her was palpable and he was saddened by what he saw but was helpless to do something that mattered that could change the situation for the better. Wes felt responsible for helping her and easing her pain but what was required was beyond what a young boy could do or even understand. There was no way Wes could get her the funds she needed to pursue her dream of a better life through a college education. He was helpless and in a bind because he saw the problem, he owned his role in helping to solve it, but had not the capacity to do so.

Black mothers like Mary often try not to burden their sons and instead turn to their own mothers, their sisters, or a girlfriend for advice and support. Nevertheless, a son sometimes becomes a close confidant and a readily available source of support. Many respond to the needs of their mothers and family without hesitation, even though at their young ages they are very limited in what they can do.

Premature Self-Reliance and Independence of Action

For many practical reasons—often related to parents' work schedules, their need for help, and their emotional distress—families value, permit, and encourage BB to be independent early. One youth reflected on his past and how he grew up too fast, succumbed to negative peer influence and in his case took on behaviors that were troublesome but that allowed him to fit in and survive:

> I just wanted to be grown and do what I wanted to do. Well, a lot of gang activity was going on in the neighborhood. I got influenced by a lot of my peers and then just not listening to my mother. And you know it just drug me down. My friends wasn't doing nothing in school, so I wasn't doing nothing too. (Demarius, 17)[36]

Chronic fighting during middle childhood is an ineffective strategy for resolving peer conflict and is often a gateway to more serious behavior problems. Most Black families teach their sons not to start fights. However, sometimes fighting is necessary to protect themselves or their siblings. However, families may encourage their sons to fight back to protect themselves and their siblings. They often advise their sons: "If someone hits you, fight back or they will continue to hit you." Too often young boys are not able to distinguish the difference between starting a fight and defending oneself. The line between the two is often blurred in peer interactions. For some BB, like Ron, fighting is part of a pattern of premature and disruptive behaviors that place them on a negative trajectory toward serious problems

> I started growing up (sic early) for my age. I started skipping school. I started fighting. Then I got kicked out for fighting and causing problems. So, then my mother put me into a counseling program for about two weeks.... then things were going all right for a couple of weeks then I started getting back bad. (Ron, 17)

BB may receive guidance about behavior at home that diverges from expectations and rules at school. At school, they are infantilized in that they are neither expected nor allowed to help themselves to food and materials or to claim a space as their own. They must wait until an adult allocates these. They cannot initiate activities on their own but must wait until a teacher signals that they may do so. If someone hits them and takes something away by force, they must not retaliate but should resolve the issue non-violently or bring it to the attention of an adult to sort out. Most families have relatively loose rules about where a child can be positioned physically, the posture they must assume, and their ability to talk to others or argue to assert their perceived rights, but in schools these social interactions are tightly scripted and controlled, carefully orchestrated, and not following the prescribed approach can result in some disciplinary action. School rules cover so many aspects of self and identity that are not subject to scrutiny or control at home. For example, school codes of student conduct dictate acceptable behavior and expression of emotions, BBY dress, their movement through space and their attitudes.[37] School rules determine where BB can be at what time, for how long, how they must comport themselves, and carry and control their bodies (sitting, standing, reclining, running, jumping, swaying; eating, drinking, and going to the bathroom) in those places. This stands in stark contrast to the freedom of movement they experience at home, where they spend a great deal of time alone and form their own rules about where to be, what to do, and how to do it. Many BB have difficulty adjusting to the tighter constraints on behavior at school. This can lead to BBY being viewed as oppositional and out of control.

Seeking and Gaining Independence

Along with the assumption of adultlike roles, parents often grant boys freedom from close monitoring. They are permitted to be out and about on their own exploring their neighborhood long before they are ready for such independence. For their part, BB often seek and relish independence that places them in settings out of the view and control of adults, settings dominated by same-age or older peers that convey a sense of freedom not afforded at home or school. BB have this independence either because parents are not around to supervise or because of gender-based practices that allow freedom of movement to males more than to their female siblings.

Often this is more freedom than BB can handle responsibly. In the absence of close supervision and guidance from parents or adult mentors, they make poor choices, place themselves in risky situations, and fail to anticipate the consequence of their actions. This is particularly true for the subset of boys who engage in predelinquent shoplifting and experimentation with alcohol, tobacco, and marijuana. They are left on their own a lot; they are allowed to wander and explore the neighborhood on their own. Parents are not there to protect them, so as a consequence they must find ways to protect and keep themselves safe. They are exposed to random neighborhood violence and left on their own and to their own wits to survive when out in the community. At the same time, although they are seen as older and take on the role of an adult, they lack life experience. In some ways, they have moved directly from the terrible twos—where responses to requests are usually an emphatic "No"—to unreachable teens who respond more to peer pressure than they do to adult proscriptions and guidance.

Self-Reliance

For BB, the quest for independence is motivated not only by the possibility of having fun that adults would not permit, but also by an awareness of having to be responsible for their own well-being. Early on, BB discover the painful truth that as much as parents may want to and try to, they cannot guarantee their sons' safety. Parents cannot protect them from random community violence and the despair of economic insecurity. Parents can no longer be the secure base and offer protection from harm, as they did for infants and toddlers. To survive in the neighborhood, BBY understand that they must master and adopt the code of the street where reputation and respect are everything—and sometimes the difference between life and death.[38]

The drive to maintain respect from others is so great that it is worth the risk of dying. Disrespect must be responded to, often lethally, if one is to survive in their neighborhoods. This realization means that boys understand that when they are out and about in the community, they are largely left to their own wits to survive. They are on their own. Because of this, at school they may overreact to perceived threats or slight provocations and attribute hostile intentions to others. They have difficulty sorting through a chain of threats, accusations, and slights that can give rise to their animosity. When fights break out between boys in middle childhood, it is common for each boy to point to the other as the one who started the fight, and they often get into trouble and are disciplined because of this inability to discern their own role in the initiation and continuance of conflict.

Loss of Innocence

As a consequence of family circumstances, Black boys accelerate toward adolescence and adultlike roles for which they are often ill-equipped and unprepared.[39] The adultification of BB strips them of the protections most children receive. They are expected to act like adults more often than their White counterparts. BBY are often not afforded the protections of childhood extended to other children, such as the presumption of innocence, dependence, and vulnerability, that call for supportive responses from adults when children are in distress or emotionally disorganized. As a consequence of these biased perceptions, even little BB are feared and perceived as threatening and adultlike instead of as frightened children who need to be pulled closer and comforted emotionally.

To some adults, their early maturity justifies treating BBY like adults themselves and imposing adultlike consequences on them for their misbehavior. At times, BBY appear so mature and secure in their masculine identity that it is easy to forget that they are children—not men—and that they are just boys often searching, playful, and unsure of themselves. Teachers may be alarmed by boys displaying masculine bravado, imitating the menacing posture of "gangsta" rappers, fighting with each other in ways that start out as consensual play, and engaging in boisterous social exchanges. Teachers may react to the tantrum of a diminutive four-year-old BB with a level of fear more appropriate to the threat of serious physical harm from an adult. Their loudness and aggressive posturing may be misinterpreted as dangerous even when it is symbolic, exaggerated, well-rehearsed, and choreographed play. As a consequence, BB lose and are deprived of the presumption of playfulness, innocence, and naivete that is granted to other children in middle childhood. BB are more likely to be labeled as "troublemakers" by their teachers and seen as deserving of disciplinary action and punishment in the criminal justice system. BBY are 18 times more likely to be tried as adults than their White counterparts.[40] Thus, there is converging evidence that Black boys are seen as older and less innocent than their White peers.

Each of these indicators is thought to be set in motion by conditions characterized by stress, deprivation, and adversity. The outcomes are especially negative when adversity is chronic and occurs from birth. Individuals exposed to more unpredictable, unstable environments during the first five years of life grow up faster, and by age 23, have had more sexual partners, engaged in more aggressive and delinquent behaviors, and are more likely to be associated with criminal activities than their peers who have not experienced the same conditions.[41]

In summary, chronic stress and adversity are major contributors to the atypical developmental trajectory of BBY that is associated with accelerated physical and psychological development. BB are given adult responsibilities at home, seek independence from adult monitoring, and come to be viewed as older and more mature and responsible than they really are. Instead of having the benefit of innocence in middle childhood, they are viewed as culpable and treated like adults outside of the family. Thus, growing up in environments that are chronically stressful arguably influences gene expression and the timing of physical maturation, brain architecture, and neuroendocrine functioning. These in turn influence the development of executive functions, emotional responses to stress, and the capacity to regulate behavior to conform to societal expectations. For some BBY these conditions, combined with their efforts to overcome material hardship, may leave them susceptible to living life on the margins—outside of school and just on the other side of legal behavior.

Notes

1. Del Guidice (2014) p. 197.
2. Evans et al. (2005).
3. Hirschi (1969).
4. Barbarin (1995).
5. Not all BB fall into this danger; some are resilient in the face of adversity and instead develop competencies which sustain their positive adaptation to school, home, and community.
6. Barbarin & Crawford (2006).
7. For example, in a nationally representative sample of Black boys, Brown, Barbarin, and Scott (2013) found that about 88% were low in internalizing symptoms and remained so from K through fifth grade. Young BB are rated highly on an absolute basis by teachers on self-regulation (Barbarin et al., 2013), and effortful control (Clincy & Mills-Koonce, 2013). Moreover, in a study that included girls and White boys, Barbarin (2013) found both that BB were rated as proficient in social competence in an absolute sense and that they did not differ from White boys. The issue here is the disparate and high levels of externalizing difficulties—not 100%, but rates two and three times that of peers.
8. Kotlowitz (1991).
9. Shonkoff (2010).
10. Shonkoff (2010).
11. Idkowiak et al. (2011).
12. Del Guidice (2014).
13. Drury et al. (2014).
14. Mundy et al.(2015); van Goosen et al. (2000).
15. van Goozen et al. (1998) p. 6.
16. van Goozen et al. (1998).
17. Strong & Dabbs (2000).
18. Robinson et al. (2013).
19. Maras et al. (2003).
20. Del Guidice (2014).
21. El-Sheikh et al. (2007).
22. Karpati et al. (2002).
23. Bleil et al. (2018).
24. The study used data from the National Health and Nutrition Examination Survey to analyze the timing of puberty in a group of boys aged eight to 19 years old. See Borges et al. (2018).
25. Mendez & Hillman (2015).
26. Ge et al. (2006).
27. Argabright et al. (2022).
28. Rice et al. (2018).
29. Klopack et al. (2020).
30. Argabright et al. (2022).
31. Wade et al.(2020) p. 3.
32. Chae et al. (2014).
33. Mitchell et al. (2014).
34. Cooke & Halberstadt (2021).
35. Moore (2014) pp.16–17.
36. This quote and all adolescent quotes are from a qualitative research project (Barbarin, 1995).
37. Ferguson (2001).
38. Anderson (1999).
39. Cooke & Halberstadt (2021).
40. See Goff et al. (2014); Okonofua & Eberhardt (2015).
41. Simpson et al. (2012).

PART IV
ORIGINS OF SERIOUS PROBLEM BEHAVIOR

8
Loss, Trauma, and Problem Behavior

Black boys and youth (BBY) who have become chronic problems have often developed reputations at school as fighters and rule-breakers. The urgency to maintain safety and order make school staff more concerned about controlling this misbehavior than understanding its etiology. Yet, unless we understand the factors that contribute to these serious behavior problems we will be unable to engage them preemptively with prevention efforts and thus confining society responses to punishment and continuing to experience exorbitant rates of recidivism and failure with repeat offenders. Understanding what drives misbehavior may contribute to success in redirecting offenders onto a prosocial path. Adversity, particularly early in life, is a major culprit and a common feature of boys who are troubled and in trouble. Life history interviews of BY involved in chronic behavior problems are replete with reports of loss and trauma, especially early in life. This chapter considers the proposition that the origins of chronic behavior problems, which seem to emerge in middle childhood and worsen during adolescence, might be linked to those losses and the emotional trauma that accompanies them. This proposition diverges from explanations offered by sociologists or criminologists who typically focus on the role of individual pathology, such as psychopathic personalities, deviant peers, or macro-level factors such as limited opportunity structures, racially disparate police surveillance, neighborhood disorganization, or antisocial values.[1] The evidence supporting these and other causes is not disputed here. Instead, this chapter offers an analysis that draws attention to the interpersonal and psychological mechanisms that explain at a deeper level and that may connect these distal or systemic causes to BBY's behavior.

Racism, poverty, and the adverse childhood events associated with them are common sources of loss and trauma for BBY. Poverty in particular is associated, for example, with parental conflict, separation, and divorce; father absence or noninvolvement; parental neglect; exposure to violence at home and in neighborhoods; while racism is associated with a loss of innocence. Many BBY experience loss due to voluntary and involuntary separations from primary caregivers because of employment, incarceration, war, hospitalization, or death. Dismissive or demeaning racial microaggressions give rise to a demoralizing loss of self-confidence and undermine a sense of personal worth.[2] These losses cause stress and trauma that can be visualized as an emotional wound, an injury that impairs healthy functioning and development. The wounds resulting from the trauma may heal but they can leave scars that undermine healthy behavioral and emotional functioning. They increase the risk of BBY landing on a path leading to serious behavior problems, disengagement from school, and involvement in illegal activity. In conceptualizing these experiences as a loss that causes psychological trauma for BBY, it becomes possible to speak to the psychological processes which connect distal social and financial disadvantages to serious behavior problems of BBY.

To have a proper, broader, and balanced perspective on the words of these BY, we must take a moment to add important context. This chapter presents observations of family life from BBY who represent an extreme minority of BY. Less than 3% of BY are involved in serious offenses involving a combination of fighting, stealing, drug-selling, and handgun possession.[3] All of the respondents whose words are presented below have been adjudicated and sentenced for serious and chronic violations of law by juvenile court to an intensive treatment program. They represent a small subset of BY and families. Their struggles are illuminating but should not be regarded as representative or typical of BY and their families. Though a tiny fraction of BBY, they provide a valuable window onto the environmental factors, including racism and poverty, that contribute to behavioral difficulties, some of which end in serious juvenile offending. These accounts of families in distress are painful to read. They reveal the difficulties and impediments some families face in caring for their sons (e.g., substance abuse, incarceration, depression, parental absence, as well as inadequate support and supervision from parents). They also include reported feelings of loneliness due to parental absence caused by multiple job commitments, premature adult responsibilities that force BB to mature too quickly, and instances of physical abuse.

It is important to allow that the approaches they take may represent families' only viable options when coping with their own trauma, loss, and financial constraints. Acknowledging these hardships and problems in Black families should not be equated with blaming these families for them. In including these observations, the intent is to represent the unadulterated accounts of BBY family life from their perspective and to contextualize these accounts within a broader framework of loss, trauma, and financial distress that families grapple with. This chapter makes no excuses for the choices families make, nor does it assign blame.

Psychological Effects of Separation and Loss

John Bowlby was among the first social scientists to theorize and gather evidence which supports the association of serious behavior problems with traumatic loss, particularly in the form of separation from and loss of primary caregivers with whom the child has developed a secure attachment.[4] Secure attachment, he argued, fosters in the child a belief that he is important and matters to someone who will look out and care for him. The assurance of safety, protection, and responsive nurturance that comes from attachment security militates against the development of serious behavior problems. To test this thesis, Bowlby completed assessments of young children, mostly boys, who were adjudicated for behaviors that included truancy, stealing, and chronic dishonesty.[5] Bowlby learned that these children were much more likely than other children to have experienced prolonged separation from their mothers or caregivers because of parental desertion, out-of-home child placement, illness, or death, especially in the first five years of life. Separation and loss, especially when it occurred before the age of 3, left children distressed, sad, despairing, detached, and angry later in life. The loss diminished their ability to express affection and left them feeling abandoned. It increased the likelihood of emotional difficulties. Disappointment connected with this loss made them hesitant to trust and to enter emotionally intimate relationships in the future. While delinquent children demonstrated superficial congeniality, they were less likely to become emotionally close to others and would push away people trying to get close to them. They displayed little warmth in interactions with others and rarely expressed genuine affection. Once bitten, twice shy. Moreover, they did not display normal affection, shame, or a sense of responsibility for their actions and were unable to sustain long-term friendships.

Black Boys' Own Perspectives

To what extent are Bowlby's theory and research on the effect of the trauma of an early loss of caregiving applicable and useful for understanding the effects of the wider array of losses and trauma BBY experience? Loss or disruption of caregiving is a critical factor linking loss, trauma, and delinquent behavior. The caregiving system for BBY can be construed as broader than just a biological parent or single caregiver. Other family members, school staff, and neighborhood residents can also be part of the caregiving and monitoring system that BBY need and come to rely on for safety, protection, and guidance. Accordingly, access to involved, nurturing adults is key to BBY positive development. Disruption, neglect, and dysfunction at home, in school, and in the neighborhood deprive BBY of relations they need to function and place them at risk of serious behavior problems.

Reflections shared by BY suggest that they perceived a link between disruptions of the care system and their status as juvenile offenders. Consistent with the research, BY attributed their delinquent behavior to factors such as stress in family life, antisocial peers, and disengagement from school. They rarely labeled these as trauma or loss specifically, but their accounts were replete with descriptions of traumatic events. They also identified factors not commonly noted by researchers: namely, loneliness, the excitement of street life, and the desire to be independent and free from the suffocating control of school and family. The reflections of BY that are presented next constitute important idiographic accounts and insiders' perspectives on the forces that pushed BY toward problem behavior as well as the supports that have enabled them to turn away from an antisocial life on the streets.

Separation and Loss at Home

For many BBY, loss takes the form of father-absence due to parental separation, divorce, or abandonment. In some cases, where fathers do not reside with a child, mothers are also absent from home during much of that child's waking hours. Many parents are stuck in low-wage work that requires them to juggle multiple jobs to cover expenses. Solo parents, usually mothers, are forced to make difficult choices between working long hours to pay for necessities and being at home enough to care for and supervise their children. For BBY, this means a loss of support and having to spend long stretches of time without an adult around.

> Mama used to always be gone. We'd be at home, just me and my brother and her boyfriend would be upstairs. She was always at work or at school. She was gone a lot. We didn't have that much time with her. (Alonzo, 13)

There is a tinge of unexpressed sadness over this loss even though Alonzo could rationalize why. In Alonzo's case, his mother was also taking college courses so that she could qualify for a higher paying job and struggle less with finances. However, this meant that she was less available to help her son when he needed her, and he had to rely on his own wit to solve the problems he encountered.

Because of their burdens, mothers who are the solo caregiver often are not able to arrange optimal childcare while they are working away from home. As a result, they have to choose between hunger, homelessness, and the risk that their children might not be well-cared-for, as in the case of Ron who reported:

> My Mom used to work a lot. She used to work at night and go to school in the afternoon. We didn't have that much time with her. We was either with my grandfather or with somebody else. I didn't like being at my grandfather's house that much.... he was mean. (Ron, 13)

Disrupted parental relationships are ubiquitous in reports by BB who have been designated as youthful offenders. Most reported losing their father at an early age. For some, like Phillip, the loss occurred as a consequence of the death of his father.

> My mother wasn't there. She wasn't there. She was working to pay all the bills and stuff because my father died. It was mostly, me and my older sister at home at night, my mom was still working late. (Phillip, 12)

Phillip seemed to accept that fact that there had been a change in the family since his father's death, and the burden of supporting the family fell entirely on his mother. Phillip experienced the loss of his father through death and the loss of his mother to work. For others like James, parental loss was due to a choice his mother made to use drugs to which she subsequently became addicted.

> My mother, she abusing drugs so she and my father separated when I was nine. I live with my father, but I didn't like to spend time at my home because my father, he work a lot, you know, after he get off work, he go to sleep. He weren't really nobody that I can feel I can go and talk to. (James, 15)

So in the end, James too experienced a double loss, his mother to addiction, his father to work.

Sometimes the tension between parents is so great that life is better and feels safer when one of the parents is not present. In the case of Jerome, this was due to his father's alcoholism.

> My father wasn't in the house. He had drinking problems. I know that he just used to come over drunk. When he would come over, him and my mom would be arguing or something like that. He used to scare me. (Jerome, 14)

For Jerome, his father is a figure with whom there is an avoidant attachment. The father is a source of fear rather than a refuge and harbinger of safety. This represents another type of disruption in the caregiving system.

Traumatic loss can also result from a significant change in the family's living situation and economic status. As another BY reports, there was a noted contrast between the good times, when his father was supporting the family before his parents divorced (due to his father's addiction) and the current difficult times after his father was no longer in the home and offering support.

> Before I entered school and I was real little? Yeah, ah, before I started school, everything was straight, I mean we all stayin' together, me and my mother, and my father and both of my sisters, everything was going well, I got nice clothes, food, stuff like that. Far as I can remember I had a great life when I was little. I think about Christmas a lot. That was always a good memory, every Christmas. It was really the toys and happy to have my family there. It is very different now. (Jamal, 15)

Disruptive changes in family life may also result from tensions and conflict between parents that leads to the loss of the presence of a parent in BB's life. These tensions may spill over into violence and violence to separation.

> My father was living with us for a while until they (my mother and father) started having fights and stuff like that, so he moved out. Well soon after that one uncle got killed, then my other uncle went to jail for second degree murder. (James, 17)

For James, the impact of the loss of a stable household is amplified by the loss of family members due to violence and incarceration. Loss and trauma are especially devastating if these occur as the result of some disruption after a stable period when life has been good. Sometimes, due to a mother's absence and the lack of adult supervision, things get out of control and siblings are left to resolve conflicts on their own, sometimes with disastrous consequences.

> My mother was almost always away at work. There was a lot of fighting between me and my sister. Like one time we was fighting, she hit me with this scale in the bathroom that you weigh yourself on. She hit me in my chest with that. I hit her with a brand new bottle of Scope (mouthwash).
> Another time she locked me out of the house, and it's like, in our door, it's like a little glass window. She wouldn't let me in, so I punched that window in. Cut myself.
> One time me and my sister was fighting, I hit her with the thing you water the plants with, and it cut her arm open. (Kobe, 15)

Kobe demonstrates the palpable effect of parental loss. In the absence of parental presence to help manage the conflict, youth may learn the lesson that aggression is an acceptable way to negotiate differences in intimate settings.

In addition to sibling conflict, parental loss can require BBY taking on adult responsibilities that go beyond their maturity and abilities. Because parents spend long hours away at work and are not able to guide and supervise their children, boys can also face increasing responsibility that alters their lives, creating a situation in which there is a reversal of roles and a loss of childhood because the caregiving system itself requires care.

My mother by herself. You know my father left, so we had to struggle, you know what I'm saying, as a family just us three, you know what I'm saying. We had to... She has been visually impaired since she was 17... for a period she couldn't do any work, you know. So, me and my oldest brother we had to do things around the house that, you know what I'm saying, normal kids wouldn't do but we had to do. (Jamari, 14)

Family Adversity as Loss

Stress in family life arises from multiple sources: parental dysfunction, weak emotional ties, and the failure of parental monitoring that leaves space for entanglement with antisocial peer groups.[6] This often means that the parent is completely oblivious to and unable to respond to and monitor the boy's needs and behavior. The BBY realizes that he must not only fend for himself but may also have to be a caregiver and perhaps rescue the parent from the effects of an overdose. In all this can be a frightening situation that is overwhelming for the child. The disruptiveness of family problems can be so complex, and come from so many directions, that a BBY's home life becomes so unpleasant and unpredictable that refuge is found in the streets.

I got adapted to the streets, and I didn't want to be at home. I rather hang out in the streets with my friends than at home. So many bad things happened when I was little... When I got about 9, 10, my mother started using drugs.... When I was 13 my oldest sister, the one that had the baby, she had got locked up in jail for murdering her boyfriend's girlfriend. She was pretty easy-going most of the time but she... her boyfriend's messing around on her so... that's what she felt she had to retaliate for. (Zach, 16)

By this point, his parents had relinquished whatever influence they once had over Zach's behavior. Zach did not accept or comply with rules which were haphazardly enforced. He ignored parental admonitions to do schoolwork and stay out of trouble. Instead, he embraced the values and behavior standards of the street. Zach's case illustrates how adverse events occur together in ways that multiply their effects. The loss of his mother to substance abuse was compounded by the effect of losing his sister to incarceration. Traumatic loss occurs in different ways—some direct, some indirect. The impact of these family events for Zach occurred vicariously in that he was not the substance user or the incarcerated one, but the sadness they created was still palpable.

Loss can also take the form of a lack of family cohesion evidenced in relationships between a child and family members that are frayed by sibling conflict and parental disengagement as described by Robert.

> Lot of us in the family kept our distance. My brother, he'd go into his room, close his door. I'd leave my door open, but my Ma, she'd go upstairs, and she'd go to sleep. That's what took place most of the time. Then my mother, when I'd do something wrong, my mother and brother would go together, and they would get me locked up; like when she beat me, they tied me up. My brother helped her. My brother would help her whoop me and stuff like that. I started disliking him. (Robert, 17)

Some of the experiences BBY recount are unimaginably horrifying, wrenching, and traumatic:

> My mom had a boyfriend. I was raped by my mom's boyfriend's son when I was little. (Robert, 13)

The experiences of violence, helplessness, and confusion from being preyed upon as a young and vulnerable child are haunting and likely to lead to enduring emotional scars that will distort a boy's view of himself, undermine his trust of others, and create resentment toward the adults who did not protect him.

Speedo Green: Loss, Trauma, and Redemption

Ryan Speedo Green exemplifies how early trauma sets the stage for later difficulty. Like many of his peers, he grew up fatherless, destitute, and in a trailer park. He was filled with sadness and pent-up anger. His troubled early life included violent conflict with family members, particularly his mother. One day, in a fit of rage, he attempted to attack her with a knife. Police were called, he was arrested, sentenced to juvenile detention, and placed in a special alternative school. At the age of 12, he found himself in solitary confinement at the juvenile facility time and again due to his uncontrolled outbursts. He was full of rage and hate. Every other word out of his mouth was a filthy, angry curse. When transferred to a special school, he was still a seething cauldron of anger. He was mad at the world. He resisted efforts by anyone to control him. He refused to cooperate and follow instructions.

On his first day at the special school, he confronted the teacher and yelled, "I will not be taught by a f'ing white woman!" In a fit of anger, he threw his chair and overturned the table where they were to work. Apparently, this was not the first time she was confronted by an angry young BB. She did not reciprocate his emotional outburst or interpret his actions as a challenge to her authority. She did not display fear, show anger, or try to leave the room. She did not yell. She did not call for the guards to come and take him away. Her response was composed, measured, and calculated. Instead, she looked at him intently, sensing the fear underlying his explosive emotional outburst, and calmly said, "OK, when you are ready not to throw your chair at anyone you may have it back." In the meantime, they worked together sitting on the floor.

That was the opening gambit for his many attempts to test, push away, and challenge her. She responded to each with calm composure. Whenever he gave her an opening, she used the opportunity to ask whether everything was all right at home and talked about what was going on with him, what was wrong, and why he was so angry. Not all at once, but over time, he opened up and things began to turn around. Eventually he broke down and admitted to her that things were not okay. He talked about a stormy relationship with his single mom, and how difficult it was to grow up next to a drug house and be surrounded by people who might steal from, threaten, or hurt you. Through their conversations, for the first time in his life, he came to feel safe and as if someone recognized something redeemable and worth saving in him. Most importantly, she seemed to like him. Indeed, after he was transferred from the alternative school to the regular public school, she stayed in contact with him and became someone he could call when things got difficult or when there was something to celebrate.

Loss and Trauma Outside of the Home

Not all the loss experienced by youthful offenders occurs in the home. It can also come from sources outside of the family, from school and from the neighborhood. Attending school offers many challenges for BBY, particularly those who enter school with few of the characteristics valued by schools, such as an easy facility with language and emergent literacy skills and the ability to manage behavior, follow rules, and get along with peers. Many BB who initially have difficulties adjusting to the routines at school learn to do so eventually. Those who need a longer time to accommodate face the risk of being labeled troubled and may be destined for a position in the preschool-to-prison pipeline described eloquently by Ferguson in her book, *Bad Boys*.[7] The behavior of these BB is often misinterpreted, and they have few opportunities to have their strengths acknowledged and their efforts and accomplishments celebrated. They suffer the psychologically numbing effect of being insignificant and invisible except when in trouble. The emotions and distress they experience from trauma and loss at home are not recognized and appropriately remediated. Schools resort to strengthening the presence of police with arrest powers rather than mental health counselors and social workers. BBY's instances of emotional distress, expressed in episodes of anger, rule-breaking, or aggression, are not seen as teachable moments. BBY face the subtle hardship of being labeled and are subjected to being sidelined academically and separated out from the mainstream into classrooms labeled "special education," which often are more like holding tanks where instruction is anything but special and educational.

> And they, they ain't learnin', they ain't learnin nothin', I got friends today, friends today, that can't, that's my age, can't even read, can't write, can't do nothin', you know, 'cause all they ever did in their life was sell drugs, you know, that's the only thing they know how to do, you know. They can't even say, well they seventeen now, they can't say, I'm gonna stop and go to school now. (Prince, 13)

The situation is even worse if they are assigned to failing schools where safety is fleeting due to bullying and other forms of violence. BBY are disproportionately referred to the office for disciplinary reasons and given in-school and out-of-school suspensions. Moreover, they are more likely than other groups of children to be arrested and referred to the juvenile justice system for behavior problems at school.

Things may be no better in the neighborhood. BB who are poor live in neighborhoods that the poor can afford. These neighborhoods often reinforce values consistent with the use of violence to maintain respect and retribution for real or perceived slights.[8]

> The neighborhood I grew up in always been rotten. Um, when my oldest sister was growin' up it was rotting but you know, for me and my other sister ... it was just, I mean wild, a lot of people, I mean basically the stuff that I'm doing now, it was going on ... back then, people shooting at people, people robbing people, people sellin' drugs, smoking weed, stuff like that. We stayed in the same neighborhood ... all my life. (Antonio, 12)

Many BBY grow up in environments which can be more stressful than peri-urban or suburban settings. High rates of violence, drug use, and crime mean that surveillance by and encounters with police are commonplace. At the same time, many crimes are never solved. Some youth feel therefore that they must take things into their own hands to get justice. Moreover, in the face of physical threats, saving face and maintaining respect represents an important way for them to stay safe. If BBY don't safeguard their reputations, they may be victimized, killed, and have RIP (Rest in Peace) after their names.

> The neighborhood wasn't rough, but we had those people who try to run the neighborhood and stuff. My sister, they tried to rape her. One time I was outside playing with my friends, and she was in the house and these guys snuck in my house through the side door and I wasn't paying attention. I was like somebody in my house, they was like, yeah. Then, I went in there. My sister was in the bathroom, and they went in the bathroom and locked the door behind them and I couldn't get in. She was just like stop, stop. I was like man what you doing? You better open the door, and he didn't say nothing. All I heard was her saying stop. I ain't calling the police, I'm just gonna make him get out. I just hit the emergency button on our burglar alarm. He just left. Ran out and left. Then, I told my mama. We pressed charges and he was sent to the Youth Home a couple of weeks later. But I didn't want him to go to jail. I wanted to take care of him myself. He was about 15 or 16. I was like 13. But I couldn't do nothing about it, at that time. (Malik, 16)

Additionally, too many of the schools serving poor neighborhoods are themselves in distress and struggling to maintain order and provide a safe environment in which students can learn. Their inability to do so is demotivating even for those students who are inclined toward learning. For those students whose lives are difficult at home and for whom a commitment to learning is tenuous, it is even worse.

And Redwood, that school is terrible you know, it's real terrible and I just couldn't concentrate in there. If I'm gonna go to school, I want to go to a school where I can concentrate. You know where I can sit down and do my work and succeed. You know what I'm sayin', at Redwood, you don't succeed in there, there's too many influences, okay, there's too many drugs in that school for one, being that that is supposed to be a drug-free zone, there's too many drugs in there.

The kids aren't obedient, you know what I'm saying, there is fighting, it's just wild, the school is wild. It's nothin' like a high school that you've ever seen before, you know? It's a public high school, you know, where kids in the neighborhood go. But once you're in there, you don't feel like it because it is wild, you know, it's fighting, It is wild, man! You can't control it. You can't even sit down and say I'm gonna do my work when you hear people schemin' over here and these people fightin' over there. (Denzel, 15)

For Denzel, going to school was exasperating and fruitless. Even though he had made up his mind to study and was motivated to concentrate and do well, his environment did not make this possible. This made it difficult to stick with his commitment to change his life from fighting and dismissing education to taking it seriously; the school environment frustrated him and made it difficult to stick to his resolution to do better. In this way the pressures of his environment kept him on an antisocial trajectory rather than facilitating his positive development.

As the accounts of the BY presented here attest, family, school, peers, and neighborhood have all played a critical role in the unfolding of their lives as juvenile offenders. Although BBY don't always explicitly make the connection to early emotional trauma, their accounts are replete with instances of early loss; and on the basis of the reflections provided by BY, trauma and loss are present on all fronts at home and in the neighborhoods. BBY experience loss due to the desperation of their families' economic situations, due to exposure to neighborhood violence, death, and the frequent disruption of family relationships.

As glaring and compelling as these tangible losses are, it is important, however, not to lose sight of other equally important losses BB experience. This includes the loss of the halcyon period of middle childhood and the loss of innocence in middle childhood that is caused by prejudice, stigma, and implicit bias. These distortions reshape how BBY and their behaviors are imagined, understood, and responded to by others. In early childhood, BB's restlessness, temper tantrums, disobedience, rule-breaking, inattention, and conflict with peers are often viewed optimistically as transient delays in the maturation of self-regulation and executive function. Parents and teachers are hesitant to characterize these early difficulties as arising from pathology and deviance out of concern for labeling them. By middle childhood, however, the narrative shifts and these behaviors come to be seen as enduring features of boys' character. At this point, BB with behavioral difficulties themselves become the problem. The cost to BBY of being viewed as a problem is paid for and settled with the currency of bravado, indifference, and living for the present moment. By adolescence, assessments of boys with difficulties tend to reflect stereotypes, such as aggressive predators that place them beyond hope and in danger of hostile reactions by others.

For BBY, the psychological effects of loss and trauma can be overwhelming. They engender the feeling in BBY that they do not matter and that their needs are not deserving of adult attention. As a result, loss may contribute to a nihilistic, devil-may-care attitude in which risks that endanger their lives are worth taking because life is difficult and ephemeral anyway. These beliefs and feelings provide a fertile ground in which behavior problems can grow and multiply. Challenging these beliefs and the environmental conditions that give rise to them are critical for promoting resilience in BBY.

Notes

1. Jessor & Jessor (1977).
2. Hoeve et al. (2012).
3. Goings et al. (2023).
4. Bowlby (1969).
5. Bowlby (1944).
6. Hirschi (1969).
7. Ferguson (2020).
8. Stewart & Simons (2010).

9
Lives in Distress

BBY experience extraordinary stress, as a consequence of loss and trauma, as they grow up. Numerous adverse conditions, occasions, or events are highly prevalent in the lives of Black boys and youth (BBY). All of them can be sources of chronic stress. These stressors and how BBY cope with them have significant consequences for their well-being in the long run. This chapter draws on data from mental health research to map BBY's emotional landscape and consider what they mean for BBY's well-being. It focuses on emotional pain occurring specifically within the social spaces in which BBY spend the most time: families, schools, and neighborhoods. (For a summary, see Table 9.1, which lists key life stressors located within family, school, and communities and Table 9.2, which identifies the negative emotions commonly elicited by these stressors.)

Distress for BBY arises from emotional trauma related to financial worries and instability in family life, unfair treatment in failing schools, physical threats in dangerous neighborhoods, and the cumulative effects of family traumas.[1] Accordingly, BBY's inner lives and emotional experiences are shaped by perceptions of threat, deprivation, and loss within these spaces. The political commentator, John Edwards, expressed it this way: "Young African American men see their options as going to prison or dying. As a result, they don't invest in their education, they don't invest in their futures."[2] These concerns for BBY are echoed in numerous policy reports that describe them as vulnerable, endangered, and disconnected. Their hopelessness and pain are evident in their rising suicide rate.[3]

Due to traumatizing events at home, at school, and in their neighborhood, BBY frequently experience emotional distress.[4] Across each of these environments, Black children are more likely to experience emotional problems, such as anxiety, than other groups of children. For example, epidemiological research estimates the prevalence of internalizing problems (encompassing fear and sadness) in Black children to be as high as 10%, while for the population as a whole, the figure is only 4.6%.[5] Black individuals have a higher lifetime prevalence of anxiety disorders than White

Table 9.1 Stressful Events in the Lives of BBY

Family	School	Neighborhood
Financial worries	Exposure to violence	Implicit bias, stigma
Food insecurity	Crime victimization	Low expectations
Family strife	Excessive police force	Unfair discipline, scapegoating
Parental drug and mental health problems	Physical confrontations fighting	Peer teasing
Loss thru separation/death	disrespect	Exclusion, rejection
Father absence	Racial microaggressions	Academic struggles
Adultification		
Loneliness		

Table 9.2 Emotional Reactions of BBY to Stressful Life Events

Sadness, hopelessness	Envy	Mistrust
Anxiety, fear	Jealousy	Anger
Guilt,	Resentment	Frustration
Shame	Uncertainty, self-doubt	Regret
Self-hatred, self-blame	Insecurity	Disgust

individuals (30.9% vs 22.7%),[6] and Black children are diagnosed with post-traumatic stress disorder more often than White children.[7] In school, BBY are disproportionately designated as requiring special education instruction in classrooms for the emotionally impaired,[8] and test anxiety and social phobias are also more common among Black school children than their White counterparts.[9] Meanwhile, data gathered on samples of children from low income urban neighborhoods have detected levels of depressed moods in non-clinical, non-referred Black children that were on average equivalent to levels found among children hospitalized for mood disorders.

Discrete Emotions of BBY

Emotions such as anxiety and sadness are complex feeling states that have parallel physiological and cognitive processes associated with them.[10] Emotions can be conscious or unconscious. Most often, they involve activation of specific neural pathways and reveal themselves overtly through telltale signs that can be detected by discerning observers. For example, BBY emotions may manifest in facial expressions or posture, frowning, crying or smiling, excessive or diminished motor activity, sustained interest, behavioral perseveration, or uncontrolled rumination. Izard and Akerman have proposed a list of discrete emotions that includes, among others, sadness, fear, anger, and shame.[11] Each emotion has specific and unique ways in which it organizes individual thinking and facilitates adaptive responses to stress. Accordingly, each emotion can give rise to positive or negative ways of perceiving and thinking about and behaving in the world.

Chronic stress affects emotions through the impact it has on brain structure, in the form of a lowered plasticity, structure, shape, and volume of the hippocampus, which plays a central role in emotion regulation.[12] It also suppresses production of new neurons which results in fewer connections or synapses that allow the hippocampus to communicate with other parts of the brain, something that creates the effect of increased sadness and depression. At the same time as these neurohormonal and physiological changes are taking place in the body, an emotional drama is also unfolding.

Troubled Behaviors and Troubling Emotions

Troubling emotions often underlie troubled behaviors. Emotional distress, while often masked, can often be observed in the misbehavior of BBY. While it is easy to see and respond to disruptive behavior in BBY, it is more difficult to discern the disturbed feelings that often drive the behavior. Nevertheless, it is important to do so if one is to understand BBY. These behaviors communicate what words and facial expressions may not. For example, sadness is associated with irritability, which can be observed in curt responses, opposition, and a refusal to comply with rules and instructions. It also often spills over into conflicts with peers. Thus, behaviors reveal a range of emotions and reactions to the world and are themselves genuine expressions of internalized problems.[13] These problems are more likely to generate concern when detected because so little is understood about their origins and the extent of their effects.[14] It is clear that the emotional problems behind these behaviors have broad consequences for BBY's school adaptation, motivation, and skill development, which not only have implications for success later in life[15] but also portend detrimental consequences for society in terms of decreased productivity.[16] When school and families fail to probe beneath the surface to find out what is really driving non-compliance or disruptive behavior, they are likely to consider recrimination, punishment, and control as the most appropriate responses and thus, unwittingly, confirm BBY's feelings that they are unseen and misunderstood.

Anxiety and Fear

When adults look carefully and try to discern the emotions driving misbehavior, they often find fear and anxiety—especially about safety. Fear is usually a response to a loss or harm that is anticipated but has not yet occurred. It is a reaction to the perception of danger and threats, such as those BBY often face in violent neighborhoods. The source of fear can be internal and psychological or external and physical. Fear can arise in times of uncertainty about the future or from guilt due to a failure to meet some standard or expectation for behavior and achievement. In a recent study about two-thirds of BBY expressed fears about getting shot, contracting HIV, getting sick, and dying young; and a small number expressed fears about getting beaten up and getting into drugs. They also reported sensitivity to and fear of rejection.[17] For BBY, community violence and school-related stress are linked to symptoms of anxiety or fear.[18] Paradoxically, perceived or imagined danger can cause arousal and fear that is even greater than the threat or danger itself.[19]

Fear activates vigilance and wariness and can cause somatic symptoms, such as muscle tension, stomachaches, restlessness, shortness of breath, headaches, and sweaty hands. It can also result in sleep disturbance, hyperactivity, and feeling restless and jittery, which may be reflected in difficulty sitting still. Fear can also take the form of social phobias or performance anxiety. Aggression may be driven by anxiety and fear. Boys who seem willing to be oppositional and fight to deal with conflict and disagreements may be anxious, fearful, and acting out of fear. BB who appear to be hostile and indifferent to the consequences of their behavior for themselves and for others may in reality be responding to their own belief that their survival is threatened or that aggression is the only way to avoid loss of something they value even if the loss is abstract or elusive such as reputation, respect, honor, and fairness. At the same time, fear can be adaptive in that it can help to heighten concentration and strengthen acuity of perception when exploring strange and novel situations. In this way, fear is adaptive in neighborhoods with a high prevalence of violence.

One BBY, Cleon, described a fatal occurrence in his neighborhood to which he had a very strong emotional reaction and, after the fact, he was able to own up to being afraid[20]:

> Yeah, one time I was afraid, ah, when my boy had got killed. He was, like, the head leader of our crew. He had got killed, ah, all the rest of us, we was standin' on our side from the spot (where he had got carjacked and shot for his car). His mama and his brother had come across the street and told us and we all got to the hospital.

Threats from larger and stronger gangs left Cleon and his friend Chris, the boy who was killed, vulnerable to multiple acts of intimidation and theft of prized possessions.

> Yeah, he had got carjacked twice, the first time he got carjacked at this gas station. He had, I think, a new Charger, with some rims on there, sounds and stuff. He had went to the gas station to get some cash. They had carjacking for his car. They had carjacking once and let him go. The second time, about two weeks later, he's like, well, they carjack me for this car, I'm going to show them, I'm going to get me another car and hook it up better than I hooked that first one up. So, he had got him a Camaro and threw some Dayton Tires on there. Got some sounds in there and stuff like that. Had a nice engine, uh-huh. He went back up to the gas station. This time, they carjack him again, the same people. This time they shot him in his back. From what we heard, they knew him and he knew them. That's why they killed him basically. They knew what we's going to get accomplished (retribution).

The event was emotionally traumatic for Cleon, in part, because it was so unexpected.

> I was playing basketball when he was shot. My sister was going with him at the time, She came running and she was crying, she was like, Chris got shot, like that, and I was like for real, you know, we went out to the hospital, his brothers and all them was out there, all us. It was about a good twenty of us, his friends, family, and stuff, we's all out there, and the doctors told us he was going to live so we went back to the neighborhood and starting getting drunk and stuff. About one thirty in the night, his daddy came outside, and

told us that he had died. After his father told us he had died, I got, I started getting afraid cause I didn't know what was going on. Cause first, okay, it's like, we was beefin'. Our side of the neighborhood was beefin' with another side of the neighborhood. And ah, this was the second murder within, I'd say, two months, that they side of the neighborhood had done on our side so. They had killed two people on our side of the neighborhood in about two months. So, you know I started getting afraid, saying well they doin' all this to us, and we ain't doin' nothin' to them, you know what I'm saying. They ain't catching me walking around by myself and ride up on me and shoot me and stuff like that. And that's when I started, you know, getting the mind frame, to where I got to get more gun power and stuff like that so when I be walking, alone by myself and stuff like that. [If] they ride up on me, then they really going to have to kill me, cause I'm going to try to kill them. (Cleon, 17)

Retribution and escalation of violence, though futile in the end, were regarded not only as a commensurate response but were also required to maintain one's respect in the eyes of others, particularly one's adversaries. As a consequence, both sides of the conflict were trapped in a spiraling retribution that only created more psychological pain and loss of life and required high levels of vigilance and fear.

Anger and Resentment

Some BBY are filled with unspeakable anger but express themselves in ways that are not understood by others. Anger is a negative state of arousal stemming from either the perception of an injustice or undeserved harm, the blocking of a highly desired goal, or the prevention from gratifying some wish or important need. Sometimes, the precipitant for anger is trivial, as in the case of Braelon:

I was angry a lot of times when I couldn't get my way, like, if I wanted to go out and buy me some new gym shoes or a new outfit, stuff like that. If I had money, and I knew it was a party I'm like, I'm saying to myself, dang, I gotta go get fresh real quick, somethin' like that. But if I ain't got no money I'll get upset, I'll get upset and I'll be takin' it out on other people but I'm really upset within myself, mad at myself because, I've spent all the money that I had, now I can't go on and get fresh. (Braelon, 17)

Other times, anger has a more serious cause, as in the case of Ethan, who was presented in Chapter 3. Recall that Ethan, a Black boy in a mostly White elementary school, was bullied by his White peers. On the way home from school, a group of White boys held and punched him, knocking him to the ground. He was angered by the attack, especially because one of the boys had seemed to befriend him. His anger boiled over when the teacher made him come to the front of the class and chastised him for starting a fight. He felt betrayed by this injustice, but he had to suppress his anger. It took him many years to get over it.

Anger is an emotion that is typically targeted outward. It is characterized by antagonism toward someone or something that has deliberately caused or done some wrong. Physiologically, anger increases the flow of blood toward muscles needed for action. Anger can lead to aggression, but more often it results in a somewhat more reasoned response, which can influence others to apologize, express remorse, or change the offending behavior. In some cases, anger can be seen as positive, as when, for example, it motivates the finding of solutions to a problem or helps an individual to sustain effort and mobilize action toward some desired goal. Excessive uncontrolled anger, however, can be a problem, as increased blood pressure and other physical changes associated with anger can make it difficult to think straight and can harm physical and mental health. Nevertheless, externalizing the blame through anger proves to be a healthier response than directing it internally in the form of shame and embarrassment.[21]

Sadness

Sadness and depression are also related to stress. Sadness is a negative mood state characterized by anguish, heartache, hopelessness, melancholy, misery, longing, feeling alone, disinterest in and lack of motivation at school, self-doubting, and becoming easily irritated by those trying to provide comfort. It often occurs together with anxiety in response to pervasive psychological distress. Sadness in young BBY means bearing pain in silence, but desperately wanting someone to notice you, to see you as worth their time and attention. For BBY, sadness is a common response to a loss or rupture in a relationship, disappointment, criticism, or failure.[22] When sadness is chronic and deep, it can include not caring about anything and losing hope about everything. As we shall see in the following section, a case study describing a BBY named Tyshaun McPhatter, when linked to trauma, sadness can spill out into anger, impulsivity, and emotional outbursts.

Tyshaun McPhatter—A Case Study in Emotional Distress

Tyshaun McPhatter, a young Black boy, is the central figure in a 2017 *Washington Post* story by John W. Cox.[23] This compelling account, which describes a variety of challenges he faced in middle childhood, including parental separation and community violence, provides a good example of how the emotions described above can affect a BB. At the time of the article, Tyshaun was a student in second grade in a Washington DC public school, and his life had been tragically derailed by the sudden loss of his father to random gun violence.

Even before the loss of his father, Tyshaun's life was not easy. Each day, there were multiple reasons for him to worry and be afraid. Frequently, the sound of gunshots firing outside his window caused him to fall to the floor to avoid getting hit by a stray bullet. There were bullet holes in the front door of his home from bullets that had traveled straight through, striking the TV in the living room. Friends of his father had been killed in separate incidents not far from his home, and when he heard gunshots at school, he often said to himself, "I hope my dad is okay." Other children, friends at school, were scarred emotionally by seeing dead bodies near where they waited at their school bus stop.

In spite of these adverse conditions, Tyshaun had been on his way to developing the social competencies typical of middle childhood. Tyshaun showed empathy and concern about the safety and welfare of his family and others in his neighborhood. He recognized and was able to verbalize his fear and uncertainty. He sought and received support and reassurance from both parents, who did all they could to protect him. He felt secure and safe when he was with his father. Nevertheless, his fledgling mastery of self-regulation sometimes failed him, and he had a tendency to explode in anger, even to the point of fighting with peers when they did something to upset him.[24] His father advised him, "never start a fight, never pick up a gun, but fight if you have to!" Tyshaun looked up to and had a strong emotional bond to his father. He listened to his father's advice not to be afraid, not to react to teasing. His parents, though not living together, effectively co-parented Tyshaun. He spent a lot of time with his father, who lived with his own mother not far from where Tyshaun went to school. Tyshaun and his father often had fun playing video games together. But it was not all play. His father also practiced Tyshaun's multiplication tables with him. In return, Tyshaun taught his father to dance to rap music. Tyshaun wanted to be just like his father, strong and brave.

One morning, after hearing gunshots at school, Tyshaun was again worried about his father. He knew something was wrong when his mother showed up at school to pick him up well before the usual dismissal time. In the car she told him that his father had been shot but had survived. Tyshaun was in shock and could not talk. He did not know what to say. His father had had no involvement in illegal activity and was sitting in a friend's car just talking. The intended victim was his father's friend. Hs father had simply been in the wrong place at the wrong time. Word spread quickly among the children that Tyshaun's father had been shot, and the next day at school a friend asked Tyshaun if he was okay. Before responding to the question, Tyshaun heard another boy laugh. He interpreted the boy's laugh as making fun of his father's serious injury. Enraged, he went over and knocked the boy down to the ground. Fortunately, the school staff understood the grief behind the anger and had Tyshaun talk with a male counselor. Later that night, news came that Tyshaun's father had died. When told of his father's death, Tyshaun slumped in a chair and again could find no words to express his feelings.

As he tried to process his loss, Tyshaun responded with coping strategies typical of a young boy whose ability to understand death and deal with trauma is still forming. He immersed himself in magical thinking, fantasizing that he could create a potion that would bring his father back from the dead. He imagined creating a time machine so that he could go back and tell his father not to get into the car. He fantasized about seeking revenge on the shooter. He sought to assuage his sadness and come to terms with his loss by seeking details about the murder. He wanted to know how, where, and by whom his father had been killed. In addition, he attempted to maintain a connection to his father by dressing like his father and sleeping with his father's hoodie, so that he had the smell of his father with him at night. He was worried about how his younger brother was handling the loss. On the day of the funeral, he wanted to feel connected to his father by wearing a piece of his father's clothing. At the funeral services, he was emotionally overwhelmed and did not want to go up to casket to view his father's body. But his family pressured him to approach the casket and make a final farewell to his father. He felt unable to manage the emotional distress of viewing his father's body because it would remove all doubt that his father was gone for good. "I don't want to look at it!" he protested to family, "I can't touch him." Finally, after considerable encouragement, he did lay a handkerchief on top of his father in a gesture that he imagined would help his father remember him.

Tyshaun had experienced unequivocal love for his father whom he idolized and on whom he was strongly dependent. Although it was not apparent, his emotional reactions to the loss of his father combined sadness, fear, and anger. These emotions, which sometimes took the form of irritability, over-reaction to others, and aggression, could easily have been misunderstood. Fortunately, Tayshaun had supportive environments at home and school that showed patience and understanding as they helped him to keep his behavior within acceptable bounds even as he worked through his initial mourning.

Coping with Loss

Tyshaun's family felt that he shut down emotionally after his father's death. He pretended that everything was normal and made an effort not to break down. However, these efforts to cope were unsuccessful. He initially argued and fought with his peers and found himself in trouble at school. Fortunately, there were men in his life—his grandfather and a school counselor—who could pull him aside to talk through what he was thinking. Tyshaun returned to school soon after the funeral. Although he continued to experience emotional difficulties, resumption of normal activities had its benefits. He could be distracted by the academic tasks that required his attention. In addition, the opportunity to play with peers brought a normal source of joy into his life.

Social support is a key factor in buffering stress and promoting resilience in the face of a loss that would otherwise be overwhelming. On this dimension, Tyshaun was extremely fortunate. The likelihood of his continued positive development is high. Given the social support Tyshawn received from family and school staff and the socio-emotional competencies he has already demonstrated, there is reason to be hopeful that Tyshaun will bounce back from the traumatic loss of his father. While Tyshaun will miss out on the support, guidance, and companionship his father would have offered, he is fortunate in having a grandfather and other adults who have stepped into the breach and provided some of the things his father would have, had he survived. Over time, it likely that he will grow stronger and further develop the social skills typical for middle childhood.

Coping with Ambivalent Sadness over Father's Death

Not all boys have the clear and unambivalent feelings about their fathers that Tyshaun did. Some have a deep ambivalence that creates emotional conflict as they try to come to terms with the death of their father. Some of the ambivalence is a consequence of the way poverty can distort family relationships. These conditions weave a complex web of emotions that are intense and confusing. This was the case for another BBY, who had mixed feelings about the sudden death of his father, which had been preceded by turmoil and a frightening conflict with his mother:

> The night my father died, him and my mama got into an argument or fight or something because, I heard them in there yelling and stuff. And I went to the door to look through the crack of the door, and I seen my father go in the kitchen and grab a shovel, and head back to the room, like he was going to hit her with it. I was so scared I just sat on the bed and started crying. I was like, I can't wait until I get older, I will kill him, like that. Just cried myself to sleep.
>
> Then, the next thing you know, I woke up. I heard my mama screaming my name. She was like: "Come out here!" to either me or my sister and I ran out there. I just seen him laying there on the floor. She was like call 911. I called 911, I didn't know what to say, so she ran and came and got the phone. I just walked back there. She said, it was either an asthma attack or a heart attack. I didn't feel bad that he died or nothing, I was just lucky, that's how I feel. Kind of miss him, but kind of don't because that night, he made me hate him to that point. (Phil, 17)

What is most striking and palpable in this description are the mixed emotions felt by this boy. On the one hand, he "kind of misses" his father; on the other hand, he feels contempt for his father and reports even wishing to kill his father in order to protect his mother.

Adversity Without Social Assets

For BBs who do not have adequate social assets to help them become resilient in the face of adversity, loss, and trauma, adversity comes not in a single event but in the form of recurrent challenges and tragedies. For them, the impact of adversity on socio-emotional development may be deeper, longer-lasting, and more detrimental than it was for Tyshaun. For them, chronic stress, economic deprivation, and social stigma set them on a developmental trajectory that is quite different than that of boys who experience middle childhood as a Golden Age with relatively auspicious conditions. Their developmental trajectories are altered by social stressors at home, at school, and in their neighborhood via economic deprivation and racial stereotypes.

The emotional struggles of Tyshaun and of other BBY and how they cope with emotional trauma and loss are important because they help us to understand how BB end on a path or trajectory that is different than other groups of children. The divergent behavioral trajectory of BBY beginning in middle childhood is arguably linked to emotional experiences shaped by perceptions of threat, deprivation, and loss that frequently give rise to negative emotions such as fear, anger, and sadness. To resolve or address the well-documented comparatively high levels of behavior problems BB exhibit during middle childhood, it is necessary to probe beneath the surface of what is going on to understand the root causes. For BB Serious emotional distressed often occurs under the guise of oppositional and aggressive behavior. Anxiety and fear engender a sense of threat that propels BB toward fighting and resisting adult authority. Perceived threat or loss may arouse anger and, in turn, hostility expressed in aggression. Moreover, high levels sadness and emotional arousal that BB experience may slow or distort problem solving and decision making leading BB to act impulsively or in anger over a perceived injustice, and resulting in making poor choices about behavior and sub-optimal coping with stress in their lives.

Learning more about the emotions underlying conduct problems that BBY exhibit and how they cope with emotional distress may provide actionable information to adults who seek to support the positive development in BBY and help more of them to become resilient in the face of adversity.

Notes

1. Evans et al. (2005).
2. MTV political forum (September 27, 2007).
3. Bridge et al. (2015).
4. Stevenson (1997).
5. Costello et al. (2003).
6. Kessler et al. (2005).
7. Last & Perrin (1993).
8. Serwatka et al. (1995).
9. Beidel et al. (1994), Silverman & Albano (1996).
10. Izard et al. (2000).
11. Izard et al. (2000).
12. Kim et al. (2015).
13. Coyne & Thompson (2011).
14. Lemery-Chalfant et al. (2007).
15. Breslau et al. (2009).
16. Beck et al. (2011).
17. Cassidy & Stevenson (2005).
18. Gaylord-Harden, et al. (2011).
19. Hall et al. (2008).
20. Barbarin (1995).
21. Dunbar et al. (2021) asked Black adolescents how frequently they experienced discrimination at school and in their communities and how those experiences made them feel. Adolescents and their mothers were also presented with a hypothetical discriminatory event perpetrated by a teacher and asked to discuss together what they would do. Although BBY reported feeling emotions such as anger and frustration in response to discrimination, these emotions were not associated with symptoms of mental health problems. However, BBY who experienced more vulnerable and self-blaming emotions, like sadness, shame, and embarrassment, were more likely to have emotional and behavior problems.
22. Gaylord-Harden et al. (2011).
23. Cox (2017, April 20).
24. Drury et al. (2014) also investigated the effects of cumulative direct and indirect exposure to violence on the externalizing behaviors of Black children (ages 4–15 years). Indirect exposure to violence was significantly associated with behavior problems.

PART V
STRUGGLES WITH ADVERSITY

10
Denying Emotions and Losing Self

Racial discrimination, social exclusion by White peers, unfair discipline, and being ignored or viewed as a threat are familiar experiences for most Black boys and youth (BBY). These experiences can cause sadness, fear, uncertainty, loneliness, boredom, and anger. When confronted with these situations, how do BBY tend to respond? How do they tamp down the negative emotional arousal they feel? What strategies do they use to feel good about themselves when they are belittled, ignored, treated as expendable, and told that their feelings do not matter? This chapter describes some of the strategies that BBY deploy to regulate their emotional distress and control how they respond. In particular, it explores how some BBY deal with adversity by hiding their vulnerability, concealing their feelings, and pretending not to be hurt.

Denying and concealing pain is understandable and consistent with the messages that BBY receive about what it means to be a man and with the concerns families communicate about the dangers of being too emotional or appearing fragile. Families often discourage their sons from expressing emotions such as anger because it may provoke powerful reactions from those who would perceive their sons as a threat. Crying and expressions of pain, meanwhile, are equated with weakness by peers who value strength and stoicism. Thus, for BBY, the expression of emotions is a liability that can negatively shape how others judge them. They learn that acknowledgment of emotional and physical pain is discouraged and could be exploited by those who might harm them. Consequently they must conceal how they feel and what they truly think.

Because expressing emotions signals weakness, BBY develop strategies that allow them to effectively deny their pain and hide their feelings. Some strategies involve taking actions targeted directly at the sources of the distress. Others are more defensive and seek to modify or ameliorate emotional reactions to stress. These often involve some combination of denial, concealment, deflection, masquerading facades, and hypervigilance. Each of these strategies distances BBY from their feelings and blocks knowledge of these feelings from others. As a rule, BBY disclose their secret fears and reveal their hurts to few. They hide the truth from others and ultimately from themselves. Adopting such defensive strategies comes with a significant cost, as it amounts to letting no one get close enough to see and respond supportively to their pain. Popular and well-liked BBY may surround themselves with many people but they are often not more than acquaintances. Few see behind the mask to know BBY true feelings. Some BBY may even have a posse, the boys they befriend and with whom they spend time. But even for the posse there are barriers erected to keep all at an emotional distance so that fears, vulnerabilities, and self-doubt cannot be seen. While these attempts at self-protection may keep the pain at bay temporarily, they do little to heal BBY's wounds or offer the relief BBY really need.

Self-Protective Responses to Adversity

Emotional Numbing

Emotional numbing is a self-protective strategy driven by the emotional exhaustion that occurs when BBY experience a series of severe stresses or traumas in close succession. It is a form of habituation in which the body has no more energy to respond, thus leaving BBY feeling drained and emotionally empty, and often occurs when multiple demands and stresses overwhelm their capacity to cope. The only solution is to shut down and zone out. When BBY are in this state, they can become non-responsive to stressful events that would otherwise evoke sadness, anger, remorse, or fear. Emotional numbing may make BBY appear to be unemotional and even callous in the face of horrendous events, exhibiting little feeling or reaction in cases where an emotional reaction would be normative and expected.

Often, BBY's emotional numbing occurs as a response to repeated loss of family or friends. Loss through homicide is so common in some neighborhoods that boys learn to cope by not letting themselves feel anything. As one BBY tells it:

> My best friend Brandon had got killed, . . . We was all like family, me, him and my other best friend Shawn, who grew up with me. We've known each other ever since we was about one. We got pictures and stuff when we was

not even a couple of months old, we was sitting in the play pen together and stuff like that.

It happened one day when I was at school. My daddy had called up there, and he was like, well 'I want to come get my son, early' And the school went: "Well all right", but they wouldn't tell me what for. When I got home my sister Taneca and my best friend Shawn they sittin' at the table, they was crying,

'Hey, what's wrong with you all?'

Everybody said, "Well, Brandon got killed last night!"

I was like, "For real?" I thought they was playing at first. But then, my daddy, he's like: "They ain't playin' like that."

Brandon, was standing out there on the corner that night about twelve thirty with two more of my friends, Boo, and Tyrone. A van rolled up and someone shot him in his back and chest."

I was like, "He's what, fifteen?" Brandon was just fifteen and I couldn't stop crying. (Donte, 15)

Not long after Brandon's murder, Donte's friend Shawn was also killed. These two tragic losses may have dulled Donte's emotional response to future stressful situations; he himself recognized that the double losses had diminished his responses. In his own words: "After the two times my friends got killed, it ain't really too many situations came up after that to make me sad, afraid and stuff like that." Emotional numbing is damaging not only because it covers over BBY pain but also because numbing makes it possible for BBY to harm others without emotions, remorse, or guilt.

Physical Dissociation

Dissociation is similar to emotional numbing, except that the suppression of emotion arises out of an attempt at distancing oneself from the unpleasant event or situation, rather than out of exhaustion or habituation. It allows one to be unaware of the immediate environment and be transported to an entirely different space. Meditation or hypnosis could be a means by which this is achieved. Dissociating helps to blunt emotional pain by keeping it out of conscious awareness, thereby allowing the individual to suffer less in the short run. It typically involves walling oneself off from the pain and the circumstances that elicit the pain. It can be an out-of-body experience through which one is transported to another place away from the stressful situation. It can seem as if you are stepping outside of your body and looking down at yourself from above. This disconnection between the mind and body can result in detachment from emotions, an unawareness of what is happening in the present moment, and memory loss. Dissociating thus allows BBY to remove themselves from threatening and harsh circumstances and occupy a safe space protected from harm. A BBY's body is there but his mind his not, and so he is not in touch with the pain.

Dissociation is described well in a passage from Jovan Haye in his memoir *Bigger Than Me.* In it he tells how, as a young boy, he overcame the stress and stigma of childhood dyslexia to end up playing in the NFL. He recounts his experience of being greatly misunderstood because people did not know how to interpret his restlessness and hyperactivity. His life was a battle to manage the expectations of others while at the same time dealing with the struggle to speak and regulate his attention.

> For The first hour (of church service) the kids had to attend children's Bible study. I didn't like that part because I had a hard time keeping still and quiet. I felt a constant urge to talk, yet I couldn't form a normal sentence like other kids my age. Our teachers made us recite verses, and I couldn't do it because of my stutter. When it came time to say prayers, I was terrible I just couldn't pay attention. . . . The adults must've thought I was being stubborn or defiant, because they yelled at me a lot and a leader often struck my hand. When things got bad, I withdrew into myself. I just stared out the window. It was like *I was there but I wasn't*.[1]

Behavioral Overcompensation

Behavioral overcompensation, also known as John Henryism, is achieved by immersing oneself fully in one's responsibilities and in taking on one burden after another without hesitation, rest, or attention to the physical cost of doing so. It is founded in the belief that effective coping requires an uncritical embrace of all the challenges or obstacles life sends your way. It is best characterized as a persistent overachieving and compensation in response to increasingly stressful demands combined with the feeling that one has no choice but to take up the tasks. It may reflect a combination of caring too much, bravado, and a sense of invulnerability.

The notion of John Henryism, first introduced by Sherman James, is based on the folk hero, John Henry.[2] Henry was a Black railroad worker, who became famous for his strength and determination. According to legend, he defeated a steam-powered machine in competition, working ever-faster until he collapsed and died. The concept is meant to capture the behavior of Black males who push themselves to the limits in order to achieve success, often at the cost of their physical and mental health. Believing that responsibility, hard work, and persistence are the only ways to overcome adversity, they often repress their emotional reactions to maltreatment and cling to the fantasy that they will be okay if they keep pushing harder. Their singular focus on the task at hand diverts attention from their exhaustion and keeps them from feeling the emotional distress of adversity. Consequently, they refuse to admit to needing help, no matter how dire the circumstances, and they convince themselves that all is well until the moment of total collapse. Like many of these protective strategies, John Henryism is effective in achieving short-term goals, but it can also lead to burnout, health problems, and other negative consequences in the long term.[3]

Consider the example of Marquis, a 16-year-old junior and one of a handful of Black students in a competitive public magnet school for the sciences. Unlike most of the other students, he has had to work after school and on weekends to help his family financially. He has no downtime to relax. Even though he is stressed out and tired all the time, he cannot admit (to himself or others) that his work and advanced courses are too much to manage. In fact, he even asks for more hours at work. Taking less rigorous classes and having time with his friends would be unthinkable. He believes his only option is to keep pushing himself and to ignore the cost to his health and to his academic performance.

Concealing Feelings from Others

From the time they are young, BBY are taught to ignore and discount pain and emotion. Social disapproval and the stigma associated with boys expressing emotions make them less likely to admit to feelings, such as fear or sadness. Because they are encouraged to man up and not to cry when hurt, many BBY dismiss, conceal, and suppress expressions of emotions that signal pain. Their masculine identity is defined as being tough, strong, and emotionless in the face of pain, and they are trapped by the desire to be seen as strong Black men. They are also taught by their parents, who fear for their safety, to suppress and control expressions of anger. Thus, anger, fear, and sadness may be repressed, though they often find expression in oppositional, explosive, impulsive, or aggressive behaviors.[4]

This kind of concealment is central to *The Butler*, a film based loosely on the life of Eugene Allen, who served in the White House for 34 years. The film makes clear that Allen's success across eight different administrations, from the presidencies of Eisenhower to Reagan, depended on his remaining nondescript, one-dimensional, and invisible to all. He had to become a lifely fixture line, a statue not noticed for his human qualities. To do this he had to present a smiling face to the world and appear as an emotionally blank slate. He could not let the people he served know what he truly thought, felt, or needed. He described his situation as requiring two faces: one for White individuals and the other for himself and the people he trusted. In order to keep his job, he could not express any opinions or feelings about the oppression of Black individuals, so he had to repress—perhaps even deny—his feelings, which left him out of touch with them. He could not afford to offend his employers by revealing to them his disappointment, indignation, or anger at the unfair practices related to pay and promotions he endured on the job. Regrettably, this mask of emotional neutrality was worn so tightly that his deeper feelings were not even apparent to his family at home. This caused deep fissures in his relations with his wife and alienation from a son, who could not understand his father's emotional acquiescence in compromising and bending his identity to conform to whatever the White "master" wanted.

In the minds of BBY, real men do not show emotions, cry when hurt, or acknowledge pain. That is what girls do.[5] In their understanding, to do so would make them appear weak and render them vulnerable to teasing by other boys. Evidence of this importance of strength and toughness is seen as early as middle childhood, where BBY take pride in flexing and showing off their biceps, or seeing who can take the most pain without wincing or shedding a tear.

This suppression of emotions and need to demonstrate strength have been described as toxic or hyper-masculinity. Toxic masculinity in middle childhood and adolescence is often expressed as defiance, impulsivity, fighting, and aggression. Some of the best evidence of emotional distress in BBY can be gleaned from observations of these behaviors. Even when boys are unable to identify their hurts and talk about their feelings, their behavior tells a story and often opens a window onto their emotions and feelings. When we witness tantrums, opposition, fighting, and conflict on the surface, emotions lurk beneath that need to be interrogated and understood.[6]

Feigning Indifference and Passivity

Cultivated indifference is the pretense that something as traumatic or frightening as violence and death has no effect on one's emotional state. It could be facilitated by emotional numbing but is more often a deliberate act to deceive others about one's inner emotional state. It is intended to convey an impression that one is unperturbed, cool under fire, indifferent to pain, and unshakeable in the face of danger and loss.[7] Feigned passivity in the form of taking a cool pose is a type of self-presentation in which one communicates in words or actions that one does not care about what others think and is indifferent to external events. Criticisms, insults, intimidation, and teasing are made to seem as though they roll off like water off a duck's back.

A BBY is socialized to be a "big man," to endure hurt without crying, and to avoid trusting anyone. Of course, this self-presentation is almost always a façade. BBY care, but they pretend not to. For example, they may display feigned indifference and pretend not to be bothered by teasing or disparate treatment at school. This is something like the "rope-a-dope" strategy made famous by Mohammed Ali. In a fight, Ali would constantly back pedal away from the blows of his opponent, pretending not to be affected by his opponent's best punches. He would strike a cool pose of indifference. No one would ever know if he was hurt or not, especially his opponent.

Some youth know this as "Fronting." It is a form of masquerading, hiding behind a façade, by striving to appear strong and convey traits such as daring and courage. By adolescence, the façade becomes an internalized script, and BBY learn to play the role with skill. They adopt a hyper-masculine posture, engage in short-term thinking, seek immediate gratification, and withhold trust from everyone. One youth described the hopelessness that drives this approach in this way:

> When I was about twelve all the people my age range except two, um, every one of them got killed. I was like forget them, they gone you know what I'm saying. I ain't got nothin' to live for, no way. Ah, that kind of gave me an excuse to continue going out with the gang. (Demetrious, 15)

Bravado and hyper-masculinity are aspects of the "fronting" masquerade behind which a BBY's true self is hidden. Cunningham and colleagues have defined hyper-masculinity as a combination of stoicism, bravado, objectification of women, and rigid adherence to stereotypic beliefs about men.[8] In their research, they found that pre-adolescent BBY in eighth grade already adopted exaggerated hyper-masculine attitudes, although these attitudes softened by tenth grade. Similarly, Santos and colleagues found that BBY endorsed attitudes favoring physical toughness in dealing with peers.[9] The same posturing is reflected in the attraction of the gangster culture glorified in rap lyrics. At the same time, BBY recognize that features of this culture invoke stereotypes that can pose physical threats to them in certain circumstances. To minimize this possibility, they may downplay things about themselves that could arouse and threaten White individuals. For example, in some situations, BBY may self-consciously alter their speech and appearance to modify how "Black," "Ghetto," or threatening they seem. They may take further steps to appear harmless by smiling excessively, joking, or speaking with an affected softness and precision. On the other hand, they may alternatively react to negative social cues by amplifying hyper-masculine stances, assuming a cool, indifferent posture of bravado just to create the impression of toughness and opposition to authority.

Although BBY may cope with social challenges by suppressing anger, they can also be hyper-sensitive to rejection and perceived disrespect from others. They may resort to angry outbursts or the direct use of aggression as a defensive reaction to actual or perceived unfairness by adults or peers. In this way, the adoption of aggressive or hyper-masculine attitudes might be construed as a form of adaptation to environments perceived as adverse or threatening. It could serve the function of protective impression management to prevent intimidation by others. In presenting himself as someone who is tough and unafraid to fight, a BBY communicates to others that he should not be messed with. It is an adaptive strategy for building respect and influencing how others see and respond to BBY.[10]

A Glimpse of BBY Fronting

Rap music offers a public window onto the fronting posture assumed by some BBY. Lyrics by artists such as 50 Cent, Drake, Jay-Z, and Lil' Wayne display the psychological vulnerability, disappointments, and bravado of BBY.

Songs such as "Late to Da Party" by Lil Nas X, "Pushin' P" by Gunna, "Prices" by Lil Uzi Vert, "Make No Sense" by NBA Youngboy, and "Bubbly" by Young Thug, Travis, Scott, and Drake reveal insights into BBY's thoughts and feelings that would not otherwise be disclosed.[11] These songs reflect their wins, material successes and excesses, their triumphs and struggles. They also reveal a dark side of hyper-masculinity in the form of the objectification of women as existing to serve the prurient carnal desires of men and the glorification of the domination of women. Rap is pridefully defiant, projecting to the world, "here I am. Like it or not, this is me." The bravado and braggadocio sometimes serves as the armor that protects BBY, counteracts racism, and transforms adversity into a strength. It is an emancipation proclamation asserting the freedom to be oneself, unchained from others' constraining expectations.

However, beneath this exterior runs a current of vulnerability. A piece by The Notorius B.I.G. (Biggie Smalls), called "Everyday Struggles" captures in stark terms the enduring strains and desperation some BY feel.

> I don't wanna live no more . . .
> Sometimes I hear death knockin' at my front door
> I'm livin' every day like a hustle, another drug to juggle
> Another day, another struggle
> Baby on the way, mad bills to pay
> That's why you drink Tanqueray, so you can reminisce
> And wish you wasn't livin' so devilish, . . .
> Sometimes I hear death knockin' at my front door

"Everyday Struggles" captures the fragility and emptiness with which some view their lives. In "Suicidal Thoughts" Biggie Smalls expresses the pathos connected to contemplating ending his life. The lyrics gain their energy and punch from an intriguing contrast of defiance and depression; between diminished worth and assertiveness, and between self-loathing and self-acceptance.

> When I die, f---' it, I wanna go to hell
> 'Cause I'm a piece of shit, it ain't hard to f---'in' tell
> It don't make sense, goin' to heaven with the goodie-goodies
> Dressed in white, I like black Timbs and black hoodies
> God'll prob'ly have me on some real strict shit

> No sleepin' all day...
> Hangin' with the goodie-goodies, loungin' in paradise
> F--- that sh--, I wanna tote guns and shoot dice...
> All my life I been considered as the worst
> Lyin' to my mother, even stealin' out her purse
> Crime after crime, from drugs to extortion
> I know my mother wish she got a f---in' abortion
> She don't even love me like she did when I was younger

These lyrics reveal being at the edge of despair and feeling undeserving of love. Other songs openly consider suicide as an option. What is most revealing in Biggie's lyrics is that in this state of demoralization at the brink of suicide, he is able to marshal strength and stay true to his identity. In death, he is determined to dictate the terms of any afterlife. No quiet slow existence in a namby-pamby, sanitized heaven for him. His heaven will be gritty, or hell will be his choice. The number of BY who opt for suicide is small but growing. There is reason to believe that risky behavior and a brash sense of invulnerability some BY display are expressions of an unconscious death wish as in the case of renown hip-hop artist Juice Wrld, who in the midst of a depression died at age 21 of an opioid overdose that was ruled accidental. Like too many BY, Biggie Smalls died at age of 24—not by suicide but by gun-related homicide.

The brash posturing inherent in the genre reveals a struggle over identity, meaning, intimacy, and trust of others. It conceals a nihilism and lack of certainty about one's true identity, which inadvertently reveals the ultimate emptiness of the people with well-appointed bank accounts, gold jewelry, and fancy cars. In the lyrics for "Over," Lucky Daye reveals various poignant emotional torment: his disappointment at a heroin-addicted father ("Like I needed my father, but he needed a needle..."), his sadness over the death of his mother ("Went through deep depression when my mama passed..."), and the raw, unresolved emotional turmoil he felt over an on-again/off-again romantic relationship that ran hot and cold:

> We're thinkin', will we get there?
> You know that I miss you But I be gettin' mixed signals
> Why you slow down? Don't stop this green light
> Now you callin' me special When you know I can't have you
> You keep on makin' believe Nightmares turned into a dream

If you're so toxic to me, what am I findin'?
'Cause I thought it was over
Got me thinkin' my feelings over
I'm just tryna get closure. But you pullin' me closer and closer.

Hypervigilance and Distrust

Historical narratives about lynchings and contemporaneous incidences of police violence against Black individuals have been seared into BBY's imaginations and reinforce their tendency to be hypervigilant in social settings. In response to the unpredictability of community violence, BBY hone their abilities to scan their environments for signs of danger and size up social situations quickly. They have learned that, if they are to avoid physical and psychological harm, they need to be on high alert—they must know where they are and be aware of what is around them at all times.

BBY encounter multiple situations throughout the day at school and in the neighborhood that can set off alarms signaling danger. Few places provide guarantees of safety. For example, even just walking alone at night in an unfamiliar or predominantly White community can be dangerous for a BBY, for whom being stopped by police can turn into a deadly encounter. Being highly cautious and risk-averse can be a logical response to growing up in a highly unpredictable environment. In addition, the multiple challenges related to racism and poverty—the disruptions of family life, parents preoccupied with their own worries, abandonment by a father, homelessness, neighborhood violence, and murders of best friends—cause some boys to feel emotionally vulnerable with little prospect for comfort from the adults around them who are overcome by their own difficulties. Over time, BBY come to recognize and accept that they are on their own in coping with their worries and pain. As a result, BBY are continually in a state of high alert.

Cultural Mistrust

Hypervigilance occurs in tandem with cultural mistrust or cultural paranoia. Cultural mistrust refers to being guarded and reluctant to share information about oneself, especially in cross-racial interactions, out of fear that anything revealed will be exploited and cause harm. It is a wariness or mistrust of the motives of White individuals, resulting from a history of racism and social denigration.[12] It is grounded in a suspicion of the malign intentions of White individuals, a feeling of personal powerlessness, and a fear of the trouble that will result if one is not careful. Cultural mistrust provides another reason for BBY to hide their true feelings and thoughts from others, as hesitation and reticence to disclose too much about oneself in social situations serve as survival tactics. With practice, BBY become adept at sizing up and reading social cues. They learn to withhold trust and not to assume the beneficence of others. Thus, cultural mistrust is an ultimate tactic of self-protection against exploitation and humiliation.

Take Jaylon, for example, a 17-year-old senior at a predominantly White high school. He suspects that while most of his White teachers give the appearance of being interested in his doing well, they are not really sincere. He is convinced that some have low expectations of him and do not give honest feedback on writing assignments because they do not think he can do better. Others, he believes, are hostile and harshly critical without explaining what he could do to improve. White administrators also pretend to care, but they punish Black students unfairly and do not recognize the good things Black students do. He finds it hard to trust any of them. In addition, he thinks his peers are prejudiced and two-faced. He has a few Black friends and sits with them at lunchtime. He does not reach out to get to know any of the White students because he believes they will pretend to be friendly but talk about him behind his back. Consequently, he is mostly on guard while he is at school and generally keeps to himself.

The Cost of Disassociation, Concealment, Hypervigilance, and Mistrust

These various strategies, although effective to varying degrees in the short run, come with serious costs. First, they often involve the potential loss of self. In suppressing their feelings, BBY construct a persona that may be so convincing that they come to believe this false image of self and are unable to identify the authentic person behind the protective façade. They get lost in the smoke and mirrors of their own creation and forget who they really are. The roles they take on become and take over reality, and they lose touch with what is going on inside themselves and establish a boundary between their feelings and the world.

Second, they risk a loss of support. If BBY cannot communicate their pain and do not allow others to know what they are experiencing, they may deprive themselves of possible supports that can help them through emotionally difficult times. Their posture of indifference and attitudes of mistrust ensure that few people see them at their most vulnerable.

Third, these strategies can often exacerbate social problems. BBY sometimes adopt behavioral strategies and coping responses that impair adjustment in a school setting.[13] Reliance on such concealment strategies can have adverse effects because they mask students' abilities, needs, and vulnerabilities. Such strategies can make them come across as unmotivated, uncaring, resentful, defiant, or combative, and as a result, they increasingly lead BBY into disciplinary actions, suspensions, and dropping out. For example, Ron, a 17-year-old BBY, used fighting as a way to deal with his anger and reduce the frustration he felt at school:

> Like I used to fight with my friends all the time. Or if I get mad that's how I could control my temper sometimes. I just fight it out that's how I'd solve it sometimes. (Ron, 17)

Unfortunately, this was also a strategy that led to numerous exclusions from school. The subsequent loss of instructional time led him to fall farther and farther behind in his studies and made it difficult for him to keep up with the rest of the class. This in turn lowered his motivation to achieve anything at all.

Some of these coping strategies are the consequences of adultification, the process of growing up too fast. They are developed in response to urgings by others to be a big man, to tough it out, not to cry when hurt, and not to trust anyone that is not family. For many BBY, the strategies are intended to protect against the vulnerability of being out in the open where weaknesses can be seen and possibly exploited, but they are neither productive nor helpful. The downside of such strategies of self-protection, which rely on concealing one's feelings, is not so much that they are maladaptive or unjustified by the circumstances, but more that they result in BBY losing sight of who they really are, making it difficult to foster authentically intimate relationships with others. Self-knowledge and social support are essential for health and well-being. They are also critical ingredients of resilience, the ability to overcome and avoid being defeated by external circumstances. Moreover, because their emotions are often concealed or disguised, BBY are often misunderstood. As one BBY, who was sensitive to the effects of being poor and how, as a poor boy, he was treated differently, put it:

> It might be different if you are a well-off Black but there is little effort to understand poor Black boys, let alone judge them in a positive light or give them the benefit of the doubt.

Notes

1. Haye & Buckner (2013), p. 22.
2. James et al. (1983).
3. James et al. (1983).
4. Lindsey et al. (2010).
5. Harris et al. (2022).
6. For example, the work of Shepard Kellam and his associates at the Johns Hopkins University Prevention Research Center has demonstrated a strikingly high correlation of emotional disturbances with problem behavior and academic underachievement. See Ialongo et al. (2004).
7. Majors & Billson (1992).
8. Cunningham et al. (2013).
9. Santos et al. (2013).
10. Hall et al. (2008).
11. Kresovich et al. (2021).
12. Ridley (1984).
13. Thomas et al. (2009) provides a compelling account of distancing coping strategies developed by BBY in response to racial provocation or perceived unfairness in treatment by BBY's teachers or peers. These coping strategies include open expressions of anger, overreaction to perceived social rejection, hyper-masculinity, blustery conduct, taking on a tough persona, and noncompliance.

11
Becoming a Knucklehead

My great-grandmother introduced me to the term "knucklehead" when she described my cousin who seemed to be constantly in trouble. She meant it neither disparagingly nor as a form of rejection but to describe behavior that was at once exasperating and tragic. Most people will understand the idea, even if they are unfamiliar with the term. It signifies a combination of frustration and enduring affection in a relationship with a hardheaded family member who is a chronic miscreant, who resists correction, and who dismisses family advice to change. Knuckleheads can't stay away from trouble; they seem drawn to it. The trouble may vary from indolence and lack of effort at school to more serious antisocial behavior that might land the knucklehead in jail. In spite of this behavior, knuckleheads are still deeply loved and often protected by the family. The word is probably derived from the old-fashioned belief that the only way to get a troubled youth to listen is to tap him once or twice on the head with a knuckle, in other words, to knock some sense into him. Judging from its effect on my cousin, this treatment does not seem to work well—at least in the short run. Warnings and imploring go in one ear and out the other. They are so set in their errant ways they are difficult to reach. Although families tend not to give up, there is much pain in the relationship. In this analysis, we equate being a knucklehead with serious juvenile offending.

Being a knucklehead is not an identity that Black boys and youth (BBY) seek or claim. No BBY wakes up one morning and aspires to become a knucklehead. There are many factors that contribute to their becoming knuckleheads, some personal, some environmental. The process occurs slowly and takes shape through association with antisocial peers and a progressive induction into inappropriate and illegal behavior. Youth march along this path by a gradual introduction and exposure to increasingly serious transgressions, an almost imperceptible progression from minor acts of silliness and mischief—such as clowning, risk-taking, and rule-breaking—to

Building Emotional Resilience in Black Boys. Oscar A. Barbarin, Oxford University Press.
© Oxford University Press 2025. DOI: 10.1093/oso/9780197747490.003.0012

a more worrying embrace of values and attitudes permissive of and justifying illegal behavior. Relatively minor infractions are a prelude to more serious ones that lead to arrest, arraignment, conviction, and sentencing as an offender in the juvenile justice system.

While most families can identify a few features of knuckle headedness in every son, true knuckleheads are a tiny minority of BBY and unfortunately tend to be clustered in families that experience the highest levels of economic hardship, adversity, and emotional distress. Despite being a tiny minority, however, this group illustrates clearly the process by which societal structures create and sustain powerful economic and social disadvantages which give rise to adaptations that, in turn, make it difficult for families, schools, and neighborhoods to function and support the positive development of BBY. As noted earlier, progress on this path is often strewn with loss and trauma, much of it occurring within family life and much of it linked to emotional processes resulting from parental absence, conflict, or ambivalence in relations with adults who would ordinarily be key to BBY sense of safety and security. Serious juvenile offending is one of the paths followed by BBY as they adapt to this loss, trauma, material hardship, and dysfunctional school and neighborhoods.

The Antisocial Pathway

The process of becoming a knucklehead normally takes several years. Loeber and colleagues, for example, have observed that there are seven years of warning before a boy settles into a chronic pattern of delinquency.[1] Their research found that minor problem behaviors begin on average at 7 years of age in middle childhood, while a BBY's first court contact occurs at around 14.5 years of age. During these seven years, inflection points arise. These are occasions when youthful offenders choose to remain on their current illicit path or seek an alternative approach to life. At such inflection points, BBY make critical decisions to persist in or desist from misbehavior—decisions that will profoundly impact the course of their life. These inflection points also represent opportunities for adults involved in boys' lives to invest and intervene in and prevent their journeys along the antisocial pathway to serious behavior problems.

Minor Infractions Are the Start

Retrospective accounts by juvenile offenders provide details about how their paths toward chronic offending began as early as middle childhood with minor and seemingly innocuous indiscretions. They ignored rules and did not respond to correction when they misbehaved. Problem behavior was often accompanied by moodiness. They were easily upset, sometimes sad and disappointed, and often angry. They frequently fought with peers. For many, the process began with a gradual initiation into misbehaving that is startlingly similar across BB growing up in urban settings.

> I was between 6 and 12 years old, I started acting up in school sometimes, getting suspended, stuff like that, disrupting the class. I started to do stuff that was bad like popping firecrackers at gas stations, stores. Doing stuff to people's windows with my friends. (Ron, 17)

Problem behaviors increased at school and expanded to difficulties with peers:

> I was doing stuff like, you know, like I was fighting at school and, you know, cussing at people, you . . . . Just stuff that ain't right, you know what I'm saying? (Damarius, 15)

At school they were more interested in socializing with friends than learning in class. They dilly-dally between classes, lollygagging and enjoying the company of their friends, unconcerned about arriving late to their next class. Tardiness with friends led to dares and compacts to leave early or skip school entirely.

> Where I started off (I) was skipping school and partying with friends. After that I started smoking weed and stuff, and getting with the people that was involved with drugs. (Antonio, 16)

At first, problem behavior takes place sparingly, but over time it becomes habitual. It also leads to more serious misbehavior, such as staying out late and using drugs and alcohol even when there is school the next day:

So, after cutting classes, I just started hanging' out all times of night, smokin' weed, running around with the people that I'd see, standing on the corners getting high. (Ray, 15)

Whereas Black girls who exhibit conduct problems are more likely to argue, act meanly toward others, and display hot tempers, BBY with conduct problems are more likely to be described as breaking rules, cutting class, and skipping school. This pattern supports assertions that boys are bored and looking for more exciting ways to spend their time. As a consequence of frequent unexcused absences and disinterest in school, BBY fall further and further behind in acquiring the skills expected for their age, and the achievement gap widens to an extent that is difficult to reverse.

Dabbling in Petty Crimes

For many BBY, illegal behavior begins with petty crimes, such as shoplifting from neighborhood markets or department stores. They tag along on joy rides in cars stolen by older peers. By early adolescence, many have honed their skills as burglars:

> I just do little things if I get together with my friends. We might say "Look, we going to go over here and we gonna steal some hub caps or somethin'. Or We gonna go over here and we gonna steal from the store."
>
> The first time (stealing), we broke into this bike shop. It had a whole bunch of bikes and money and stuff. We went through the roof. Me and a couple other people. Went in there and got some bikes and money, inner tubes and stuff to keep our bikes up. Then, as I got older, people start learning how to, . . . we started breaking in other people's houses. Like, let's go see what they got. Then, some people moved on to stealing cars. (Kyan, 15)

To earn more money, BBY diversify their criminal activity, often selling drugs:

> After I turned twelve, I started selling drugs, selling crack and stuff like that . . . I did all these things for money. We wanted the guns, we had to have them, just in case we got into it. (Tabari, 15)

Many are introduced to selling drugs by older felons who take them under their wings and teach them the rules of the game. The older men see this as a mutually beneficial arrangement, one in which they gain an accomplice, and in return, they protect the BBY from using and becoming addicted to drugs:

> With you being so young, (you have to) get with somebody that, get with the guy that's sellin' your mother them drugs. And when you get with him, he say, "Well," he look at you and say "I ain't gonna leave this young guy here with these crack heads and then one day he be doin' the drugs (himself) so I'm gonna put him out here and show him how to make some money selling." (Jamar, 15)

However, mentorship and tutelage in drug-dealing clearly exploit BBY. They are recruited because they are minors, who, if caught, would not be prosecuted as adults. By enlisting BBY to sell drugs, older patrons can avoid direct involvement in a trade that violates their parole and carries the risk of more severe sentences.

> Older guys (twenty and twenty-three) leading younger guys (fourteen and fifteen) to do stuff for them. These older guys that have already threw their life away, and they get these younger guys and they tell them, "Well, this is how you survive. This is how you make your money." So, we started hanging together, and all the other people I was hanging around with when I was thirteen about nineteen, twenty, some were thirty. After that, we all just got established and we, we all just established a house, um, in the neighborhood, about six of us, selling crack out of it. I was smoking weed and drinkin' every night, but that was it. The main things that made me get into and stay in trouble [were] me being able to walk around with eight hundred or thousand dollars in my pocket; um, runnin' around in nice cars...
>
> This is how it's done on the streets nowadays which it (should) not (be) done like that. It shouldn't even be like that. But them young kids, man, they get, they get pulled in, so a lot of them get pulled in. It's hard to pull them back out 'cause I know how hard it was once I was pulled in. Once I got out, I looked back and said, you know, there's people leading me to do stuff like. There is a lot of people nowadays that lead these kids. (Deion, 16)

As BBY progress from minor to major criminal activity, they become known to law enforcement and have increasing contact with the juvenile justice system.[2]

> I was riding in a stolen car. My friend stole a car, he came and got me and we was riding around. We went to the weed house. We was down the street and the Narc [undercover narcotics police] pulled up behind us. They was following us for a little bit and my friend turned in the driveway, so we could get out and run. It was like four or five cars behind us then. Then, they just ran up like, "don't move." I was like, "alright." Then, they hit my friend in the head with the gun. With the barrel. Almost could have shot him. I was like, "Don't shoot me!" (Jameel, 15)

By the time families become convinced that their sons' minor infractions have become more serious problems, finding a solution can be difficult to impossible. And schools that follow policies beginning with a series of in-school punishments, like detention or (in-school) suspension but eventually leading to (home) suspension of the student, have little effect and fail to disrupt the antisocial course of development.

Imitating Antisocial Peers

> At about 12, I started hanging around with all the people around my age range except (for) a couple people. My two best friends that I grew up with and I knew that they were coming to the life that I wanted to be in as far as selling drugs, smoking weed and stuff like that. (Keshaun, 16)

The escalation to more grievous and illegal behavior is made possible by a series of bad choices BBY make, without thought to their consequences, and are justified in their minds by an antagonistic view of society. Such behavior, as well as the underlying worldview that rationalizes it, is often reinforced by antisocial peers. One youth commented on the negative attitudes of younger boys that led them to feel as if the entire world was out to get them:

> But it's, these kids nowadays, they don't want to do right, because they feel everybody's against them. They feel like the police against them, they feel like their parents against them, that's why they run away from home, they

doin' drugs and they sellin' drugs and then they get around these older guys that already threw their life away. (Jameel, 15)

When youthful offenders consolidate their reputations as risk-takers by skipping school, they are often attracted to opportunities to hang out, cultivate social connections, and party with friends. Stealing food and alcohol become a necessary adjunct to sustaining truancy and partying. Drinking and smoking weed become part of the fun and a necessary antidote to boredom. From the standpoint of BBY, their social connections with other truants represent an attempt to assuage their loneliness, boredom, and despair, and offer them support and protection that families could not and did not. Unfortunately, these connections also make it much more likely that they will continue down a dangerous path.

Inflection Points

The developmental sequence moving toward juvenile offending is predictable. It is not, however, inevitable. Hope can be found in the multiple turning points or occasions where change is possible. As Sroufe et al. observe, "Development turns at each and every stage of the journey on an interaction between the organism as it has developed up to that moment and the environment in which it then finds itself."[3] Supportive environments can help BBY change by offering prosocial activities and alternative ways of socializing to cope with and fill in the emotional gaps BBY experience as a consequence of loss and trauma.

The idea of inflection or turning points is used in this section to denote various points along the line of progression toward serious offending that present an opportunity for a reversal of direction toward prosocial development.[4] Inflection points vary from youth to youth. They include specific events, such as an arrest, the death of a friend from violence, having a child, or the start of an important relationship with a romantic partner or mentor. But they can also occur when a BBY hears or experiences something that alters their perception of themselves or their behavior. Something happens during an inflection point that moves BBY to evaluate their behavior and reflect on its consequences for themselves and those they care about. The inflection points that were described most often in our ethnography of youthful offenders can be categorized as:

- an initial arrest or frightening encounter with police.
- a blossoming relationship with a caring adult or mentor.
- a change of physical environments, such as school or neighborhood.
- transition to adult status (e.g., birth of a child, employment).

When an inflection point is managed effectively, it can become an occasion to challenge and redirect BBY's ways of thinking and behaving toward a more promising pathway. At these points, BBY will accept responsibility for their behavior rather than blame others. They will consider and begin to care about the harm they do to others and desire to make amends.

Disturbing Encounter with Police

A BBY's initial police contact can be overwhelming and traumatizing. The coercive and seemingly unrestricted power wielded by police officers is intimidating. Most BBY are aware of generic policies that allow police to frisk and search without specific cause and the ill-defined limitations on police use of force. Even by middle childhood, they are aware that police stops for minor violations can lead to injury and even death:

> It scared me when the police pulled us over, because the first cop that jumped out, he was like, "Move and you die!" I was like, ah, we out here in a white neighborhood, we all black in this car, and they are about to kill us. I'm like "oh, my God." He was like, "Stick your hands out the window." I'm sticking my hands out the window, he just yanked me out the car and threw me in the back seat of the police car and searched me and stuff. I didn't know what they were going to do. (Jameel, 15)

In his book, Wes Moore describes an event that was fraught with similar uncertainty and fear, and that left an indelible impression on him.[5] He recalls the police officer pointing a finger at him and admonishing him that he was too young to be in this trouble. If Wes did not get smart, the officer warned, he would see him again.

> I was wincing because the handcuffs were beginning to hurt my wrists, but I was sincerely fearful... Something about this situation had soured me on romantic rebellion... It may have been the moment when the officer finally

pulled my second arm behind my back and tightened the handcuffs. I became aware of how I had put myself in this unimaginably dire situation—this man now had control of my body... more than that, he had control of my destiny... All I wanted to do was turn around, go home and never find myself at this precipice again for such a stupid reason (i.e., spray-painting graffiti).[6]

Wes Moore's mother, his only advocate, was so disappointed by the event that Wes wanted to make sure he was never in this situation again. Other BBY report similar epiphanies:

I ain't never, I said I ain't never want to get locked up no more. It was like, I don't want nobody else, I just, you know, it was just you wake up, you eat, you do what they tell you to do. You eat at a certain time, you go to school, you do what they tell you to do. I was like, man, they stricter than my mother. At least I can get some leeway with my mother... When I was in there, I just used to think at night, like man, when I get out of here, I'm just going to go to school and get me an education. Without it you ain't nothin'. Got to help these children out here today I'm tellin' you. You got to just get hard on them you know? (Tyrell, 16)

By implication, Tyrell is underscoring the elements of supervision and control that were missing in his life. He was able to bargain for too much freedom in negotiating life with his solo mother. She was working so much that she did not know what he was doing and the trouble he was getting into when she was not home. For Tyrell, the turning point came when he entered court-ordered residential treatment that altered his environment and imposed structure that was missing before.

Relations with Caring Adults

Just as acts of abandonment, the loss of primary caregivers, and uncaring relationships with family and school can push BBY toward antisocial peers and juvenile offending, the introduction of a caring nurturing adult, no matter how late in adolescence, can pull BBY back from the precipice. The entry into BBY's lives of people who sincerely value and mentor them can be very impactful, as can the establishment of meaningful bonds. One youth describes the absence and recovery of his father in a positive way:

> My father left when I was three. So, I didn't know him that well. but I know him well now. But I didn't know him that good. I didn't think about him until like about two years ago before I was locked up. He came back and he's takin' me to his house for Christmas and holidays, birthdays, you know. He shows he cares... this meant a lot to me. I'm his only child. (Daren, 15)

Another BBY described how he worked at building a positive affirming relationship with his stepfather:

> Well, we got a strong relationship you know, being that he's my stepfather (i.e., not my father). He help me a lot. He's a mechanic. So, you know, we, me and him we get into it a little, we don't argue or nothin' like that. We got the same kind of thoughts. We like cars, me and him both, so you know that's a lot, that's how me and him get our relationship together. (Keion, 16)

Sharing a common interest is one way caring adults link to and build relationships with BBY. While parents, stepparents, and close relatives often provide the impactful mentoring and guidance, professionals that enter BBY's lives and invest in them can also help direct them back onto a more positive developmental path. Such was the case for Ryan Speedo Green (the opera singer), introduced in Chapter 8. After leaving a special education program, Green attended a public school in his community. The school had a music program, and a Black male teacher led the choir program. Although Ryan had shown no previous interest in singing or in music, the director encouraged him to join. Ryan identified strongly with this nurturing man who took an interest in him and helped him to recognize and develop his talent. This was the beginning of a sustaining relationship that redirected him onto a positive path that led to a career in opera and the stability of marriage and children.

Changing Environments

Getting away from a negative family, peer, school, or neighborhood environment can also give BBY a chance to reimagine themselves, to start over, and to establish a new identity. Sometimes, such changes are voluntary, as when a family moves to a different neighborhood, decides to change schools, or sends a youth to live with relatives in a different city or state. At other times, changes in a BBY's environment may be involuntary, as when a youth is convicted and sentenced to a residential treatment facility (this was the case for the youths who participated in our ethnographic interviews). These programs are designed to create a positive peer culture, help youths deal with their emotional trauma, and challenge the antisocial attitudes and values they were living by when they were arrested. Time spent in a treatment program can offer an opportunity to deal with earlier unprocessed trauma and help youths envision a different "possible self."

Wes Moore's story is an example of how moving to a new environment can change a BBY's trajectory. Although he promised to change his ways after being caught by the police, his reform was short-lived. He continued to skip school, set off a smoke bomb at school, and generally ignored his education. Out of boredom, he attempted to punch his sister on the arm to get her attention and accidentally hit her in the face, causing her to bleed. Fearing the worst for his future and even his survival, his mother took on a heavy financial burden to send him away to Valley Forge Military Academy in PA. She hoped that the structure of the school would teach him to accept discipline, follow instructions, and develop self-control. Before deciding to enroll Wes in the school, she met with a senior Black student and leader at the school, Ty Hill, and asked him to look after Wes if he were to enroll. At first, Wes hated the school and resented being there. As one of the few BBY at the school, he was lonely and missed his family and his troubled friends. He ran away from the school several times but never made it very far because of the surrounding woods. After one attempt, he was confronted by his chain of command at the academy and challenged to snap out of it. In time, the school administrator formally introduced Wes to Ty Hill, who Wes later described as having a frighteningly serious demeanor, an old soul in a teen's body. In keeping with the pledge made to Wes's mother, Ty became Wes's guide and mentor. Wes looked up to Ty and sought to emulate him. In time Wes grew to love the Academy and rekindled an interest in learning.[7]

Transition to Adult Status

The transition to adult status occurs late in the formation of a juvenile offender, but it can also serve as an inflection point. It comes with the development of the prefrontal lobe of the brain, which is responsible for mature reasoning and a reordering of priorities. This transition often begins with a realistic appraisal of the risks taken and their impact on others, something that is often missing earlier in life. It may involve taking on responsibility for another person by, for example, beginning to work to contribute to the household financial resources, getting married, or caring for a child. During such transitions, change in behavior and outlook almost always involves the collision of past experience with a vision of fresh possibilities that motivate a youth to set off in a new direction. These inflection points provide an opportunity for BBY to choose between committing themselves further to the deviant way of life or turning themselves around and engaging in more prosocial behaviors. These life-changing events generally result in a reconsideration of life on the streets.

> I'd say I turned around when I had my son. It's like all the stuff I was doing before that, it was like I really didn't care, what happened to me. When I had my son, my momma was like, "you know, you got to get a job, you have to start doing better, you have to go to school." (Deondre, 19)

Realizing the Impact of Delinquency on Family and Self

Sometimes, a turning point is triggered by the realization that one's behavior has been deeply troubling for one's family. This realization can be enough to give the youth pause about what they are doing:

> I know my behavior affected my father a lot, 'cause my sister would tell me that he wouldn't even act the same, he would come home from work, and sit down at the table and listen to sad songs all the time and drink and sit there and cry and then he would go to bed. So, I knew it was hurting him a lot. So that kind of helped me push myself to and say, "I don't want to have my family walkin' around miserable like this." (Phil, 19)

More broadly, adolescents on the cusp of adulthood will sometimes come to recognize the consequences of their negative behavior, how their life has gone, causing them to regret their past behavior. In retrospect, it all seems senseless and futile:

All that stuff we did in the past, like shoot at each other and kill each other, boys, not worth it. We wouldn't allow rivals to walk on our side of the block and stuff like that. All that madness, you gotta get to the fact, it ain't even worth it. I mean, it ain't going to get you nowhere where like my friends ended up, couple of their boys ended up, you know where I'm saying, I ended up, and some more of their boys ended up: either dead or in jail. That's only place it's going to . . .

I wish I could start all over, from day one when I was first born, um, maybe I feel I have a better chance of starting off right than I did, well, than I did when I started doin' what I was doin', you know. I would like to be little again; I would do things different. (Eric, 17)

Wisdom Comes Late

"Too soon old, too late smart" is a proverb of uncertain origin that captures a fundamental tragedy of life in which wisdom often comes late. We grow old more quickly than we grow wise. For some, a bit of wisdom comes with experience.

To try changing my life, I'm going to sit there, and I'm going to think like, well, how long am I going to sell drugs now, uh? Till I turn what fifty, you know what I'm saying, I'm going to run from the police until I turn fifty, and you think, and I just start thinking you know what I'm saying, and I just say, man I ain't doin' it? (James, 16)

Reflections about adulthood and what a future might look like can also mark an inflection point in which BBY become motivated to change the direction of their lives.

This tragedy of growing smart late is all too common for BBY caught up in juvenile offending. Their circumstances thrust them into situations that require them to grow up too soon. They take on adultlike responsibilities to care for and protect others and must make sophisticated judgments or engage in self-regulation before their reasoning abilities have developed sufficiently to equip them to make such judgements. Many BBY gain wisdom too late to undo mistakes and reverse the processes that have led them to incarceration and a life of being under the control of others, a form of modern-day slavery, where many of their rights have been taken away and their human dignity diminished by others.

A combination of external and internal factors can divert BBY from a prosocial trajectory onto the path of juvenile offending. This combination involves the interaction of poor individual choices, family dysfunction, material hardship, poor schools, and neighborhood violence. BBY are failed by under-involved parents, detached fathers, and a lack of connection to their extended family or spiritual communities. Disorganized schools are unable to understand and engage BBY with inspired instruction and emotionally available teachers. Problem behaviors are also linked to dysfunctional neighborhoods with high levels of substance abuse, easily accessible guns, violence, and glaring resource deficiencies. These risk factors render BBY vulnerable to problem behaviors. They created an environment where choosing a prosocial path is difficult.

Although our analysis highlights numerous external influences that contribute to juvenile offending, BY are not faultless. They ultimately bear responsibility for the choices they make. As we have seen, decisions to commit to an antisocial path and to associate with peers who model and encourage antisocial behavior are motivated by loss, loneliness, and a need for acceptance and protection that their families and other adults cannot provide. These decisions are fueled by BBY's low academic engagement, which leads to a self-reinforcing deficit of academic skills. BBY remain on this negative path because for a while they enjoy the freedom and excitement that comes from escaping the controlling presence of adults. They covet the material goods that their families cannot give them and that they cannot afford to provide for themselves through legal means. They lose hope over what they see as a dead-end life with a premature death.

Understanding these internal and external risk factors can help identify strategies for intervening with BBY before they have embarked upon a path leading to serious problem behaviors. If we can improve the environment by minimizing some of these risk factors, boys will be less vulnerable and have a greater likelihood of coping with trauma and developing social competencies. As has been discussed in this chapter, there are various inflection or turning points in BBY's lives where access to social connections and mentoring make it possible to prevent them from progressing from minor to major transgressions, and can enable them to turn their lives around. Love not retribution, caring not punishment, and inclusion not exclusion are the solutions to prevent boys viewed as challenging, disruptive, aggressive, and oppositional from becoming juvenile offenders.

Notes

1. Loeber et al. (2003).
2. Barbarin & Soler (1993); Barbarin (1999); Farmer et al. (2002).
3. Sroufe et al. (2010).
4. It has been previously used in Sampson & Laub (2005).
5. Moore (2010).
6. Moore (2010), p. 83.
7. Moore (2010), p. 94.

PART VI
SOCIAL ASSETS AND EMOTIONAL RESILIENCE

12
Emotional Resilience

Emotional resilience refers to a state of equilibrium that results from coping with adversity without the emotional distortions or stunting that are associated with denial, emotional numbing, dissociation, or faking emotional indifference. This chapter describes several coping strategies that can help BBY become resilient in spite of distress arising from economic hardship and racism. Emotional resilience involves a capacity to withstand or recover from such adversity and to mitigate the risks they pose to positive development.[1] However, life is messy, and emotional resilience does not imply a complete avoidance of pain associated with adversity or guarantee a state of saintly perfection in responding to it. Emotional resilience often means that residual flaws or problematic responses to hardship coexist with robust social competencies. Emotional resilience my not break the adverse sequelae of racism and economic hardship, but it does suggest that they can be bent enough that resilient BBY are able to acquire a fundamentally prosocial stance toward life.[2]

The emotional cost of dealing with strains of racism and economic hardship do not place a productive and meaningful life out of reach. BBY can cope with loss, trauma, and emotionally demanding situations through self-awareness, self-regulation, and social awareness. These enable strategies by which to offset negative emotional arousal associated with trauma. They do this by enabling the setting and achieving of meaningful goals, cultivating friendships, giving and accepting help, and constructing a sense of purpose that lends meaning to their existence. They enable BBY to manage distress, for example, through active problem solving, encouraging feelings of gratitude, optimism and joy; or finding some good in an otherwise painful situation.

Self-Awareness and Resilience

In dealing with chronic distress, BBY face a choice. They can either disregard their pain, become fatalistic about danger, succumb to inaction, and fail to take steps that might make their lives better; or, alternatively, they can become reflective, and resist stereotypes. They can draw on social competencies related to self-awareness by acknowledging pain and avoiding threatening situations, affirming self-worth and personal efficacy, and rejecting stereotypes and stigma. Self-awareness is exemplified in reflecting on and analyzing emotional reactions to events of the day. To do this, resilient BBY focus on what they are feeling and express those feelings in words instead of denying them or acting them out.

Acknowledging Emotional Pain

Acknowledging emotional pain is singled out for consideration here because it poses a unique and difficult task for BBY. As noted elsewhere, BBY are often pushed to disregard their pain when they are hurt. Pain is hard for BBY to acknowledge, especially BBY who have cultivated a hyper-masculine identity and reputation. To overcome the pressure to deny pain requires being in touch and admitting pain related to traumatic experiences of loss, such as homicide of a friend, father-absence, scapegoating at school, belittling by peers, intimidation, and social rejection. Recognizing and admitting the pain and fears to themselves and others are important first steps in moving toward emotional resilience. Adopting this stance means admitting to themselves when they are hurt. For BBY to do this, they must cultivate the practice of introspection. They also must be courageous enough to disregard being considered weak, teased as girly, or criticized as oversensitive. When BBY are sufficiently reflective, they become aware of persons, places, and situations that pose some physical or emotional danger and, as a consequence, are able to identify what makes them angry, despondent, hopeless, or afraid.

Affirmation of Self-Worth and Personal Efficacy

Affirmation is an active cognitive strategy in which BBY identify and articulate for themselves their values, strengths, and abilities. Affirmation combines a realistic but positive self-regard and personal agency, a proactive approach to solving problems steeped in the belief that they can do it. Resilient BBY engage in self-affirming dialogue within themselves. For example, they might give themselves a pep talk just before addressing a serious problem. They use internalized speech to lift themselves up with statements delighting in their talents and reviewing their past accomplishments. They understand that persistent effort is required, and that it will make the difference between success and failure and failure is not an option.

Resisting Racism Stereotypes and Discrimination

Confrontation is an active problem-focused strategy using assertive behaviors to challenge discrimination and affirmative statement to counter racist stereotypes. To do so, BBY may push back against persons in authority who discriminate and refuse to comply with rules that are unfair. This may involve calling out adults who enforce rules that are patently unjust or impose standards that are unreasonable. Angry outbursts, indignation, and non-violent protest may be employed to agitate for and demand fair treatment. Resilient BBY resist internalizing negative messages and cultivate ideas that contradict claims of Black inferiority by pointing to models of Black excellence and achievement. They critically analyze the self-serving motivation of those who discriminate and believe the stereotypes. This approach can be seen in the self-description of Austin, one BBY in our study:

> I see myself as strong-minded. I speak for myself in a way that you know how I feel. I speak up for myself a lot. If I'm gonna speak up for myself, I feel like a lot of people should be like that. Anyone around me should speak up for themselves too. (Austin, 17)

These strategies can be taught. For instance, Smith and Hope describe an action research project that transformed BBY's social and political attitudes and led them to challenge racist tropes and stereotypes of BBY as intellectually inferior, aggressive, out of control, or socially inept.[3] These attitude changes were fostered within an afterschool program conducted at a suburban, predominantly White high school. It encouraged BBY to think deeply and analyze their experiences at school using photography and discussion. The goal of these reflections was to provide the boys with an opportunity to consider what their school could do to better support them. The program helped boys counter the negative narratives about BBY and, over the year, its consciousness-raising discussions and activities wore away at the negative representation of BBY and created space for more positive views of BBY to take hold. Participants in the program became leaders in the school, aspiring and working hard to achieve success.

Fortunately, by middle childhood, many BBY in their responses to emotional distress have matured beyond the extremes of angry outbursts on the one hand and concealing and suppressing the display of emotions on the other. They adopt strategies that reflect an ability to inhibit inappropriate behavior and anger, to manage frustration, and to develop more positive relations at home, in school, and in the community. These strategies, part of BBYs' ability to self-regulate, enable BBY to assume responsible prosocial roles and benefit more fully from the guidance of adults. Examples of these strategies include toning down speech, judiciously using humor, avoiding sudden movements, and sidestepping conflicts and aggression. In particular, self-regulation enables specific strategies that facilitate coping with adversity: accommodation, redirecting emotions, and reframing.

Accepting and Accommodating Adversity

Acceptance is a cognitive strategy by which moderate emotional distress when faced with unexpected and uncontrollable stressful life events that can range from minor events such as disappointment over a teacher's reprimand or peer rejection, to more serious setbacks, such as dealing with life-threatening illness, parental divorce, incarceration, or death. Acceptance is a passive strategy that is more effective than active strategies because BBY have little or no power to alter or stop the stressful event. Acceptance means acknowledging the reality and the pain these events cause, avoiding self-blame, and the realization that one will do better if one can adjust to one's reality from a position of emotional equilibrium and peaceful resignation. Cognitively, acceptance is a positive calm indifference based on the conviction that adversity will not break you and that you can learn to live with it, as bad as it may seem and feel at the time. Acceptance strategies can be enacted through yoga, mindfulness exercise, meditation, or prayer.

Behaviorally, acceptance involves accommodation or behaving in a way that reflects resignation to the situation in order to stem the sadness it causes. This can take various forms, such as changing oneself to fit into a social group that would otherwise reject one. Accommodation may be observed in changes in various aspects of self, such as language, dress, response to peer pressure, generally, or the alteration of work habits to fit in and be accepted by peers. For BBY, it may mean giving up on trying to excel academically and win the approval of teachers in order to overcome the label of "bad boy," and shifting instead to seeking approbation from other sources, such as peers, or pursuing recognition in other domains, such as athletics. While this might seem fatalistic, the response itself is adaptive, as it allows BBY to invest energies in pursuits that are more likely to yield desired results.

Redirecting Feelings

The redirect strategy refers to channeling one's energy away from negative impulses and toward more positive and productive activities. It is similar to the defense mechanism of sublimation, in which socially unacceptable impulses or feelings are transformed into socially acceptable behaviors or activities. Using redirection, an unpleasant emotion such as anger can be transformed and redirected toward athletic competition, while anxiety might be redirected toward academics or debates. Though the stressful events that gave rise to the emotions may not change, redirecting minimizes the likelihood of unproductive or antisocial responses that might make the situation worse. For example, sadness and remorse at the loss or absence of a father might be channeled into volunteering and serving men at a Veteran's hospital. Thus, the energy and force of an emotion can be redirected from an antisocial response, such as hostility and aggression, toward socially acceptable behavior that reflects altruism or kindness.

Reframing Adversity

Often BBY can do little to get at the root of intractable problems. They can, however, alter how they interpret and feel about a problem and, in doing so, help themselves to moderate their emotional responses. In some circumstances, solving an emotion-ladened problem requires looking at it in a different way. A frame is the lens through which we see the world, the fixed assumptions that shape our interpretation of an event. Reframing is the act of reinterpreting a situation so that it is no longer viewed as a loss, a threat, or a source of adversity, but rather as an opportunity with positive features or a challenge to overcome. It means shifting from seeing a glass as half empty to seeing it as half full.

Reframing requires opening up to an alternative way of thinking about a problem or situation. It involves assigning purpose and meaning to events that might otherwise appear to be meaningless and futile. Reframing involves shaking up and questioning assumptions. It begins with considering and questioning what we believe to be true about life and people. This can be achieved by discovering opportunity in a loss and attaching a larger meaning or purpose to a traumatic event that otherwise provokes sadness or anxiety. For instance, adversity can sometimes be interpreted as a lesson to be learned, or a skill to be mastered.

For BBY, reframing often involves forming different ways of thinking that counter prevailing stereotypes about their supposed inferiority and deficiencies. Disparagement and rejection by a circle of close friends at school might be reframed as a chance for BBY to branch out and form new relationships that offer a more authentic acceptance. BBY growing up in severe poverty might shift their focus from the material things they cannot afford to gratitude for the things they have that allow them to feel satisfied. Rather than envying what others have that they do not, they might focus on the fact that they have all that they need.

Social Awareness and Resilience

In many cases adverse events related to racism and economic hardship have complicated social features that are difficult for one person to understand and address on the basis of their knowledge, experience, and own resources alone. They will need help to cope effectively. This is especially true for young BB who have yet to develop the competencies and knowledge to deal with many of the problems they face. In such cases, it is important for BBY to have people they can count on for help and that they learn to look for and reach out to potential helpers.

Avoidance of Danger

Avoidance is a human response to pain and danger. It can be a reflex like pulling one's fingers away from a flame, or a learned response, like knowing to avoid a flame in the future. It is an attempt to minimize one's exposure to dangerous situations, whether they be social, psychological, or physical, by staying away from certain places and people that threaten or cause harm. This is a strategy that is often endorsed by parents as a way of preventing injury. Beyond merely avoiding certain situations entirely, it can also mean backing away from a fight, de-escalating a conflict by an apology, or conceding that the person on the other side of the argument may be right. Avoidance is a common response BBY use to cope with sources of unpleasant arousal, such as anxiety or sadness.[4]

Cultivating Friendships and Positive Social Ties

Loneliness is aversive and unpleasant. Loneliness and the effort to cope with it were a major reason some BBY joined gangs. Although BBY may seek to withdraw into their own world when in pain, many find value, safety, comfort, and pleasure in the presence of others. Those who do typically have better mental health than those who are socially isolated. Reaching out to others and developing friendships satisfy a need for emotional connection. The ability to reach out and develop positive peer relations is marked by spending time and engaging in fun activities together. It also means feeling empathy and trying to comfort and reassure others who are in pain. Secure attachment of BBY facilitates interpersonal trust and emotional intimacy that is advantageous in giving and receiving emotional help. As a consequence, BBY who master this strategy have fewer conflicts and are more able to repair relations when conflicts arise.[5] Creating and maintaining positive social ties and friendships can be hard work. However the rewards are great and come in the form of supportive peer relations,[6] reduction of interpersonal conflict and prejudice,[7] and joyful intimacy in dyadic relationships.[8]

Accepting Help

Accepting help is an active problem-focused strategy that BBY can use to seek emotional support, external intervention, material aid, or advice in addressing difficulties they face. Accepting help involves the ability to recognize one's need for aid and the willingness to reach out to others for assistance in dealing with problems. Many difficulties faced by BBY can be overwhelming and present issues that BBY cannot manage alone. At the same time, there are multiple obstacles that BBY must overcome before they are able and willing to accept help. Doing so requires revealing one's pain, vulnerability, and inadequacy to others. Accepting help requires the humility to recognize that one is unable to resolve the problem alone. Moreover, relying on help from others belies the myth of masculine strength. For some boys who have been socialized to see themselves as independent or responsible for others, it may be particularly difficult to ask for or accept help. If BBY can overcome the idea that they must remain independent and struggle alone, they can benefit from encouragement, affirmation, empathy, and direct assistance from others.

Helping Others

Helping others refers to acts of kindness and service from which no benefit is expected save the joy that comes from helping others. It is a form of altruism and is associated with better emotional functioning, the ability to cope with stress, and reduced aggression.[9] Research has shown that attending to and responding to the needs of others offers psychological and social benefits. Tashjian and colleagues, for example, have demonstrated that performing acts of altruism resulted in increasing positive affect, decreasing negative affect, and reducing stress.[10] Practicing altruism has also been associated with lower levels of violence and substance abuse among youth who grew up in adversity.[11] Research on positive youth development also points to the importance of opportunities to help others for emotional development. Under normal circumstances, helpers receive positive reinforcement and gratitude from those receiving help. In addition, they come to develop a positive image of themselves and often become embedded in a prosocial community that models and reinforces positive coping behaviors.

For some BBY, close family relationships provide an opportunity to undertake such altruistic acts. For example, Rashad was profoundly sad for his mother whose visual impairment prevented her from doing things that others take for granted.

> Yeah, a lot of times in my life I felt, you know, sad that my mother couldn't see, you know, that she can't even get around by herself, you know what I'm saying? But, it just made me sad that some of the things that I knew she wanted to do. Like I knew she wanted to drive, you know what I'm saying.

> I knew she wanted to do things that any other ones wanted to do.... it made me sad that she can't do what she plans. (Rashid, 17)

Rashad adapted and coped with his sadness about his mother by reframing and viewing his mother's condition in a different light. He began to see it not as an occasion for sadness but as an impetus for altruism. This perspective strengthened his resolve to be with and help her to overcome the obstacles presented by her limited vision.

> But me and her get together and talk and we move on and find larger things, you know what I'm saying, greater things, you know, than what she can't do. I'm gonna be here for my mother, you know what I'm saying ... all my life, no matter what, I'm gonna be there for my mother.

Participation in a Spiritual Community

Participation in a spiritual community refers to joining and becoming actively engaged in a religious or spiritual organization such as a church, temple, or mosque. This strategy has two important facets: social and spiritual. First, it provides connection with a social group that is likely to offer care and support. Second, it offers a set of beliefs about life that places human existence within a larger framework overseen by a caring and providential being. This providential and powerful other, who cares about and is invested in the well-being of individuals, is someone in whom BBY can trust and on whom they call for help in coping with life's challenges. Spiritual beliefs offer a worldview, a framework for understanding self and one's place and purpose in the universe. These religious beliefs have long contributed to how Black families have coped with adversity. Attending church services and prayer have been a source of consolation in difficult times and an emotional release for Black families in times of anxiety and worry. For example, a relationship to God developed and solidified through prayer and reflection can serve as a source of solace, comfort, and guidance, as expressed by one BBY who identified his biological and heavenly father as the individuals on whom he relied for help:

> I would say I get most of my help from my father, then the Lord. (Phillip, 13)

Another BBY noted that belief in God was his source of hope for a better future:

> I do believe that God is with us. I depend on the Lord a lot, to help me through my problems. I believe that it is going to be a world after this one ends. I feel the Lord going to make a better world after everybody leave this earth, it's going to start all over from the beginning again. (Traevon, 15)

Social Competence and Effective Coping Foster Resilience

BBY respond to emotional distress in a variety of ways. Some are active in the face of threats; others are passive. Some cope with loss and trauma by denying and concealing their impact. Some fight, others avoid conflict. When criticism, invisibility, and rejection become too much to bear, some express anger, adopt the "cool pose," or pretend not to care. Some dissociate and others use self-affirmation to counter stigma and shame. Some deal with the devaluation and lack of respect they feel at school by seeking opportunities to excel elsewhere or by seeking relief from their despondence in mood-altering substances.

Coping strategies arising from social competencies enable BBY to moderate arousal, deal with emotional trauma, and find their way in the world. These strategies help them to deal with the realization that while their power to change things overall may be limited, they do not need to fall victim to resignation, fatalism, or acceptance of the status quo as normal. This in turn can help them avoid internalizing hopelessness or seeing themselves as victims. Effective coping can make the difference between BBY becoming indifferent to meeting societal standards of success and becoming resilient in spite of adversity.

Hip-Hop as a Resource BBY Use for Emotional Coping

BBY utilize many of the coping strategies described above by listening to the lyrics of hip hop artists. Hip hop artists, such as Biggie Smalls, Juice Wrld, Kid Cudi, and Kendrick Lamar seem to appeal to different generations who anoint them as the authentic voices of their era. These artists are successful because they capture the tempo and express the mood of their generation.

BBY listen to and find resonance in the emotions expressed in their favorite artist's lyrics. These artists give voice to the feelings many BBY cannot put into words themselves. The lyrics often occupy the gray zone between fantasy and reality, between the world they aspire to and the world they live in. BBY see themselves represented in the music and can imagine that they overcome their struggles just as the protagonists in the lyrics do. They experience emotional relief through the songs. Listening to and singing along with the music is calming and helps BBY down-regulate chronic emotional arousal. In this way, hip hop poets not only open a window onto the inner lives of BBY through their representations of Black life but also serve as a principal medium through which BBY achieve emotional resilience.

Socio-emotional Competence

Socio-emotional competence is the thread that binds together elements of healthy development, mental health, coping, and psychological adjustment. Together, social awareness, self-awareness, and self-regulation contribute to resilience.

Because they are generally agreeable, easy-going, and easy to please, socially competent BBY make friends readily and have positive relationships with adults. Among peers, they may be trend-setters and peacemakers who help to de-escalate conflict. Though they can be assertive and push the limits to get what they want, in the end they comply with rules and try to meet behavior expectations especially from the people whose respect they seek to earn. Social competence is also associated with a positive racial identity, optimism, self-acceptance, and a realistic sense of personal efficacy. Resilience is also evident in interpersonal trust. Socially competent BBY develop optimistic views about the world. Unless experience proves otherwise, they do not assume hostile intentions in others, anticipate threats everywhere, or fear getting close to others. Instead, they expect that others will be friendly but also understand that racist views and discrimination do exist and are likely to touch their lives.

Social competence in BBY arises from the deployment of effective coping strategies and the development of social skills. Both are highly dependent on BBYs' access to social assets in the form of supportive relationships at home, school, and in the community; and both draw on cultural practices and beliefs. These strategies strengthen emotion self-regulation and help BBY to be civil and accommodating, to bounce back from disappointment, or to maintain performance in the wake of some personal loss or other source of distress. They enable BBY to endure life challenges, overcome setbacks, strengthen relationships, and meet the expectations society holds for mature and responsible individuals. Social competencies and effective coping provide a foundation on which academic and psychological adjustments are built. They are a metaphorical ladder with which to scale a wall of burdens, or the lubricant needed to minimize friction and glide gracefully over life's bumps and hurdles.

Becoming Emotionally Resilient

Progress toward resilience requires personal agency, transcendence, optimism, an appreciation of who one is, and gratitude for the people who care about one. BBY can adopt an optimistic and active posture that reflects a conviction that no matter how bad a situation might seem, one can act to reduce the stress, limit its effects, and perhaps improve the situation. They can choose to explore and seize opportunities and opt to seek help, rather than sleepwalk through life because it all feels too hopeless and painful. These choices begin with self, a willingness to look inward and to acknowledge rather than deny emotional pain. Resilient BBY reject as untrue stigma and negative characterizations. They marshal their attention, willpower, and psychological resources to manage behavior and emotions so that a bad situation is not made worse.

At the same time, while resilience begins with self, it does not end there. To become resilient means that BBY must build connections with others and recognize both that the path through life is much easier to traverse with help, and that there is benefit in responding when others need assistance. No single strategy or approach is perfect or correct in all situations. None can guarantee a desired outcome. However, the social competencies discussed in this chapter make it possible to overcome adversity and achieve positive prosocial outcomes. BBY rarely acquire these skills on their own. Instead, social assets such as supportive relationships with peers and adults increase the likelihood of resilience and the capacity to manage arousal, adversity, and stress in their lives.[12]

Notes

1. Masten & Cicchetti (2016). Also see the report of the APA Task Force on Resilience and Strength in Black Children and Adolescents (2008) for an exhaustive and excellent review of the issues and evidence pertaining to resilience in BBY.
2. Barbarin et al. (2022).
3. Smith & Hope (2020).
4. Gaylord-Harden et al. (2011).
5. Busby et al. (2013).
6. Jensen-Campbell & Graziano (2001).
7. Sibley & Duckitt (2008).
8. Busby et al. (2013).
9. Thulin et al. (2022).
10. Tashjian et al. (2021).
11. Thulin et al. (2022).
12. Kraag et al. (2006).

13
Social Assets Build Resilience

Economic deprivation and racism pose significant risks to Black boys and youth (BBY) development and emotional well-being.[1] They impose material hardship, expose BBY to adverse events and trauma, and can push BBY toward negative representations of self as threatened, vulnerable, and helpless victims. Even though growing up under adverse conditions has few apparent advantages, healthy emotional functioning is still possible. Adverse conditions notwithstanding, many BBY draw on psychosocial competencies and strengths to become emotionally resilient. But resilience depends on more than the individual efforts of BBY. It cannot form apart from the contributions of families, schools, and communities. Emotional resilience is much more likely to form with the participation of these social assets than in their absence.[2] This chapter presents examples of social assets and explains how they build resilience.

Although scholars initially thought that emotional resilience resulted from personality traits, choices, and behaviors of BBY, in time they came to learn that these individual characteristics could not account for emotional resilience on their own. Instead, the research revealed that access to social assets in the form of supportive relations at home, at school, and in the community were potent predictors of resilience in children growing up in adverse circumstances.[3] This chapter explains the importance of supportive experiences, interactions, and relations that BBY have in their families, schools, and communities. These supports help BBY become emotionally resilient by developing their ability to tamp down emotional distress and keep their behavior within acceptable bounds. Accordingly, this chapter describes how these social assets prevent psychological injury and heal wounds of adversity by supporting the development of social competencies.

Social Assets

To develop resilience, BB, and indeed all children, need networks of caring persons that are activated when BBY become emotionally dysregulated and distressed as well as when they need reassurance, respect, encouragement, support, and safety. BBY also need structures of control that are activated to take charge, set limits, give directions, and impose consequences to augment boys' self-regulation when they are out of control or when they are about to make poor decisions, act irresponsibly, or do things that may harm themselves or others. These networks of care and structures of control ideally exist at home, at school, and in the neighborhood and constitute social assets that facilitate prosocial development and resilience. Social assets that come in the form of involved supportive families and communities can make a big difference in how well BBY function in adversity. More precisely, these social assets include loving family relationships, which can be evident early in life in the form of attachment security, connections to teachers who demonstrate interest, and friendships that grow closer during middle childhood and adolescence. As noted in Chapter 5, secure attachments to primary caregivers provide protection and safety for young children when they are upset. Similarly, responsive care and guidance from family and mentors in the community are extraordinary resources for reducing and managing stress and negative emotional arousal in middle childhood and adolescence. These relational assets may expand to include networks of extended family and affinity groups based on common ethnicity, culture, language, or heritage. Together, families, schools, and communities comprise a "3-legged stool" of social assets, as described in the Introduction.

Social assets, as networks of caring, include supportive relations with parents, teachers, and community mentors. Social assets are recruited as part of structures of control when they monitor, supervise, and set behavior standards and consequences for violation of those standards. Social assets may also include the cultural values, spiritual beliefs, and practices that are intended to strengthen racial identity and affiliation. Cultural beliefs and practices offer comfort and affirmation when experiencing stressful life events, such as loss through death or worries about economic security. For BBY, cultural values, beliefs, and practices can include a positive racial identity, a vibrant spirituality, and a body of rituals—used to give meaning to important life transitions between birth and death—that aid in coping with hardship, struggles, and stressful life events. Social assets can also contribute by providing interpretive frameworks through which BBY transcend their immediate situation, make sense of the world, and claim personal agency over events and outcomes in their lives. Access to these social assets provides emotional comfort, instrumental aid, and guidance that enable BBY to cope with stress, self-sooth, moderate their impulses, and meet the social demands of getting along with others.[4] These social assets offer an antidote to social conditions and events that might otherwise impede or overwhelm BBY's capacity to cope and stunt their development of social and emotional competences. At the same time, social assets in the form of control structures establish limits and reinforce standards about what constitutes acceptable behavior. Together, social assets in the form of networks of caring and structures of control can offset the negative impact of adversity, provide a foundation for psychological well-being, and redirect boys onto a positive developmental trajectory, especially if they are available to BBY at critical turning points.

Roles of Social Assets

Social assets perform several important roles in assisting BBY to overcome adversity and become emotionally resilient. Family and community mentors can reassure BBY when they are distressed by racial bias, material deprivation, or adverse events, such as parental absence. Schools can offset the effects of material hardship by providing material assistance in the form of supplies and clothing and by connecting children with relevant services when their lives are disrupted by housing instability or homelessness. Schools can also address the psychological distress of violence and loss by offering a place of refuge and safety, support emotional resilience by offering socio-emotional learning that teaches children skills for coping with distress, and encourage recovery by offering individual counseling for acute situations and instructional accommodations to help children who have fallen behind academically to catch up. Beyond the support provided by family and school, communities can promote resilience through a variety of after-school, weekend, and summer programs that provide enrichment, the opportunity to develop talents and leadership skills, and a chance to engage in prosocial activities helping others. Finally, cultural values, beliefs, and practices can help BBY cope with loss and distress, while interpretive frameworks can help them reframe their understanding of adverse experiences they encounter in their lives.

Recovery from Effects of Adversity

By healing injuries caused by adversity and restoring BBY to health, social assets can overcome and compensate for the damage done by adversity. To illustrate how this works, consider a swimming pool with an optimal water level. During a heat spell, evaporation may cause the water level to fall below what is needed to use the pool safely. Adversity is like this process of evaporation in that it depletes BBY's emotional resources to a level where the they cannot cope well. Social assets, however, function like a hose that adds more water to bring the pool to an appropriate level and compensates for the effects of the earlier water loss. In other words, social assets act in a compensatory manner to make up for and help BBY overcome adversity and reduce its long-term impacts on development.[5] For example, support and encouragement from fathers, in particular, has been shown to moderate and lessen depressive symptoms and suicidal ideation in BBY. Similarly, cultural beliefs and interpretive frameworks reinforced by school and community social assets can imbue children with an appreciation of self that helps them recover from negative messages of their inferiority. Such support is essential in helping BBY to manage the threats that they face in the world, and social assets facilitate coping in ways that help BBY bend but not break in the face adversity.

Protection against Effects of Adversity

Social assets might also immunize or protect against injury and thus prevent harm from adversity occurring in the first place. Continuing with the example of the swimming pool, social assets can be likened to a covering placed over the pool to prevent evaporation of the water, thus maintaining the water at a level suitable for swimming. Secure attachments—with primary caretakers, as well as those found in the relations with teachers and community mentors—establish an important foundation for social and emotional development by immunizing children with representations of constructive relationships that reflect positively on themselves and encourage their ability to trust the good intentions of others. In doing so, they shield BBY from the detrimental emotional effects of adversity. They provide comfort so that the child never becomes overwhelmed and distraught.

Family life, particularly when it is characterized by warmth, parental involvement and investment, and responsivity and succor is the crucible for positive early development. As previously noted, a family's function as a social asset begins with the establishment of a child's secure attachment to primary caregivers. This provides the child with assurance of physical safety and emotional support, which in turn are the foundations on which social and emotional competence rest. Attachment to adult caretakers becomes the gateway through which BBY arrive at strong emotional bonds, social maturity, and the ability to manage challenges.

With support and guidance through positive relationships, children can acquire the ability to cope with stress, moderate their impulses, focus attention, and develop the executive functions needed for the cognitive/academic demands of school and the social demands of getting along with others. The compensatory and protective benefits of social assets allow BBY to capitalize on their strengths. Emotional resilience of BBY can thus be viewed here as the result of two competing forces: the centrifugal force of adversity from poverty and racism, which pushes boys onto an antisocial and negative path; and the centripetal force of social assets, which can correct their course toward resilience and social competence.

How Social Assets Enable Resilience

Socio-emotional development is as much a collective enterprise, involving socialization practices and support from family, school, and community, as it is a product of an individual's response to environmental opportunities and challenges. Social assets figure prominently in BBY's development of social competencies, coping strategies, and prosocial attitudes. Social assets set a foundation for self-regulation by transmitting cultural norms for expression and repression of emotions, and by modeling healthy relationships that build on mutual trust and caring. More specifically, social assets promote emotional resilience through several distinct pathways: teaching self-control of behavior, demonstrating emotional regulation, instilling social awareness, fostering self-awareness of hidden strengths, and altering the environment.

Establishing Limits to Augment Self-Control of Behavior

Structures of control activated when BB are misbehaving are more effective in setting limits for BBY when made up of the same people who are part of the network of care. When family, teachers, and community mentors have acted as sources of support and caring, BBY are more likely to accept correction and guidance from them regarding misbehavior. This dual role allows them to steer BBY away from slacking off at school, indulging a whim or giving in to a temptation to break rules. Parents and mentors, as social assets, can guide BBY and help them realize the importance of inhibiting impulsive behavior and emotional arousal in order to adapt to life in public spaces. Supportive parents can also help their BBY navigate adverse situations by passing down wisdom and advice. For example, advice about racism is so frequently given it has become defined as simply "the Talk." In the Talk, or more accurately, through a series of conversations or interactions, parents and caregivers discuss how to avoid risky situations, whether they involve violence in the streets or at school, emotionally toxic and critical peers, or the temptation to follow along with peers engaging in illicit or illegal behaviors. The evidence regarding the effectiveness of mothers as social assets is especially impressive. Maternal awareness/vigilance, acceptance/support, and coaching/guidance have been associated with greater social competence and better self-regulation of behavior by BBY.[6] BBY are less likely to replicate and follow the behavior of aggressive or antisocial peers when they have a strong supportive relationship with their mothers. Similarly, the quality of relations with teachers is also helpful. Teachers' trustworthiness, caring, and high expectations are crucial to BBY's decisions to comply with rules and yield to their authority.[7] Supportive parents, teachers, and mentors emphasize to BBY the importance of remaining engaged and sustaining effort to meet behavioral and academic standards at school. They discourage association with antisocial peers and encourage relationships with role models who can inspire BBY to visualize a promising future and to take the steps needed to reach it.

Modeling and Demonstrating Emotional Regulation

BBY's ability to regulate their emotions is associated with their mothers' regulation of her own sadness and anger. Often through modeling, parents convey rules for emotional expression and demonstrate emotion regulation. They teach by example when, where, and how to express emotions in a socially acceptable way. Sometimes they may engage in explicit discussions of these rules and react punitively when BBY violate these rules through a display of emotions that are inappropriate or socially unacceptable. For example, parents may discuss emotional displays such as anger and indignation and explain why some emotions are appropriate to express and others are not in specific situations. Conversely, they may criticize and sanction BBY for expressing emotions they were taught to restrain. Parents may, for instance, sanction the open expression of negative emotions, such as anger, out of concern that BBY might appear threatening to others and invite preemptive attacks from those feeling threatened by BBY.[8]

Parents are especially likely to try to suppress defiant behavior and expression of negative emotions, such as anger, in young children because such expressions may blossom into conduct problems in BY and thus place them at risk of violent reprisals or harsh punishment from others. Parents therefore model how to be civil and accommodating, while suppressing the their own anger, sadness, or anxiety. BB are less likely to exhibit behavior problems when mothers modeled control of anger (except in neighborhoods with a high risk of violence).[9] For example, mothers often exhort BBY not to express anger or even rambunctious excitement, so as not to draw unwanted attention to themselves or be labeled as aggressive.[10] By contrast, Black fathers are sometimes inclined to warn boys of the danger of concealing and bottling up their feelings. They are more likely to be accepting of BBY's feelings of anger but value recognizing and expressing both positive and negative emotions appropriately.

Black parents identify as one of their responsibilities knowing how their sons are feeling and helping them to work through negative feelings. At the same time, they also recognize that they should give their sons space and time and wait patiently until they are ready to talk.[11] To do this, they engage in heart-to-heart discussions that invite BBY to reveal what they are feeling and to share their reactions to daily events, particularly situations that trigger strong emotional reactions. Parents then follow up and discuss ways to anticipate and avoid situations and people that might cause them to feel frustrated and express anger.

Instilling Social Awareness

Family members, teachers, and community mentors also promote social awareness. They do this by teaching BBY to read people from the cues they give and to size up social situations that may lead to danger. They reinforce notions that the thinking, intentions, and feelings of others may be different than their own. They help BBY interpret others by learning to read nonverbal cues and parse their language to understand what is really going on. Throughout middle childhood and adolescence, parents, teachers, and community mentors also encourage a belief in personal agency regarding BBY's ability to control and achieve the outcomes they desire. They convey beliefs and implement practices that offer interpretive frameworks that elevate awareness of the role racism plays in our society, and they provide a self-affirming narrative that counters racist stereotypes and denigration.

Families, schools, and communities can all prepare BBY for future experiences of discrimination, but BBY must recognize and accept that the dangers are real. Adults who perceive racial discrimination as robust and salient are more likely to speak with young BB about the dangers of racism. They teach BBY that uncontrolled expression of some emotions is a problem because of the danger that it might lead to negative evaluations by their teachers and place them at risk of violent encounters with police or antisocial peers. These talks lead BBY to develop greater awareness of their social environments and the likelihood that race might play a role in their social interactions. Family members and mentors discuss historical accounts of Black oppression and advancement to increase awareness of discrimination and knowledge of Black resilience. They retell stories of family achievements that became a source of pride and a hopeful signal that social and economic progress is possible. Black families teach their sons about Black heroes who exemplify strengths and whom BBY can imitate. They point out how negative stereotypes are contradicted by these examples. They encourage their sons to stand up to those who attempt to suppress them with unfair treatment or demean them with disparaging or critical comments. All of these practices are designed to instill positive views of Black individuals, promote pride, strengthen Black social identity, and help their sons develop the counter narrative that BBY are strong and resilient.

Fostering Self-Awareness of Unrecognized Strengths

Families and mentors can be especially beneficial to BBY in identifying and acknowledging the underappreciated talents and the hidden strengths that BBY develop in response to adversity. Frankenhuis and colleagues have observed that adversity often heightens cognitive, affective, and social competencies that are useful and adaptive in unstable and adverse environments.[12] For example, children who experience chronic adversity become sensitively attuned to others' emotions. They correctly identify and remember aggressive stimuli. They recognize expressions of anger or fear and are better able to detect and evaluate risk and the potential of a situation to harm them. Other strengths or hidden talents may include leadership, assertiveness, and determination. Their behavior may be driven by a refined sensitivity to fairness and justice; they may develop independence and an ability to care for themselves, as they are thrust early into adult roles that only increase with time; and they are able to remain cool and collected under pressures and environmental demands that rattle and disorient others.

Effects of Social Assets

Social assets are a metaphorical ladder with which to scale a wall of adversity and misery. They help BBY move gracefully past life's hurdles. Thus, social assets are the basis of the social competence and coping that lead to emotional resilience. This resilience, in turn, can position BBY to accommodate to difficult circumstances and enable them to take advantage of the opportunities that life may present.

Earlier chapters presented examples of BBY, such as Wes Moore and Ryan Speedo Green, whose early lives were marked by loss and trauma and for whom oppositional behavior was no stranger. Both grew up without the support of their fathers in socially toxic, physically unforgiving environments. Recall that Wes Moore's father died when he was young, and Ryan Speedo Green was removed from his home due to ongoing fights with his single mother. They had a difficult time controlling their impulses to misbehave and, by the time they reached middle childhood, they were headed toward serious trouble with the law. In middle childhood, neither had a well-developed capacity for self-regulation. Wes Moore was a chronic truant known to police for delinquent behavior, and Ryan Speedo Green was placed in a juvenile detention facility for fighting. However, by adolescence, they both eventually took a turn for the better.

Wes Moore and Ryan Speedo Green are examples of resilient BBY, who were able to overcome early adversity, loss, and trauma. Their transformations might be partially attributable to personal qualities such as social intelligence, flexibility, affability, confidence, and the ability to connect with others.[13] These qualities unquestionably reflect increases in social competencies and adoption of effective strategies for coping with adversity. However, the roots of the two men's transformations go much deeper than their individual character. Their resilience also depended on social assets, especially key persons in their families, schools, and neighborhoods—people to whom they mattered and who provided them with support, guidance, and a solid socio-cultural identity and moral grounding. For Wes Moore, it was his mother. She was constantly caring for and correcting him, provided tough love, and made significant financial sacrifices to place him in a more controlled school setting, a military academy. As we have seen, he initially resisted school rules and regimes and tried to run away several times with no success. However, with the supportive presence of an older Black cadet at the school whom he admired and desired to emulate, he eventually accommodated to life there. Ryan Speedo Green was fortunate to have a no-nonsense but caring teacher in juvenile detention, who happened to be an experienced White female, and a supportive mentor, a Black male choir director, who discovered and honed Green's talent as a singer after he was released to attend public school. These relationships, which took both men's lives in a more positive direction, illustrate the crucial role that social assets can play in lives of BBY. These social assets facilitated their resilience and allowed them to overcome their circumstances, regain their balance, and find a way to lead satisfying lives in spite of the struggles they had had earlier in life. Access to social assets, such as these nurturing or supportive relationships with peers and adults, is essential for children to develop social skills and the capacity to manage arousal, adversity, and stress in their lives.[14]

Emotionally Resilient BBY

Emotionally resilient BBY tend to have high levels of social skills. Not all resilient BBY are outgoing extroverts, but they frequently exhibit behaviors and have dispositions that make them attractive to peers and well-liked by adults. They connect to others with a flexible, easy-going, even-tempered style. In interactions, they come across as friendly and sensitive. Others respond well to them, as reflected in their popularity and ability to influence other children. It follows that BBY with high psychosocial competence typically have favorable peer relations and get along well with adults. BBY who are flexible, empathic, caring—and who conversely are not argumentative

Table 13.1 Social Assets Build Emotional Resilience by Promoting Social Competencies

Self-regulation: behavior	Increase acceptance of and compliance with rules and behavioral expectations through adult support, consistent discipline, supervision, and invoking spiritual values
Self-regulation: emotion	Strengthen emotional well-being and appropriate expression of emotion by modeling effective coping, invoking culture and spiritual values
Self-awareness	Nurture strengths, Black identity, self-esteem, and personal agency by disputing stereotypes and affirming expectations of personal control
Social awareness	Prepare for racism, "the Talk," changing the school or neighborhood, instilling paradoxical attributions, and interpersonal trust

or aggressive—are likely to be more successful at forming and sustaining positive relationships.[15] These social competencies in turn influence and increase the likelihood that others will respond to BBY positively and provide the support they need to ward off the effect of adversity.[16]

While acknowledging the impact of adversity, we have also observed that many BBY manage to avoid the most deleterious outcomes. They eventually overcome their circumstances, regain their balance, and find a way to lead satisfying lives in spite of early difficulties. Resilient BBY endure and overcome cumulative stress from multiple, chronic adverse sources. As we have seen in this chapter, access to social assets—most importantly, supportive relationships—increases the likelihood that BBY will overcome adversity.[17] Social assets at home, at school, and in the community foster BBY resilience by supporting the coping and social skills that help them avoid or recover from the negative effects of adversity. The match between the contributory actions of social assets and the domains of social competence which they target are presented in Table 13.1.

Notes

1. Financial hardship is especially associated with adverse childhood experiences, such as parental substance abuse, mental health problems, and incarceration, which make it difficult for families to provide an environment that promotes the cognitive and emotional development of children. The strains of economic hardship may also impact emotional availability. Work schedules may require parents to be away from home for much of the time. Inability to be home physically makes it difficult for parents to invest time in their sons, monitor their activities, and provide direction and guidance for their behavior. In addition to loneliness, BBY experience deep sadness and must cope alone with fears and the distress of seeing people killed.

2. Barbarin and colleagues analyzed data from a nationally representative sample of BBY collected as part of the 2019 National Health Interview Survey by the CDC. Even though adversity gave rise to conditions, such as parental substance abuse, mental health problems, and incarceration, that are usually inauspicious for development in the form of emotional and behavioral difficulties, evidence of social competences, such as altruism and affability, were found under these conditions. Barbarin et al. (2022).
3. Werner & Smith (1982).
4. Sandler (2001).
5. This framework of social assets integrates concepts from developmental, social, and clinical psychology. Social and developmental theories explain how adverse extrinsic factors negatively influence development and how supportive social relations can counter those influences. From attachment theory we learn the importance of relationships, particularly the caregiving system through which children's needs for emotional safety and security are met. From social psychology come insights about how control of attributions and social identities structure individuals' understanding of their social worlds and their places in it. From clinical psychology conceptualizations of stress, coping, and emotional functioning are helpful and relevant.
6. Cunningham et al. (2009).
7. Gregory & Weinstein (2008).
8. Dunbar et al. (2015).
9. Kliewer et al. (2004).
10. Dow (2016).
11. Labella (2018).
12. Frankenhuis & de Weerth (2013).
13. Jensen-Campbell & Graziano (2001); Masten & Tellegen (2012).
14. Kraag et el. (2006).
15. Hintsamen et al. (2010).
16. Kraag et al. (2006).
17. Luthar et al. (2000).

PART VII
HOW FAMILIES, SCHOOLS, AND NEIGHBORHOODS HELP

14
Preparation for Racism and Adversity

As discussed in Chapter 13, it is difficult for BBY to become resilient on their own. The likelihood that BBY will overcome the debilitating consequences of adversity increases when they draw on the social assets made available within their families, schools, and communities. In this chapter we will examine the role of families in ensuring BBY resilience; in the next chapter, we will look at the part schools and communities can play.

The value of families for BBY success in adapting to adversity is incontrovertible. Familial environments and practices are especially important early in life because they lay a foundation for the development of social competence and emotion regulation by supporting, nurturing, and conveying to BBY that they are valued, understood, and loved unconditionally. Accordingly, BBY are much more likely to experience positive development when they are able to access social assets arising from family. This chapter builds on those ideas to pinpoint the practices and functions of families as social assets in preparing BBY to cope specifically with racism. Through discussions that anticipate the challenges, supportive responses that soothe the pain of racist encounters, and guidance on ways to avoid the dangers, families (and others) can mitigate the risks to BBY development.[1] This task is not as straightforward as it sounds, and programs have been developed with the aim of guiding families on ways to develop the skills to accomplish this goal.

Families' Strategies to Prepare BBY for Racism

Many of the worries Black parents have about their sons involve the hurtful impact of racist stereotypes, implicit biases, and disparate treatment that their sons will inevitably face, which have the potential to inflict significant psychological pain and even cause physical harm. Parental concerns are both about their sons' physical safety and also about how BBY might feel when they are treated unfairly, disparaged by negative messages, or excluded socially just because of who they are. In addition to concerns about the treatment of their sons, parents may feel a lack of trust in a school's procedures due to a poor match between the home and school, with respect to socialization goals and discipline practices.

Families can cultivate BBY's ability to cope with racism during opportunities provided by mundane daily interactions during mealtimes, travel, TV viewing, holiday celebrations, extended family get-togethers, and shared play. Families can help BBY frame how they think about race and racism by cultivating awareness of how racism manifests in daily life and describing ways to overcome its effects. Family members can analyze the racial dynamics of events that they have experienced or witnessed, share insights about how they navigated these situations, and express pride in the accomplishments and triumphs of Black people in spite of the obstacles. Families can also make use of cultural rituals and celebrations and nurture world views that equip boys with a favorable lens through which to view their lives. For example, families can foster emotional resilience by passing on a legacy of spiritual beliefs and cultural practices that give meaning to life; they can also firm up BBY's sense of identity by developing connections with extended family networks. In addition, there are several specific practices, which I will discuss in the following sections, that families can engage in to help BBY overcome the consequences of racism. Each of these practices enhances BBY's ability to regulate arousal over racist slights, boosts pride in Black identity, and nurtures a sense of personal responsibility and efficacy.

Support, Monitoring, and Control

Support, monitoring, and control strategies are the principal tools with which parents and family members can help BBY develop emotional resilience. Supportive relationships affirm BBY, reinforce positive behavior, correct misbehavior, and convey to them that they are valued and worthwhile. Family discussions are used to help BBY adopt ways to get along peacefully with others, feel good about themselves, and understand the role of race and gender in determining how others will evaluate and treat them. Intensive close monitoring, which involves supervising where their sons are, who they are with, and what they are doing, is another way that parents minimize actions and activities that might place their sons in harm's way. By strengthening families' abilities to function in these ways, family assistance programs make families an even more valuable social asset for BBY.

Talking about Racism and Economic Inequalities

Families often engage their sons in conversations about recent events at school or in the neighborhood that exemplify racism and that can be used as an occasion to illustrate effective ways to cope. They may discuss literature or online stories that illustrate the forms that current day racism take. There is an array of children's and youth's books that present age-relevant moral dilemmas, such as how to act when a friend is teased because of race or how to cope with interpersonal stress, such as that stemming from rejection by White peers. In these interactions, many families find it helpful to explain the causes of racist attitudes and behaviors and discuss alternative strategies for responding to the event. Parents may answer BBY's questions or allay their concerns and fears. They may scaffold on to BBY's existing knowledge by elaborating and offering additional information, and sensitively responding to BBY's emotional difficulties. Probably the most helpful strategy occurs when parents respond to BBY's distress in a way that allows BBY to vent frustration in socially acceptable ways. This conveys to BBY the message that "you are seen, and you are understood." In these discussions, parental optimism and presentations of BBY as capable of coping successfully with problems are associated with social competences in dealing with stress.[2] These strategies are most impactful when parents channel the child's focus of attention, comment on their activity, and expand on the subtle themes and unspoken fears embedded in their son's responses to "the Talk."[3]

Self-Acceptance and Racial Identity

A positive racial identity can protect against the negative pressure of racism. Distress due to discrimination has been shown to be lessened when BBY possess a positive Black identity.[4] By emphasizing a connection to an African heritage and a history of Black contributions and successes, families offer an alternative positive version of Black males and what they can accomplish. Families can prepare BBY to cope with racism through stories that celebrate achievements of extended family members, inform BBY about the strengths of ancestors, and point to ways to that they stand on the shoulders of their ancestors and must maintain their legacy. These stories and traditions prepare BBY for insults and assaults to their dignity and self-worth by offsetting and undermining racist narratives. They help cultivate worldviews that reframe and neutralize societal messages that belittle, devalue, and denigrate. In doing so, they make it easier for BBY to discount or ignore hurtful messages, thereby reducing their impact. These worldviews also allow BBY to experience and give voice to their anger and rage about their racist experiences and acknowledge the worries about being victimized. Familiarity with and imitation of effective Black men makes it possible for BBY to push pass the constraints imposed by racism. In an essay entitled "The Uses of The Blues," James Baldwin, a well-known Black author, has argued that self-acceptance and self-regard are key to the well-being of Blacks in a racist society. He argues that Black children must be convinced that they have a right to exist and achieve great things. The most fundamental way to achieve this self-acceptance and self-regard is to embrace a positive racial identity. Promoting racial identity therefore should be a major socialization goal of Black parents. They must, in fact, convince their children that they have a right to exist and to pursue happiness.[5]

Foster Self-Affirming Expectations of Personal Control

Strengthening BBY beliefs about personal control is another way families can mitigate the impact of racism and material disadvantage. BBY often make sense of adversity by adopting worldviews or beliefs that shape how they interpret discrimination. Do they understand discrimination as threats of bad things about to happen, as losses already experienced, or as setbacks that can be overcome with effort? Families help BBY interpret, evaluate, and explain the underlying causes of race-related stressors. They can foster self-affirming ways of interpreting the causes of events. In this way, BBY are able to affirm their strengths and appropriately resist self-blame. They come to adopt realistic expectations about the control they possess over their life outcomes. Belief in the importance of their own efforts, in contrast to belief in the idea that their lives are overwhelmingly controlled by others, may also moderate cultural distrust. This enables them to enter social relationships without anticipating malevolence or having suspicions about the negative intentions of others. Instead, they approach social encounters with openness and the belief that others are not out to harm them.

Instill Paradoxical Beliefs about Personal Responsibility and Control

Optimism and self-confidence are necessary to offset disparagement and marginalization in a world where racism is virulent. In order to reinforce trust in others and convictions about one's ability to sidestep prejudice and racism, Black parents must entertain and hold in mind two contradictory beliefs and transmit them to their sons. They must teach their sons to account for life outcomes in terms of both personal control and control by powerful others. This means that they must develop the practice of making contradictory or paradoxical attributions for their outcomes in terms of both high personal responsibility and strong conviction about the impediments imposed by race-based structural inequalities on their lives. BBY can be taught to be trusting but not naively blind to inequality and discrimination. These paradoxical beliefs involve attributions about the control over the outcomes in life that are, at the same time, internal and external. External control is attributed to dominant groups who design and maintain racial hierarchies that rest on the fictions of White superiority and merit. The external locus of control involves a belief that some external force—fate, destiny, powerful others, institutional structures of racism—determines outcomes in one's life and can block success in spite of one's efforts. As a consequence of this external locus of control, Blacks are dominated and relegated to positions of inferiority. Beliefs in an internal locus of control assert that BBY themselves and their personal efforts are the primary determinants of what happens and of the success they achieve, including the attainment of personal goals. The extent to which BBY believe that they are in control of outcomes will determine the effort they exert to achieve some desired goal. In holding paradoxical beliefs simultaneously, BBY recognize and accept limits on their control over important aspects of life but at the same time acknowledge that goals and outcomes depend largely on personal effort. Paradoxical attributions suggest that although BBY believe they lack full control, they believe they have enough control to make a difference in whether or not a desired outcome occurs.

Cultural Practices, Spiritual Values, and Extended Family Networks

The moral sensibilities of Black families and their children are often founded on participation in religious communities, prayer, and a belief in the ubiquity and providence of a benign, all-powerful Divine Presence who is active in the world. This Divine Presence is the ultimate source of protection and support, as articulated in the teachings of the Abrahamic religions. In addition to helping to foster these cultural beliefs, participation in religious communities or churches also offers moral guidance, coaching, and development of civic virtues. These religious or church communities instill prosocial values. They foster virtues, such as patience, kindness, fortitude, temperance, humility, hope, charity, justice, simplicity, and gentleness. Spiritual guidance from trusted adults in a religious community can also support self-control and prevent engaging in risky and antisocial behavior as well as help to maintain positive attitudes that sustain engagement and motivation to do well in school.

Alter the Environment

Families also act as gatekeepers over their sons' experiences outside of the home by choosing and monitoring early care, school, and the community settings in which they place their sons.[6] This requires careful observation of children's environments and selectively placing them in settings that will care for them, protect them, teach them, keep them safe, and match their needs. Parents can, for instance, influence the environment in which their sons grow up by moving the family to a less dangerous neighborhood, if family finances can support it. Alternatively, in the past parents sent their sons to live with relatives in the rural South where the temptations and dangers of an urban environment used to be uncommon, although this is less true today. In some cases, this move is done just to get BBY away from the neighborhood during the summer. In other cases, the move is for longer periods of time to separate them from antisocial peers and continuing encounters with police.

Families are particularly attentive to minimizing their sons' exposure to racism and teaching them ways to respond when they do encounter it. When a school or neighborhood is so toxic that families cannot successfully counter those effects, parents may see an environmental change as the only or most feasible option. This may mean requesting a transfer from one public school to another, or, if family finances permit, pulling a son out of the public schools altogether. It could mean finding a school that is more supportive, or even just one with different peers. It could mean sending their son to a boarding school that offers a structured environment and where his movement is closely monitored. In the case of Wes Moore, for instance, his mother responded to chronic misbehavior in the community by deciding to enroll him in a military boarding school, even though doing so involved a great financial sacrifice.

Programs to Help Families Support Their Sons

Several programs have been designed to strengthen the capacity of families to be an asset to BBY as they experience racism and adversity. These programs focus on ways families can help BBY to anticipate and offset the effects of racism and economic disadvantage and to cope with their effects. These interventions help parents with communication skills, encouraging their retention of closeness to their sons, monitoring children's physical and psychological status, and meeting BBY's need for encouragement and support. They also help families understand how best to help their sons confront negative stereotypes and buttress their self-esteem, as well as address ways to extol Black cultural values and use traditions and practices to strengthen a positive racial identity. They train families to communicate about racism, counter stereotypes, foster beliefs in personal efficacy in spite of racism, and impart cultural and spiritual values.

Several programs have been designed to help families deal with the challenges of racism with specific suggestions for racial socialization. Four of these programs are described here: Strong African American Families (SAAF), Pathways for African American Success (PAAS), Black Parenting Strengths and Strategies (BPSS), and Engaging, Managing, and Bonding through Race (EMBRace).

Strong African American Families Program (SAAF)

SAAF provided training designed to increase the family's use of involved–vigilant parenting strategies. These strategies included intensive monitoring, consistent reinforcement of behavioral expectation, caring, and provision of instrumental assistance when youth needed it. This program was specifically developed for parents of BY and has demonstrated its utility as a program for the prevention of risky adolescent behaviors related to sexually transmitted diseases (STDs) and substance use. SAAF consisted of seven weekly sessions for parents based on a curriculum that fostered what the developers labeled "regulated, communicative parenting behaviors." In addition, it suggested activities or strategies that might strengthen family cohesion. Simultaneous sessions were offered to youth on topics designed to build their social competencies. These sessions were followed by joint parent–child sessions, in which parents and sons were given the chance to use the communication skills. Parent training focused on consistency of support and involvement in their sons' lives, complemented by close monitoring, communicating, and reinforcing behavioral expectations. Discussion of racial socialization strategies were also included in the training sessions. Skill development focused especially on helping parents to understand their impact and value as active listeners. When BBY are convinced that their family will listen to them on sensitive and difficult issues, they are more likely to listen to and adhere to parents' expectation for their behavior.[7] Parents viewed pre-recorded presentations that covered the suggested strategies and provided examples of family interaction that demonstrated how to implement them. Trained facilitators led discussions of the material and answered questions.

The effectiveness of the program was assessed in terms of parents' consistency in discipline, knowledge of their sons' companions and whereabouts when outside the home, ability to deal with and solve problems that came up between parent and child, and their explanations of rules and behavioral expectations. Racial socialization was assessed in terms of talking about stereotypes in the media, discrimination, and Black traditions, history, and achievements.[8] McBride-Murry created an interactive CD-ROM and online version of the program. It has been used in a six-week format to strengthen parental functioning and tested for its efficacy in preventing early sexual initiation and substance use in Black youth growing up in rural settings or minimal control conditions.

Black Parenting Strengths and Strategies (BPSS)

Black Parenting Strengths and Strategies (BPSS) [9] is a strengths- and culture-based parenting program designed to improve aspects of parenting associated with the early development of conduct problems and the promotion of social and cultural competences.[10] The program goal is to increase monitoring, positive parenting, and proactive racial socialization. Parenting practices that are based on such proactive racial socialization and cultural norms and values strengthen identity in youth and protect them against the development of conduct problems and later antisocial and high-risk behavior. The program addresses some of the causes of poor behavior and emotional difficulties, including inconsistency in disciplining, parental criticalness, unclear rules and commands, lax parental supervision, and cycles of coercive parent–child interactions. Racial socialization, which refers to messages about the significance and meaning of race and ethnicity, is central in BPSS because it shapes children's beliefs about themselves and the world and helps them develop skills for coping with racism, impacting their interactions within and across racial groups.

The BPSS curriculum was administered over the course of 12 weeks (12 two-hour sessions provided once a week). It was led by two facilitators. Although BPSS is an adaptation of the Parenting the Strong-Willed Child (PSWC) program, which focused on dealing with problem behavior,[11] BPSS adds the sociocultural context of race and cultural differences as important considerations. Sessions included standard topics on social and emotional development in Black children, combating teacher implicit bias and increasing children's confidence about achievement at school, positive racial identity, and dealing with hurtful interactions such as name-calling and exclusion by peers, discrimination, and microaggressions. Sessions also helped parents reflect on their own experiences as Black individuals and illustrated the use of African proverbs, sayings and affirmations, poems, quotes, symbols, pledges, prayer, role-playing, storytelling, extended family participation, and humor. Parents learned strategies for discussing race-related content in a developmentally appropriate manner, as well as how to access culturally affirming resources in their communities. The parent groups also discussed ways to strengthen and connect to informal support networks.

Engaging, Managing, and Bonding through Race (EMBRace)

EMBrace is an intervention program whose goal is to help Black caregivers and youth ages 10–14 by training them to use tools and strategies that mitigate the stressful effects of racism and promote healthy coping.[12] It was inspired by theories on race-related stressors, coping, and healing. In addition, it bases its intervention strategies on evidence-based behavioral programs designed to reduce trauma and behavior problems and improve parent–child interactions. Its primary goal is the strengthening of racial socialization practices. Specifically, the program aims to improve communication skills, strengthen the caretaker–youth relationship, and increase skills with which parents and children can discuss and cope with the stress of racist encounters.

The intervention is organized around five 90-minute sessions that are conducted by trained clinicians with individual caretaker and youth dyads, rather than in groups. Each session is devoted to a single topic such as cultural pride and preparation for bias. The coping skills portion of the training focuses on increasing parents' ability to recognize racial discrimination, accurately appraise how it impacts self and others, reduce stress, and confront microaggressions. After each session, *funwork* described in the participant manual is assigned to give participants a chance to practice. *Funwork* might include an assignment to watch a program or film related to the topic, or it might involve an activity, such as "Brainstorm about your family and cultural tree," or "Try to recall people, places, and things that are important in your immediate family or in your heritage."

Fatherhood Programs

Fatherhood programs are intended to support and encourage fathers in their roles as caregivers, role models, and positive influences in the lives of their children. The specific goals and activities of these programs vary, depending on the needs of the fathers they serve but some common goals and activities include:

- Improving the Quality of Father–Child Relationships: Many fatherhood programs aim to improve the quality of relationships between fathers and their children. Activities may include parent–child bonding activities, coaching on communication skills, tips for spending quality time with children, and bringing fathers and sons together around a fun and engaging activity, such as a sporting event or video games and competitions.

- Promoting Responsible Fatherhood: Fatherhood programs often aim to promote responsible fatherhood by encouraging fathers to take an active role in their children's lives, provide financial support, and be positive role models.
- Improving Parenting Skills: Some fatherhood programs focus on improving fathers' parenting skills, including strategies for managing children's behavior, setting boundaries, and promoting positive child development.
- Encouraging Employment and Economic Stability: Many fatherhood programs recognize the importance of economic stability and employment in supporting father involvement. These programs may offer job training, financial literacy training, and other services to help fathers secure stable employment.
- Supporting Healthy Relationships: Some fatherhood programs aim to help fathers develop healthy relationships with their partners, co-parents, and other family members. Activities may include counseling, mediation, and conflict resolution training.

Overall, fatherhood programs aim to support fathers in their roles as parents, partners, and providers, and help them build strong, positive relationships with their children and families. These approaches appear to be effective in making a difference for children.[13]

Examples of fatherhood programs that specifically target Black fathers include:

- Black Fathers Rock is a non-profit organization that aims to empower and support Black fathers through fatherhood conferences, workshops, mentorship, and community events that focus on building strong father–child relationships and promoting responsible fatherhood.
- The Black Dad Initiative: The Black Dad Initiative offers workshops, coaching, and mentorship that focus on improving parenting skills, building healthy relationships, and promoting positive fathering attitudes.
- 100 Black Fathers: 100 Black Fathers is a fatherhood program that offers mentorship, coaching, and support to Black fathers in the Chicago area. Their programs focus on building strong father–child relationships and addressing issues, such as violence prevention and economic stability.

- Black Dads Matter: Black Dads Matter is a fatherhood program that offers workshops, support groups, and mentorship to Black fathers and families in the Philadelphia area. Their programs focus on promoting positive fathering attitudes, improving parenting skills, and building strong father–child relationships.

In light of the potentially devastating effect of racism and its associated adversities on BBY emotional functioning, preparing sons to deal with racism and adversity is a direct and helpful way for families and mentors to promote emotional resilience. As we have seen in this chapter, this can be accomplished by promoting the development of BBY's social competence through the following steps: providing emotional support, close supervision, and consistent discipline; providing a positive narrative boys can adopt about themselves that counter negative stereotypes; bolstering their racial identity and sense of personal agency; helping boys understand racism; and teaching them to draw on cultural practices, spiritual values, and extended family networks for support; and, when all else fails, changing their environments.

Doing each of these tasks effectively can be difficult and challenging for families. Family intervention programs such as the ones described above can help. Even with the availability of such programs though, it is impossible to guarantee that every BBY will have a cohesive, attentive family that protects and nurtures development, or the financial resources sufficient to afford living in a safe, adequately resourced, and efficacious neighborhood that engages BBY in prosocial activities. However, the situation is not hopeless. There is reason for optimism even when one of the legs of the stool described earlier is a bit wobbly, as the other legs of the stool may offer enough stability to support positive development. Just as it is unlikely that BBY will become emotionally resilient on their own, it is unlikely that weaknesses in one area of life will inevitably lead to problematic outcomes. Strong families, a responsive school, and a propitious neighborhood can sometimes compensate for what may be missing in the others. Conditions for development are promising if at least two of the legs of the stool function in a way that meets BBY developmental needs.

Notes

1. Hughes et al. (2006).
2. Slaughter & Epps (1987).

3. Murray & Hornbaker (1997).
4. Zimmerman et al. (2013).
5. This idea was explored fully in James Baldwin's essay on "The Uses of The Blues." See Baldwin (1968).
6. Chase-Lansdale & Pittman (2002).
7. Brody et al. (1998).
8. Brody et al. (2004); Molgaard & Spoth (2001).
9. Coard (2003).
10. Coard et al. (2007).
11. Forehand & Long (2002).
12. Anderson et al. (2019).
13. Hawkins & Dollahite (2017).

15

Strengthening Schools and Neighborhoods as Social Assets

The question of what BBY need from their schools and neighborhoods to become resilient is straightforward but not easily answered. And from what has been learned, desirable results are not readily achieved, as BBY need a great deal more than our society has been willing to provide. From schools, BBY need effective and developmentally appropriate instruction, fair discipline, a deeper understanding of and respect for their culture, and stronger coordination and collaboration with their families. From their neighborhoods, they need safe spaces to play and explore; stimulating activities to fill the wasteland of time after school, on weekends, and during summers; and opportunities for civic engagement to serve others and develop leadership skills.

Transform Classroom Pedagogy

Schools, which make up the second leg of our supportive stool, play an increasingly important role in the emotional development of BBY. They have traditionally been judged more by the academic growth of students than by their contribution to students' socio-emotional development. And while most schools still consider building literacy and numeracy skills central to their mission, students' emotional well-being and their development as informed responsible citizens are critical to the schools' success. To be effective, schools must consider and incorporate methods that help students develop socio-emotional skills and executive functions. Moreover, they need to adopt instructional practices that match the developmental competencies of the child and address misbehavior in less punitive ways. A dual focus on academics and emotional development can be facilitated by using principles of restorative justice in addressing misbehavior and negotiating conflicts with students, and by developing closer partnerships with families around meeting the needs of the whole child.

Focusing on Socio-emotional Learning

For BBY, school engagement and academic achievement are closely intertwined with emotional functioning. Accordingly, conduct problems and deficits in self-regulation, attention, behavior, and emotions can impede BBY's progress and contribute to achievement gaps. To improve academic achievement, schools must figure out ways to buffer the effects of adversity—associated with economic disadvantage and racism—on behavior and emotions and increase BBY emotional resilience. Some teachers, however, observe that a focus on students' emotional well-being and mental health requires time and attention that reduces time available for academic instruction. They argue, correctly, that they were trained to be educators—not psychologists or social workers. At the same time, many concede that while as a group BBY possess the required cognitive abilities to succeed, their academic achievement suffers due to personal, familial and socio-emotional difficulties. To resolve this dilemma, teachers should seek creative ways to integrate socio-emotional issues and skills development into classroom instruction (in the curricula for literacy and social studies particularly).[1] In addition, certain interventions do not require additional time or resources. For instance, rather than using inappropriate and punitive approaches to address incidents of student behavior, which often exacerbate underlying problems, such incidents might be dealt with more effectively by re-envisioning them as "teachable moments." This means responding to BBY misbehavior with empathy and fairness, while striving to bridge the cultural divide between schools and families and engaging families as partners in working with their sons.

Emotionally Responsive Classroom Instruction

Effective instruction is an under-appreciated contributor to children's emotional well-being at school. Good instruction sets off the imagination of students, strengthens motivation, and enables them to experience a sense of mastery and accomplishment when they learn something new. In addition to good instruction, the emotional climate of the classroom is critical to children's well-being. Emotionally responsive classroom climates are characterized by warmth and mutual respect. These demand little time but require a positive orientation toward students. This means providing reassurance when the child is uncertain, comfort when the child is distressed, and joint satisfaction and joy when the child is successful in mastering new skills. In emotionally responsive classrooms, teachers use developmentally appropriate pedagogy. They create a space where children feel cared for and emotionally and physically secure. Emotionally responsive classrooms are attuned to BB's distress and cries for help. They rely more often on affirmation and positive reinforcement than on coercion, shaming, or punishment. While these classrooms are organized and predictable, they also avoid feeling rigid and regimented. Students are often given choices of activities and permitted freedom of movement. In these classrooms, BB's difficulty in regulating behavior can be minimized by setting clear expectations from the start, using activities that rely on gross motor skills, engaging boys' interests with relevant reading material, and redirecting (rather than overreacting to) potential behavior problems before things get out of hand. All of this is, of course, easier said than done. However, the benefits to be reaped are great. Such auspicious classroom environments represent the fertile soil in which the social competencies of BBY germinate and blossom.

Address Problems in BBY Transition to Kindergarten

In contrast to the progress BBY make in socio-emotional functioning during the pre-K year, as we have seen earlier, disappointing reversals in emotional competencies are often observed during the kindergarten year. Such transition problems, which are not unique to BB, are likely a consequence of: kindergarten's accelerated demands for self-control of attention and movement that boys do not yet have; its shift from self-initiated and individualized learning to group instruction that place greater demands on uniformity and the ability to regulate attention; and its greater regimentation with rules and routines that bring to light boys' difficulty with discontinuing highly engaging activities. Eventually, most BB accommodate to the higher expectations they face in kindergarten. However, for some BB, kindergarten is the beginning of a downward spiral where they surrender the belief that they can please adults and be successful. They begin to internalize their designation as a problem, and this designation becomes a sticky part of their identity throughout their primary school years. Some BB might benefit from school reforms that offer a more gradual introduction to highly structured classrooms and that model the early primary grades after high quality pre-K classrooms. These ideas are being tested in *Transitional Kindergarten* classrooms and in some newly established schools that just go from pre-K to third grade. The P–3 school is a promising innovation that attempts to address the transition problem by integrating developmentally appropriate practices throughout the early primary school years, by aligning learning standards across pre-K to third grade, and by introducing the structure of elementary schools more slowly. This approach can help to improve BB performance in both social and academic areas. Unfortunately school districts encounter many logistical problems in finding appropriate campuses to house the schools and integrating its students into other schools p-5 elementary schools when they move on to fourth grade. As a result, this promising innovation has been difficult to bring to scale.

Making the Empathic Shift in School Discipline

Kindergarten transition problems often set the stage for behavior problems that ultimately land BB in the principal's office on a disciplinary referral by teachers. How schools treat these emergent problems can influence whether they are resolved or persist. School discipline for behaviors considered disruptive or oppositional often involves some form of punishment, such as time in a timeout room for misbehaving students, after school detention, in-school suspension, and other forms of punishment that exclude the child from instruction. Black boys experience these forms of punishment at an extraordinarily high rate compared to other children. For example, BBY are suspended and expelled at a rate that is three to eight times higher than that of White students.[2] Instead of exclusionary punishment, most problem behaviors in school would be better handled if they were framed as teachable moments in which supportive guidance was provided to get at the root of the difficulty expressed in misbehavior. Sometimes, the underlying cause of the problem lies within the child; however, more often than not, the underlying causes stem from complex interactions between the boy, the teacher, the time, and the situation. Punishment does little to resolve these. This is especially true for BB in pre-K and elementary school. Exclusion may be necessary when the BB in question may be a danger to self or others, but exclusion compounds rather than solves the problem. For example, exclusion generates unintended consequences by depriving BBY of needed instructional time. It can inflame BBY's disposition toward schooling and school staff, reinforce staff negative views of BBY, and amplify Black–White gaps in achievement. These unintended negative consequences have motivated some school districts to implement policies that ban student suspensions and expulsions and utilize alternative approaches designed to assess and remediate misbehavior and emotional difficulties. Such bans on exclusions, particularly for students from pre-K to sixth grade, represent a sensible and developmentally appropriate policy. To be successful with BBY, schools should prioritize patience and support over punishment and retribution and make empathy, respect, and fairness integral to disciplinary practices and policy process.

A related issue, concern about student mental health, has given impetus to the implementation of Socio-Emotional Learning (SEL) programs, Positive Behavior Interventions and Supports (PBIS), and Restorative Justice Practices (RJP) in schools. SEL and PBIS programs are educational interventions targeted at changing student behavior. In SEL programs, students receive training on identifying, labeling, and managing basic emotions (anger, fear, sadness, delight). SEL is often embedded in classroom instruction or is offered on a pull-out basis by a behavior specialist. When implemented as intended, PBIS is a whole school intervention in which behavioral expectations are made explicit, and rewards are offered for individual and group compliance with those standards. Positive reinforcement of compliant behavior is the key strategy. PBIS emphasizes predictable classroom routines, breaks and respite from work, quiet correction of student misbehavior that avoids reprimand but instead articulates the desired behavior, and tangible reinforcement that follows compliance. Finally, Restorative Justice Practices (RJP) is a form of intervention widely used as an alternative to punitive discipline. RJP is fundamentally about improving coping and adaptation by increasing the supportiveness of relations between students and teachers. It is a relation building and repairing strategy, used to reduce the exacerbation of conflict and misbehavior caused by harsh and disparate discipline. Anecdotal reporting suggests that it improves student behavior, promotes healing, and sustains healthy emotional development. RJP offers a less punitive way to respond to the emotional difficulties of BBY that often manifest themselves in rule-breaking and conflict with peers.

One goal of RJP is to repair the damage done to targets of misbehavior and to allow the perpetrator to acknowledge responsibility and make amends. RJP practices are intended to help individuals learn from their mistakes and restore acceptance of the wrongdoer by the school community. In addition, RJP creates a space to discuss the consequences of misbehavior for all parties. The concern for reconciliation and healing of affected individuals represents an important departure from the focus on punishment and exclusion that is typical in school discipline. Implementation of RJP often begins by raising staff awareness of the role of adversity and trauma in BBY's emotional functioning and the potential for implicit bias to color how they evaluate and respond to BBY rule-breaking. Teachers and students learn and are encouraged to use *affective statements* to express their emotional reactions and to use *open-ended questions* to understand the transgression. Response circles or conferences bring together the parties involved in an offense or incident to discuss it, ascertain people's reactions, and generate self-care activities following the discussion. The goal of the circles and conferences is to encourage participants in a conflict situation to explain their actions and perspectives and to reflect on the impact of their behavior on others. Student-led tribunals utilize a model of participatory democracy in which peers listen to both sides of a disagreement or problem and apply standards they have previously developed to evaluate student conduct. The tribunal is made up of students with a school staff member serving as a consultant. Peer members of the tribunal are trained as mediators to listen to both sides and to recommend a course of action for addressing injury. Restorative conferences are used when problems are especially intransigent, affect more than a few students, or when it seems necessary to widen the circle of people to solve the problem. They sometimes include parents and other community members. Trust and mutual respect between teachers and students are essential for the success of RJP.

Partnering with Families

For most children, family is the first place they experience teaching and learning. Before they ever set foot in a school, children acquire language, social skills, and emergent skills in literacy and math. This learning context is shaped by cultural practices, language use, interactive styles, and methods of discipline that may differ from what children are likely to encounter at school. This is more often true for children of color than White children. Whereas White middle-class children find schools quite syntonic with what they experienced at home, BB often find that the cultural practices, expectations, discipline, and approaches to learning at school do not match what they are accustomed to at home.[3] Moreover, as the first teachers, families have learned a great deal about the strengths their sons have, the challenges they face, what they respond to, and what they seem most interested in.

This knowledge could be invaluable in helping boys acclimate to school. It can be accessed if schools set out from the beginning to work closely with families to smooth boys' transition to school. Such partnerships depend on schools' willingness to reach out and exchange information with families. To be effective, communication should not be limited to semi-annual parent-teacher conferences. Newsletters, texts, invitations to visit classrooms are helpful, as are joint social events, like "ice-cream Sundays," and joint training on topics of interest to both teacher and parents. Home visits provide the ultimate connection.

Effective collaboration consists of more than periodically informing parents about the progress of their children. It includes a two-way exchange of information in which schools solicit input from and listen to families. The State of California Department of Education has published very helpful guidelines for schools about how to build partnerships with families. This well thought-out approach considers multiple issues that arise in serving families who differ in culture and ethnicity from educators.[4] Building the school–home relationship requires cultural respect, openness to learning, and a continuous effort to appreciate cultural similarities and differences. School staff should strive to become learners before trying to teach. In addition, schools should check the tendency to unthinkingly accept that the dominant culture approach to children and education is always better.

Bridging the gap between home and school is undoubtedly a difficult task. However, the California guidelines offer practical suggestions for connecting with families who may be difficult to reach due to language, time, mobility, or prior negative experiences with their own schooling. For example, they suggest using grass-roots organizations to learn about the needs of families and ways to connect with them. Though difficult, the effort will pay dividends. By understanding the differences between home and school, teachers can overcome what at first appears to be intransigent difficulties with students. By partnering together, schools and families can support each other's efforts to help BBY adapt to the expectations and demands at school.

Expand Culturally Informed and Affirming Programs

Cultural differences are important to consider in developing programs to improve outcomes for BBY. A program called Preventing Long-term Anger and Aggression in Youth (PLAAY) is an example of an effort to take into account ethnicity and culture in teaching BBY to cope with emotional stress, control anger, and prevent aggression. The program identifies athletic competitions, such as basketball, as a natural setting in which to observe and intervene in BBY emotional distress and anger. The continuous motion, quick-thinking, and high-skill team sports, such as basketball and soccer, have refined rules and require decision-making, cooperation with, and accommodation to others. Participation in these sports can also elicit a range of positive and negative emotions such as excitement, joy, anger, frustration, and envy. BBY must deal with adulation or criticism from teammates, trash-talking from opponents, the perception of unfair treatment, and even being injured or hurt by an opposing player.

PLAAY teaches BBY how to deal with these challenges by first understanding themselves and then understanding how others see them and respond to them. These sports offer the chance to teach coping skills as tempers flare and disappointment over poor performances flourishes. The program uses "in the moment" intervention to teach BBY to accept their anger, rather than disown it. Instead, they are taught to view it as counterproductive because their anger undermines their performance. Timeouts are used to help boys identify their feelings, develop an understanding of their emotional triggers, and teach them strategies for using their emotions positively. Taking a timeout to cool off and reflect on feelings respects BBY's culture of masculinity without relying so much on talk therapy, which may not be effective for boys who avoid touchy-feely displays. In addition, PLAAY uses methods, such as role-playing student–teacher conflicts, practicing assertiveness, and offering feedback, to help BBY improve their socio-emotional competencies. In all, PLAAY is an innovative way to utilize BBY culture and identity to provoke thinking about and managing their emotions in an adaptive way that contributes to resilience.

Promoting Academic Success for Boys of Color

Not all schools are prepared to act as a social asset in support of BBY's emotional development. Some schools struggle to provide basic instruction due to a lack of order and safety for students or staff inexperience, instability, and low morale. Others are handicapped by weak, distrustful relations with families, and limited family attention and involvement. These weaknesses are particularly detrimental for low-income BBY students already facing emotional and academic challenges.[5] The Promoting Academic Success for Boys of Color (PAS) project was designed to help schools strengthen their capacity to serve as social assets that could better support development of resilience in Black and Latino boys.[6] PAS partnered with four large school districts that served Black and Latino students from mostly poor households and was a multi-component initiative with programs designed to improve the academic experience and socio-emotional climate for boys at school, increase family engagement in their sons' education, and expand boys' access to nurturing male role models.

Support for Teachers

Because teachers have the most immediate and direct impact on the quality of boys' experiences at school, most of the PAS program's efforts were devoted to deepening teachers' understanding, confidence, and skills to help BBY. This support began with frank discussions about boys' problems and potential, the need to work closely with families, instructional approaches that might motivate and engage boys, strategies for managing boys' challenging behavior, and ways to help boys to be caring and get along with others. The training provided information about trauma that might underlie boys' behavior, in order to cultivate empathy but not pity, dissipate fear, and neutralize resentment of boys' disruptive behavior. The program also emphasized the difference that teachers could make, in order to offer hope about their ability to teach boys and about the boys' ability to learn.

Beyond providing hope, the program also offered specific practices. Here, the main focus was on developing close one-to-one relations with each boy. Teachers discussed how to connect daily with each boy using their unique personal styles. Playfulness, humor, and affirmations were recommended. Hugs or "safe" touch could be used if boys seemed to welcome it. Ideas for deepening these relations included taking turns having lunch or reading one-on-one with each boy. This person-to-person connection should be characterized by warmth, unconditional positive regard, positive emotional expression, and a no-excuse-accepted demand for excellence. Teachers learned to use boy-friendly pedagogy that included hands-on learning experiences, self-directed inquiry, and intentional exposure to new information and language-rich give-and-take conversations. The ideal relation was that of a "warm demander" who expected a lot with respect to academic effort and compliance with rules, who celebrated boys' successes, and who was caring, discrete, and gentle when boys' behavior needed to be corrected.

Focusing on Emotional Resilience in Education

Most educators recognize that learning and emotional functioning are intertwined. Academic progress slows when boys struggle with emotional and behavioral difficulties. Consequently, many schools are adopting what is called a "whole child" approach, in which the prevention of emotional problems and the development of social competences are embraced as integral to their educational mandate. They have incorporated SEL programs into their curricula and attended to the effectiveness of policies and fairness of practices to deal with misbehavior. Accordingly, they are taking steps to assist students coping with distress, improve behavioral regulation, and instill civic virtues. These steps include:

- working to improve teacher-student communication and problem solving;
- prioritizing respect and support in administering school discipline;
- providing BBY opportunities to develop leadership skills;
- considering cultural differences in programming and curricula;
- and involving families as partners in the education of their sons.

These efforts convey to BBY that schools recognize their competence and innate goodness and have their best interest at heart. When done well, these efforts will contribute to BBY resilience.

Neighborhood Supports for Emotional Resilience

Neighborhoods, the third leg of the supportive stool, can also be settings that nurture emotional resilience in BBY. Efforts to promote emotional resilience in BBY are often undertaken by community-based organizations. Many adopt a framework that has been described as positive youth development (PYD).[7] Examples of Neighborhood-based programs include:

- Boys and Girls Clubs: These after-school programs offer young people a safe and positive environment where they can engage in educational and recreational activities, build positive relationships with peers and adults, and develop life skills.
- Sports and Recreation Programs: These programs promote physical fitness, teamwork, and social skills through organized sports and recreational activities.
- Arts and Culture Programs: These programs expose young people to different art forms and cultural experiences and promote creativity, self-expression, and cultural awareness.
- Service-Learning Programs: These programs combine community service with academic learning, giving young people opportunities to make a positive difference in their communities while developing skills and knowledge.
- 4-H Clubs. These programs, which typically focused on nurturing skills and interests of young children related to farming, are being expanded to increase their relevance to urban areas.

These programs nurture positive development by creating safe settings that give BBY a sense of belonging and the belief that they matter. They provide young people with the skills, resources, and support they need to become healthy, successful, and responsible adults. In general, these programs aim to do the following:

Promote healthy development: PYD programs aim to promote healthy physical, cognitive, emotional, and social development in young people.

Build positive relationships: PYD programs emphasize the importance of positive relationships between young people and adults, peers, and their communities. They provide opportunities for young people to build positive relationships and to develop social skills.

Foster resilience: PYD programs aim to help young people develop resilience by counseling them about ways to overcome challenges, learn from failures, and develop coping skills.

Develop skills and competencies: PYD programs aim to help young people develop skills and competencies that will help them succeed in their personal and professional lives. These skills may include leadership, teamwork, problem-solving, decision-making, and communication skills.

Encourage positive behaviors: PYD programs aim to encourage positive behaviors in young people, such as community involvement, civic engagement, and responsible decision-making.

These goals are accomplished through diverse activities that offer BBY opportunities to form close, durable human relationships with peers who support and reinforce healthy behaviors. They also ensure access to adults who can provide sage advice and reinforce moral/ethical behavior.[8] Activities may include tutoring younger children, participating in neighborhood clean-ups, or visiting the sick and isolated in their neighborhoods.

Such programs also pair young people with adult mentors who provide guidance, support, and positive role modeling. The National Research Council has noted that mentors are especially valuable as an extra-familial resource to guide boys through difficult times and at critical decision points in their lives.[9] Mentors may help young people with academic or career goals, social and emotional issues, or other challenges. A long-term mentoring relationship can be especially beneficial for BBY who skip over the Golden Age of childhood and are on a trajectory toward chronic behavior problems. The supportive relationship of a mentor may inspire them to remain on a prosocial path and develop the competencies they need.

BBY not only need the guidance of adults; they also need the opportunity to develop their abilities to guide and lead others. They might, for instance, observe and take part in community governance and rule-making, such as attending a meeting held for members of the neighborhood to voice their perspectives on critical problems. Participation in such activities develops BBY's understanding of how decisions are made, while also cultivating their interest in issues that affect their communities. These activities also expose BB to positive peer and adult role models, help them develop a sense of community, and offer opportunities to explore areas of interest. These types of engagement activities and leadership opportunities foster resilience by activating BBY's internal motivation—the initiative that is catalyzed and sustained by efforts to attain a challenging or difficult goal.[10] These activities are also effective in promoting prosocial attitudes and behavior, altruism, and caring about others, as well as helping prevent teen pregnancy, substance abuse, and juvenile delinquency. Moreover, working on community problems and helping others holds promise for promoting civic virtues in BBY who will themselves become valuable assets to their neighborhoods and nurture emotional resilience in others.

Overall, PYD programs aim to provide young people with a variety of opportunities for growth, development, and engagement. There is mounting evidence that programs that provide mentoring, community service, and leadership opportunities are effective and contribute to positive outcomes for BBY.[11] In particular, it has been shown that programs that provided academic support, mentoring, and leadership opportunities improved academic achievement and behavior at school.[12] They are especially helpful with respect to fostering social competencies and reducing substance use and aggressive behavior.[13] Overall, there is convincing evidence that positive youth development programs are effective ways to promote emotional resilience and socially desirable outcomes in BBY. To be effective, the programs must be correctly targeted, intensive, comprehensive, and coordinated with the efforts of others.[14] They must be intensive enough to make a difference and comprehensive enough in scope to address the wide range of possible impediments that stand in the way of its success. Finally, coordinated implementation is necessary so that the resources employed will be used efficiently and build on one another. In short, although the task of promoting emotional resilience BBY may seem like a lofty goal, family-, school-, and community-based efforts can make a difference.

Notes

1. For example, see New York State Department of Education (2018) and U.S. Department of Education, Office of Special Education and Rehabilitative Services (2021).
2. U.S. Department of Education's Office for Civil Rights (2016).
3. Rogoff (2003).
4. California Department of Education (2016).
5. DuBois et al. (1994).
6. The PAS project was an initiative funded by the W. K. Kellogg Foundation.
7. Onyeka et al. (2021).
8. National Academies of Sciences... (2002).
9. National Academies of Sciences... (2002).
10. Larson (2006).
11. Catalano et al. (2004).
12. Al-Dabbagh & Banikowski (2016).
13. Sánchez et al. (2012).
14. Durlak et al. (2011).

Conclusion

Reimagining Black Boys and Youth

For Black boys and youth (BBY), experiences of racism, economic hardship, homelessness, and traumatic loss are common. To adapt, many must grow up quickly and skip past the carefree innocence of childhood's Golden Age, an important time for the consolidation of social competencies related to self-regulation and self and social awareness. Middle childhood appears to be a critical time when boys establish a direction for their behavioral development for good or for ill. Some become hypervigilant and suspicious of others, resist adult direction, and clash openly with peers. Others become flexible, optimistic, trusting, and persistent in working toward goals they set for themselves. Loneliness and the absence of prosocial outlets during their out of school time play a key role in the direction of their development. The availability of social and cultural assets that provide caring, direction, and meaning are also critical. Social assets are evident in the concern, involvement, and encouragement of family, school staff, and community mentors. Accordingly, they form social environments with three defining features: (a) caring networks, (b) flexible control structures, and (c) frameworks of meaning and purpose. Together, these networks, control structures, and frameworks foster effective coping, promote positive self-regard, and reinforce personal agency. In doing so, they help explain why some BBY are resilient in the face of adversity and others are not. Specifically, they are key to understanding the divergent the outcomes of the two Wes Moores, one a Maryland governor, the other a Maryland inmate. Both were Black boys facing similar adversities, without their biological fathers and growing up in households experiencing financial hardship. They both encountered racism and lived in rough neighborhoods. Both misbehaved and shared a dislike of school in middle childhood. Both associated with antisocial peers. By the time they approached adolescence, both were on a track leading to serious juvenile offending. But one Wes Moore had greater access to these social assets than the other. The presence and involvement of a father is one key. On the surface they appeared to be the same in that both grew up without the physical presence of a father. However, the cause of their father's absence was not the same, and this was momentous. The resilient Wes Moore's father, a broadcast news journalist died unexpectedly due to medical malpractice when Wes was three; the other had a father who was so removed and distant that he could not even recognize and did not acknowledge Wes the one and only time they met. A deceased father could be valorized and admired. His memory and his accomplishments could inspire and be emulated. The "other" Wes Moore wanted nothing to do with his father, the thought of whom generated feelings of rejection, shame, sadness, and anger. In addition, the resilient Wes Moore lived in an extended family with a maternal grandfather who was a retired minister. The "other" Wes Moore lived with a loving mother preoccupied with financial worries and an older brother caught up in life on the streets. The resilient Wes Moore was embedded within an involved and extended family network, the other in an isolated household that was under continuous financial duress. The two Wes Moores' had different access to caring networks, structures of social control, and worldviews that reflected a sense of purpose, of meaning, and of being valued.

Caring Networks

Caring networks for BBY refer to persons across multiple settings, such as schools and neighborhoods, who display concern and provide care and support for BBY. They constitute environments in which BBY feel safe physically and emotionally. These networks foster introspection, reflection, and a willingness in BBY to disclose the pain they feel. These caring networks often provide emotional support and practical assistance without being asked. They create a protective culture of empathy, understanding, and kindness around BBY, particularly those who might otherwise feel ignored, isolated, lonely, or stigmatized. This network of trustworthy people engenders the feeling of belonging to a community in which adults act like parents and peers, like kin who go out of their way to be an empathic presence. Attending a school that offers a caring network means that BBY can identify at least one person who can be counted on to empathize, affirm, and solve problems when BBY are overwhelmed and unable to cope on their own. These caring networks are evident when someone in the setting acknowledges BBY's emotional distress, comforts them, and assures their safety. Caring networks listen and soothe BB's pain, help them feel grounded when their lives are in turmoil, under control when frustrated, encouraged when they fail, and celebrated when they succeed. A caring network responds, for example, to disputes and fighting among BBY the way a cohesive community or well-functioning family would. Namely, instead of knee jerk reactions to punish, they attempt to repair breaches in relations, salve bruised feelings, and address the underlying causes of the difficulty but only after flaring tempers have cooled down and hurt feelings have largely dissipated. Because of this caring network, BBY feel connected to a community in which they are worthy enough to deserve the solicitous attention of others. When a caring network is active, BBY feel valued, understood, and emotionally safe. The resilience of one Wes Moore could be attributed to the caring network across family and school. They offered encouragement and assistance without excessively indulging his whims. Wes Moore trusted that he could rely on them during troubling times as when he faced racist threats in a rural Pennsylvania community. School staff contributed to this system of care by setting high expectations and creating emotionally secure, organized, and responsive classroom environments. Wes's high school, in particular, recognized and celebrated his achievements, while also providing comfort and guidance when he felt lost or confused. Although neighborhoods were not central to Wes's transformation, they could be part of a system of caring for others. For example, they can offer opportunities for prosocial activities, community service, and leadership development. Additionally, communities can instill civic virtues and ensure basic needs like food, shelter, and health care are met. By involving a broader range of people in these caring relations with boys, communities can become a crucial asset for promoting resilience.

Control Structures

Control structures refer to actions, routines, and norms intended to direct BBY toward positive behavior and correct or prevent misbehavior. The structures of control set expectations, articulate rules, promote values, enforce behavioral limits, and, most importantly, involve processes for correcting misbehavior. Effective control structures monitor and redirect behavior when necessary. They constrain and regulate behavior when BBY capacity for self-regulation has not yet fully matured. When an effective system of control is in place, it establishes clear expectations and provides contingencies and consequences that guide behavior toward positive outcomes. Thus, control structures serve important functions of preventing misguided behavior when boys are unable to foresee, or seem not to care about, the negative consequences of their choices and stubbornly insist on having their way. Control structures can be explicitly activated when adults closely monitor behavior, intervene to encourage positive behavior, redirect risky behavior, or step in to stop behaviors before they result in harm to self or others. They forewarn of consequences and follow through when BBY misbehave. Control structures can also be implicit and embedded in the culture through unarticulated norms, expectations, and modeling of prosocial behavior by peers and adults. In the long run, successful control does not need to be imposed externally because the desired behaviors are imitated and prosocial norms are internalized by BBY. This was ultimately the case for the resilient Wes Moore. Wes's mother, sister, and school were swift to express displeasure and disappointment when he misbehaved. Wes's family and school employed subtle methods to get him to attend and reinvest in schooling. However, they took more drastic measures when these efforts failed. His mother enrolled him in a residential military high school when he was just on the precipice of serious problems. This was to be a turning point, though he did everything in his power to resist the move in the beginning. Wes felt the impact of their disapproval and, over time, came to feel more comfortable and accepted in his new school setting. Effective structures of control also allowed for his redemption and repairing of ruptured relationships with his family. It is through support and care that Wes Moore internalized expectations and accepted control. Wes was fortunate in having a Black upper class mentor at the high school who took an interest in him at the request of Wes's mother. This was the beginning of Wes's transformation. Wes admired and wanted to emulate this mentor though he was strict and had high expectations of Wes. In this way, the mentor functioned as a part of both the caring network and control structure. The relationship with the mentor revealed that control is more effective when the person implementing control is also perceived as part of a network of caring than when it stands alone.

Frameworks that Provide Meaning and Purpose

Frameworks are ideas, attitudes, and beliefs about self and one's place in the world that convey meaning, affirm purpose, and undergird personal worth. Interpretive frameworks can encompass values like familism, respect for others, justice, equity, responsibility, and noblesse oblige. They can also include psychological perspectives that provide self-protective and paradoxical explanations for outcomes influenced by racism. They combine to form worldviews and explanatory models for life and how the world functions for BBY. They are transmitted to BBY through racial socialization conversations, selective books, cultural norms, and spiritual practices. They can also be conveyed through family stories that highlight the struggles and successes of past generations.

These frameworks help boys comprehend what it means to be a Black person, appreciate their history, traditions, and culture; and anticipate the obstacles they will face and the ways they will be perceived in the world. These interpretive frameworks underscore the existence and ubiquity of racial discrimination and microaggressions as well as the importance of developing ways to look beyond them. By conveying these interpretive frameworks, families and even schools establish the basis on which BB can acknowledge the existence of racial oppression and, at the same time, accept personal responsibility for their own behavior. They contribute to the formation of racial identity, pride, and an understanding of racism. And they reinforced Wes Moore's belief in personal control of one's destiny in spite of racism.

By adolescence, BBY like the two Wes Moores are drawn toward trouble and "easy" money, feeling lost, ungrounded, trusting few, and lacking direction or a clear understanding of their identity and what truly matters beyond the quest for immediate gratification. BBY who get into trouble are often adrift and suffer from a lack of purpose and meaning. Interpretive frameworks may expose for some the futility of nihilistic "codes of the street" that define justice as retaliation for perceived disrespect or injury. They help BBY find significance, a sense of belonging, and the understanding that they are valuable. They can be motivational, emphasizing the value of sustained effort. They may also convey spiritual or religious values, emphasizing a relationship with a benevolent higher power that offers protection. They convey a greater purpose in life beyond materialism, wealth, and power. They are a moral compass that points toward empathy and service to others. They offer the possibility of imagining themselves as loveable, worthy, and efficacious.

Building Emotional Resilience

It may be tempting to lay the blame for Wes Moore's incarceration on his poor choices, his absent father, his failing schools, his antisocial peers, and neighborhood violence. However, it is important to recognize that each of these was sustained by greater social forces. Racism and poverty are major sources of distress for BBY and their families, schools, and neighborhoods. Poverty and racism are linked to adverse experiences and chronic emotional stress that undermine the health and well-being of BBY. Although families, schools, and neighborhoods possess social assets that could mitigate these effects, they are often depleted and fail to function effectively. We could do better as a society by combating poverty and material hardship, which drain the capacity of families, schools, and neighborhoods to raise BBY.

Combating Poverty Robustly

Significant improvements in family environments and the ability to support the positive development of Black boys could be achieved if all families had access to jobs that offered living wages, health care, and stable, affordable housing. Creative policy interventions exist that could make a substantial impact if implemented more robustly. Duncan has outlined a comprehensive approach to reducing poverty in the United States, developed by a National Academies of Sciences, Engineering, and Medicine panel. This approach includes sensible, evidence-based poverty reduction strategies. Some income support programs, such as the Earned Income Tax Credit (EITC), and health insurance programs, such as CHIP and Medicaid, have been implemented successfully in the past but could be even more effective if they served more of the families that need them. Other efforts target homelessness. The problem of affordable housing may seem insurmountable because for decades we have not increased the supply of housing to match population growth. However, the problem is solvable if we attend to local and regional impediments, such as restrictive zoning regulations, and increase federal subsidies for renting and building homes. The political will to address the financial disadvantages affecting Black boys will require transformations in how we think about what they and the poor deserve.

Reimagining Black Boys to Overcome Stereotypes and Bias

Impediments to improving the life outcomes of BBY are not just fiscal but also problems of imagination and spirit. While poverty reduction policies may be well-intentioned and successful, they do not directly go to the heart of racial bias. Even if such policies were implemented successfully, discrimination, prejudices, and implicit bias against Black boys prevail. Reversal of these biases will require addressing the anxiety that many White individuals have about Black boys who are seen as a threat. Preemptively viewing BBY as dangerous and intellectually incompetent stems from a failure to envision them as transcendent over their adverse circumstances. It is a failure to recognize the untapped potential hidden beneath the surface. To combat and neutralize these negative perceptions, it may be helpful to deliberately entertain alternative images of Black boys and reimagine them as leaders, caregivers, or defenders. For instance, consider Barack Obama's photo from his adolescence, where he strikes a cool pose with a cigarette. What do people see in this image? Do they perceive a defiant troublemaker? An academically mediocre student? A potential thug? These negative images and fears permeate the imaginations of many when they look at BBY. These images overshadow more promising possibilities and block out a vision of the potential within every BBY. How difficult is it to see in Obama and other BBY an eloquent, promising, rising star who would inspire hope and lead the world through challenging times? To reimagine BBY, we must engage in self-critical reflection and look beyond fear-based facades to see young individuals, sometimes in need of support and guidance. Solving these problems requires the belief that BBY can and will succeed if we invest in them.

This reimagining can begin with Wes Moore, the inmate. The final chapters of his life have not been written. If we reimagine Wes Moore as something more than a felon and a threat to society, if we recognize his humanity and affirm his value as a person, we can imagine him having another chance to find his footing and carve out a path toward a meaningful, purposeful, and satisfying life after all. However, to do so, he will need the same social assets that made the transformation of Governor Wes Moore possible: people who care, who empathize and provide the social support and instrumental aid needed to get his life on track while he serves his time.

Efforts to support the resilience of BBY must begin by confronting stereotypes that deem them dangerous and incompetent. We must actively resist the stereotypes that undermine the confidence, sense of purpose, and personal efficacy. We must stop regarding them as too troubled and easily disposable. We must envision a future where Black boys are liberated from intergenerational trauma, transcend the barriers of institutional and structural racism, and are set free to soar. Hope and optimism are essential to reimagining this bright future for all BBY. With the right environmental supports, the lives of many more BBY will converge onto a path that offers meaning and personal fulfillment. This is possible if the world can reimagine their humanity, foibles and all, full of possibilities and worthy of investment, nurturance, guidance, care, and support. This is what we all need to thrive.

Bibliography

Aber, J. L., Brown, J. L., & Jones, S. M. (2003). Developmental trajectories toward violence in middle childhood: Course, demographic differences, and response to school-based intervention. *Developmental Psychology*, 39, 324–348. doi:10.1037/0012-1649.39.2.324

Achenbach, T. M. (1991). *Integrative guide for the 1991 CBCL/4–18, YSR, and TRF profiles*. University of Vermont, Department of Psychiatry.

Adkins, D. E., Wang V., & Elder, G. (2009). Structure and stress: Trajectories of depressive symptoms across adolescence and young adulthood. *Social Forces*, 88(1), 31–60.

Ainsworth, M. D. S. (1978). *Patterns of attachment: A psychological study of the strange situation*. Lawrence Erlbaum Associates.

Al-Dabbagh, S. A., & Banikowski, A. B. (2016). The effects of a positive youth development program on middle school students' academic achievement, school behavior, and self-efficacy. *Journal of Youth Development*, 11(2), 22–33. doi: 10.5195/jyd.2016.420

Allard, S. W. (2008). *Out of Reach: Place, Poverty, and the New American Welfare State*. Yale University Press.

American Psychological Association, Task Force on Resilience and Strength in Black Children and Adolescents. (2008). *Resilience in African American children and adolescents: A vision for optimal development*. American Psychological Association. http://www.apa.org/pi/families/resources/resiliencerpt.pdf

Anderson, E. (1999). *Code of the street: Decency, violence, and the moral life of the inner city*. W.W. Norton & Company.

Anderson, R. E., McKenny, M. C., & Stevenson, H. C. (2019). EMBRace: Developing a racial socialization intervention to reduce racial stress and enhance racial coping among Black parents and adolescents. *Family Process*, 58, 53–67.

Angold, A., Erkanli, A., Farmer, E. M., Fairbank, J. A., Burns, B. J., Keeler, G., & Costello, E. J. (2002). Psychiatric disorder, impairment, and service use in rural African American and white youth. *Archives of General Psychiatry*, 59(10), 893–901. https://doi.org/10.1001/archpsyc.59.10.893

APA Task Force on Resilience and Strength in Black Children and Adolescents. (2008). *Resilience in African American children and adolescents: A vision for optimal development*. American Psychiatric Association. http://www.apa.org/pi/cyf/resilience.html

Argabright, S. T., Moore, T. M., Visoki, E., DiDomenico, G. E., Taylor, J. H., & Barzilay, R. (2022). Association between racial/ethnic discrimination and pubertal development in early adolescence. *Psychoneuroendocrinology*, 140, 1–6. https://doi-org.proxy-um.researchport.umd.edu/10.1016/j.psyneuen.2022.105727

Baldwin, J. (1968). The uses of the blues. In E. S. Burt & W. K. Wimsatt Jr. (Eds.), *Anthology of the American Negro in the theatre* (pp. 297–305). Dodd, Mead & Company.

Bandura, A. (1986). *Social foundations of thought and action: A social cognitive theory*. Prentice-Hall.

Barbarin, O. A. (1995). *Development and evaluation of family and community oriented programs for children and adolescents with serious conduct disorders*. Unpublished Research Report. Boysville of Michigan.

Barbarin, O. (1999). Social risks and psychological adjustment: A comparison of African-American and South African children. *Child Development*, 70, 1348–1359.

Barbarin, O. (2002a). African American males in kindergarten. In J. U. Gordon (Ed.), *The African-American male in American life and thought* (pp. 1–12). Nova Science Publishers.

Barbarin, O. (2002b). Culture and ethnicity in social, emotional and academic development. *The Kauffman Early Education Exchange*, 1, 45–61.

Barbarin, O. (2013). A longitudinal examination of socio-emotional learning in African American and Latino boys across the transition from pre-k to kindergarten. *American Journal of Orthopsychiatry*, 83, 156–164. DOI: 10.1111/ajop.12024

Barbarin, O. (2015). Creating auspicious environments for positive youth development in communities of Color. *American Journal of Orthopsychiatry*, 85(5) (Suppl), S45–S54. http://dx.doi.org/10.1037/ort0000109

Barbarin, O. A. (2019). African American boys in early childhood: Facing the challenge of diversity. In B. H. Wasik & S. L. Odom (Eds.), *Celebrating 50 years of child development research: Past, present, and future perspectives* (pp. 53–74). Paul H. Brookes Publishing Co.

Barbarin, O., Copeland-Linder, N., & Wagner, M. (2022). Can you see what we see?: African American parents' views of the strengths and challenges of children and youth living with adversity. *Prevention Science*. https://doi.org/10.1007/s11121-022-01469-y

Barbarin, O., & Crawford, G. (2006). Acknowledging and reducing stigmatization of African American boys. *Young Children*, 61(6), 79–86.

Barbarin, O. A., Hitti, A., & Copeland-Linder, N. (2019). Behavioral and emotional development of African American boys growing up in risky environments. *Child Development Perspectives*, 13(4), 215–220. https://doi.org/10.1111/cdep.12341

Barbarin, O., Iruka, I. U., Harradine, C., Winn, D. C., McKinney, M. K., & Taylor, L. C. (2013). Development of social-emotional competence in Boys of Color: A cross-sectional cohort analysis from pre-K to second grade. *American Journal of Orthopsychiatry*, 83, 145–155. DOI: 10.1111/ajop.12023

Barbarin, O., & Soler, R. (1993). Behavioral, emotional and academic adjustment in a national probability sample of African American children: Effects of age, gender, and family structure. *Journal of Black Psychology*, 19(4), 423–446.

Beck, A., Crain, A. L., Solberg, L. I., Unützer, J., & Glasgow, R. E. (2011). MacArthur Foundation's initiative on depression and primary care at Dartmouth and Cornell medical schools. *Journal of Occupational and Environmental Medicine*, 53(5), 511–518. https://doi.org/10.1097/JOM.0b013e318217e8f3

Berry, D., Blair, C., Willoughby, M., Garrett-Peters, P., Vernon-Feagans, L., Mills-Koonce, W. R.; Family Life Project Key Investigators. (2016). Household chaos and children's cognitive and socio-emotional development in early childhood: Does childcare play a buffering role? *Early Childhood Research Quarterly*, 34, 115–127. doi: 10.1016/j.ecresq.2015.09.003

Beidel, D. C., Turner, M. W., & Trager, K. N. (1994). Test anxiety and childhood anxiety disorders in African American and White school children. *Journal of Anxiety Disorders*, 8, 169–179.

Blair, C. (2010). Stress and the development of self-regulation in context. *Child Development Perspectives*, 4, 181–188.

Blair, C., Berry, D., Mills-Koonce, R., & Granger, D. (2013). Cumulative effects of early poverty on cortisol in young children: Moderation by autonomic nervous system activity. *Psychoneuroendocrinology*, 38, 2666–2675. PMID 23890719 DOI: 10.1016/J.Psyneuen.2013.06.025

Blair, C., & Raver, C. C. (2012). Child development in the context of adversity: Experiential canalization of brain and behavior. *American Psychologist*, 67, 309–318. doi:10.1037/a0027493

Blake, W. M., & Darling, C. A. (1994). The dilemmas of the African American male. *Journal of Black Studies*, 24(4), 402–415.

Bleil, M. E., Adler, N. E., Appelhans, B. M., Gregorich, S. E., Sternfeld, B., Cedars, M. I., & Rees Clayton, E. M. (2018). Early life adversity and onset of puberty in black and white girls and boys. *Journal of Adolescent Health,* 63(4), 458–465. https://doi.org/10.1016/j.jadohealth.2018.05.015

Borges J., Lee M., Lee P. A., Gantry M. E., & Housman E. J. (2018). Timing of puberty in boys in the United States: Implications for clinical care and research. *Proceedings of the National Academy of Sciences,* 115 (4). https//doi.org/10.1073/pnas.1708934115

Bowlby, J. (1944). Forty-four juvenile thieves: Their characters and home-life (II). *International Journal of Psycho-Analysis,* 25, 107–128.

Bowlby, J. (1969). *Attachment and loss: Vol. 1. Attachment.* Basic Books.

Bowlby, J. (1973) *Attachment. Vol. 2, Separation Anxiety and Anger.* Basic Books.

Bowlby, J. (1982). Attachment and loss: Retrospect and prospect. *American Journal of Orthopsychiatry,* 52(4), 664–678. https://doi.org/10.1111/j.1939-0025.1982.tb01456.x

Breslau, J., Miller, E., Breslau, N., Bohnert, K., Lucia, V., & Schweitzer, J. (2009). The impact of early behavior disturbances on academic achievement in high school. *Pediatrics,*123(6), 1472–1476. https://doi.org/10.1542/peds.2008-1406

Bretherton, I. (1992). The origins of attachment theory: John Bowlby and Mary Ainsworth. *Developmental Psychology,* 28, 759–775.

Bridge, J. A., Asti, L., Horowitz, L. M., Greenhouse, J. B., Fontanella, C. A., Sheftall, A. H., Kelleher, K. J., & Campo, J. V. (2015). Suicide trends among elementary school-aged children in the United States from 1993 to 2012. *JAMA Pediatrics,* 169(7), 673–677. doi:10.1001/jamapediatrics. 2015.0465

Bridge J. A., Horowitz, L. M., Fontanella, C. A., Sheftall, A. H., Greenhouse, J., Kelleher, K. J., & Campo, J. V. (2018). Age-related racial disparity in suicide rates among US youths from 2001 through 2015. *JAMA Pediatrics,* 172(7), 697–699. doi:10.1001/jamapediatrics.2018.0399

Brody, G. H., Flor, D. L., Hollett-Wright, N., & McCoy, J. K. (1998). Children's development of alcohol use norms: Contributions of parent and sibling norms, children's temperaments, and parent–child discussions. *Journal of Family Psychology,* 12, 209–219.

Brody, G. H., Lei, M.-K., Chae, D. H., Yu, T., Kogan, S. M., & Beach, S. R. H. (2014). Perceived discrimination among African American adolescents and allostatic load: A longitudinal analysis

Brody, G. H., McBride Murry, V., Gerrard, M., Gibbons, F. X., Molgaard, V., McNair, L., Brown, A. C., Wills, T. A., Spoth, R. L., Luo, Z., Chen, Y., & Neubaum-Carlan, E. (2004). The Strong African American Families program: Translating research into prevention programming. *Child Development,* 75(3), 900–917.

Brody, G. H., Murry, V. M., Chen, Y., Kogan, S. M., & Brown, A. C. (2006). Effects of family risk factors on dosage and efficacy of a family centered preventive intervention for rural African Americans. *Prevention Science,* 7, 281–291.

Brody, G. H., Yu, T., Chen, E., Miller. G. E., Kogan, S. M., & Beach, S. R. H. (2013). Is resilience only skin deep? Rural African Americans' socioeconomic status-related risk and competence in preadolescence and psychological adjustment and allostatic load at age 19. *Psychological Science,* 24, 1285–1293.

Brody, G. H., Yu, T., Miller, G. E., & Chen, E. (2015). Discrimination, racial identity, and cytokine levels among African American adolescents. *Journal of Adolescent Health,* 56, 496–501. https://doi.org/10.1016/j.jadohealth.2015.01.017

Broidy, L. M., Nagin, D. S., Tremblay, R. E., Bates, J. E., Brame, B., Dodge, K. A., Fergusson, D., Horwood, J. L., Loeber, R., Laird, R., Lynam, D. R., Moffitt, T. E., Pettit, G. S., & Vitaro, F. (2003). Developmental trajectories of childhood disruptive behaviors and adolescent delinquency: A six-site, cross-national study. *Developmental Psychology,* 39(2), 222–245. https://doi.org/10.1037/0012-1649.39.2.222

Bronfenbrenner, U. (1979). *The ecology of human development.* Harvard University Press.

Brooks-Gunn, J., & Duncan, G. J. (1997). The effects of poverty on children. *The Future of Children,* 7(2), 55–71.

Brown, J., Barbarin, O., & Scott, K. (2013). Socioemotional trajectories in Black boys between kindergarten and fifth grade: The role of cognitive skills and family in promoting resiliency. *American Journal of Orthopsychiatry*, 83, 185–193.

Bub, K. L., McCartney, K., & Willett, J. B. (2007). Behavior problem trajectories and first-grade cognitive ability and achievement skills: A latent growth curve analysis. *Journal of Educational Psychology*, 99(3), 653–670. https://doi.org/10.1037/0022-0663.99.3.653

Busby, D. R., Lambert, S. F., & Ialongo, N. S. (2013). Psychological symptoms linking exposure to community violence and academic functioning in African American adolescents. *Journal of Youth and Adolescence*, 42(2), 250–262. https://doi.org/10.1007/s10964-012-9895-z

Calabrese, R. L., & Barton, A. M. (1995). Mexican-American male students and Anglo female teachers: Victims of the policies of assimilation. *The High School Journal*, 78(3), 115–123.

California Department of Education. (2016). *Family partnerships & culture*. Author, Early Education Division.

Campbell, S. B. (1995). Behavior problems in preschool children: A review of recent research. *Journal of Child Psychology and Psychiatry*, 36(1), 113–149. https://doi.org/10.1111/j.1469-7610.1995.tb01657.x

Cassidy, E. F., & Stevenson, H. C., Jr. (2005). They wear the mask: Hyper vulnerability and hypermasculine aggression among African American males in an urban remedial disciplinary school. *Journal of Aggression, Maltreatment & Trauma*, 11(4), 53–74. https://doi.org/10.1300/J146v11n04_03

Cassidy, J. (1994). Emotion regulation: Influences of attachment relationships. *Monographs of the Society for Research in Child Development*, 59(2-3), 228–249.

Cassidy, J., & Berlin, L. J. (1994). The insecure/ambivalent pattern of attachment: Theory and research. *Child Development*, 65, 971–991.

Cassidy, J., & Shaver, P. R. (2016). *Handbook of attachment: Theory, research and clinical applications* (3rd ed.). Guilford.

Catalano, R. F., Berglund, M. L., Ryan, J. A. M., Lonczak, H. S., & Hawkins, J. D. (2004). Positive youth development in the United States: Research findings on evaluations of positive youth development programs. *Annals of the American Academy of Political and Social Science*, 591(1), 98–124. doi: 10.1177/0002716203260092

Chae, D. H., Nuru-Jeter, A. M., Adler, N. E., Brody, G. H., Lin, J., Blackburn, E. H., & Epel, E. S. (2014). Discrimination, racial bias, and telomere length in African-American men. *American Journal of Preventive Medicine*, 46(2), 103–111. https://doi.org/10.1016/j.amepre.2013.10.020

Chase-Lansdale, P. L., & Pittman, L. (2002). Welfare reform and parenting: Reasonable expectations. *The Future of Children*, 12(1), 167–185.

Chavous, T. M., Bernat, D. H., Schmeelk-Cone, K., Caldwell, C. H., Kohn-Wood, L., & Zimmerman, M. A. (2003). Racial identity and academic attainment among African American adolescents. *Child Development*, 74, 1076–1090.

Chess, S., & Thomas, A. (1996). *Temperament: theory and practice*. Brunner/Mazel.

Clincy, A. R., & Mills-Koonce, W. R. (2013). Trajectories of intrusive parenting during infancy and toddlerhood as predictors of rural, low-income African American boys' school-related outcomes. *American Journal of Orthopsychiatry*, 83(2-3), 194–206. https://doi.org/10.1111/ajop.12028

Coard, S. (2003). *Black parenting strengths and strategies program (BPSS): Trainer's manual* (unpublished). Duke University.

Coard, S., Foy-Watson, S., Zimmer, C., & Wallace, A. (2007). Considering culturally relevant parenting practices in intervention development and adaptation: A randomized controlled trial of the Black parenting strengths and strategies (BPSS) program. *The Counseling Psychologist*, 35, 797–820.

Coker, T. R., Elliott, M. N., Kanouse, D. E., Grunbaum, J. A., Schwebel, D. C., Gilliland, M. J., Tortolero, S. R., Peskin, M. F., & Schuster, M. A. (2009). Perceived racial/ethnic discrimination among fifth-grade students and its association with mental health. *American Journal of Public Health*, 99, 878–884. 10.2105/AJPH.2008.144329

Colarusso, C. A. (2011). *The Golden Age of childhood: The elementary school years*. True Nature Productions. http://amzn.to/calcolarusso

Cole, D. A., Martin, J. M., Peeke, I., Henderson, A., & Harwell, L. (1998). Validation of depression and anxiety measures in Euro-American and African-American youth: Multi-method analysis. *Psychological Assessment*, 10, 261–276.

Conger, R. D., Conger, K. J., & Martin, M. J. (2010). Socioeconomic status, family processes, and individual development. *Journal of Marriage and Family*, 72(3), 685–704. doi: 10.1111/j.1741-3737.2010.00725.x

Congressional Black Caucus Emergency Task Force on Black Youth Suicide and Mental Health. (2019). *Ring the alarm: The crisis of black youth suicide in America: A report to Congress from The Congressional Black Caucus*. Author. https://watsoncoleman.house.gov/imo/media/doc/full_taskforce_report.pdf

Cooke, A. N., & Halberstadt, A. G. (2021). Adultification, anger bias, and adults' different perceptions of Black and White children. *Cognition & Emotion*, 35(7), 1416–1422. https://doi.org/10.1080/02699931.2021.1950127

Cooke, C. L., Bowie, B. H., & Carrére, S. (2014). Perceived discrimination and children's mental health symptoms. *Advances in Nursing Science*, 37, 299–314.

Copeland, W. E., Shanahan, L., Hinesley J., Chan, R. F., Aberg, K. A., Fairbank, J. A., van den Oord, E., & Costello, E. J. (2018). Association of childhood trauma exposure with adult psychiatric disorders and functional outcomes. *JAMA Network Open*, 1(7), e184493. doi:10.1001/jamanetworkopen.2018.4493

Costello, E. J., Mustillo, S., Erkanli, A., Keeler, G., & Angold, A. (2003). Prevalence and development of psychiatric disorders in childhood and adolescence. *Archives of General Psychiatry*, 60, 837–844.

Cox, J. W. (2017, April 20). "Did your father die?" For a second-grader, gunfire, school lockdowns, then the worst violence of all. *Washington Post*. https://www.washingtonpost.com/sf/local/2017/04/20/tyshaun/

Coyne, L. W., & Thompson, A. D. (2011). Maternal depression, locus of control, and emotion regulatory strategy as predictors of preschoolers' internalizing problems. *Journal of Child and Family Studies*, 20(6), 873–883. https://doi.org/10.1007/s10826-011-9455-2

Cunningham, J. N., Kliewer, W., & Garner, P. W. (2009). Emotion socialization, child motion understanding and regulation, and adjustment in urban African American families: Differential associations across child gender. *Development and Psychopathology*, 21(1), 261–283. https://doi.org/10.1017/S0954579409000157

Cunningham, M., Swanson, D. P., & Hayes, D. M. (2013). School- and community-based associations to hypermasculine attitudes in African American adolescent males. *American Journal of Orthopsychiatry*, 83(2-3), 244–251. https://doi.org/10.1111/ajop.12029

Del Giudice, M. (2014). Middle childhood: An evolutionary-developmental synthesis. *Child Development Perspectives*, 8(4), 193–200. https://doi.org/10.1111/cdep.12084

Dodge, K. A. (1986). A social information processing model of social competence in children. *Minnesota Symposium on Child Psychology*, 18, 77–125.

Dodge, K. A., & Coie, J. D. (1987). Social information-processing factors in reactive and proactive aggression in children's peer groups. *Special Issue: Integrating Personality and Social Psychology. Journal of Personality and Social Psychology*, 53, 1146–1158.

Dodge, K. A., Greenberg, M. T., Malone, P. S.; Conduct Problems Prevention Research Group. (2008). Testing an idealized dynamic cascade model of the development of serious violence in adolescence. *Child Development*, 79(6), 1907–1927. https://doi.org/10.1111/j.1467-8624.2008.01233.x DO - 10.1111/j.1467-8624.2008.01233.x

Dow, D. M. (2016). The deadly challenges of raising African American boys: Navigating the controlling image of "the thug." *Gender & Society*, 30, 161–188. http://dx.doi.org/10.1177/0891243216629928

Drury, S. S., Mabile, E., Brett, Z. H., Esteves, K., Jones, E., Shirtcliff, E. A., & Theall, K. P. (2014). The association of telomere length with family violence and disruption. *Pediatrics*, 134(1), e128–e137. https://doi.org/10.1542/peds.2013-3415

DuBois, D. L., Felner, R. D., Meares, H., Krier, M. (1994). Prospective investigation of the effects of socioeconomic disadvantage, life stress, & social support on early adolescent adjustment. *Journal of Abnormal Psychology*, 103, 511–522.

Dunbar, A. S., Perry, N. B., Cavanaugh, A. M., & Leerkes, E. M. (2015). African American parents' racial and emotion socializations profiles and young adults' emotional adaptation. *Cultural Diversity and Ethnic Minority Psychology*, 21, 409–419. http://dx.doi.org/10.1037/a0037546

Dunbar, A. S., Zeytinoglu, S., & Leerkes, E. M. (2021). When is parental suppression of Black children's negative emotions adaptive? The role of preparation for racial bias and children's resting cardiac vagal tone. *Research on Child and Adolescent Psychopathology*, 50, 163–176.

Duncan, G. J. (2021). A roadmap to reducing child poverty. *Academic Pediatrics*, 21(8), S97–S101. 10.1016/j.acap.2021.04.028

DuRant, R. H., Getts, A., Cadenhead, C., Emans, S. J. (1995). Exposure to violence and victimization and depression, hopelessness, and purpose in life among adolescents living in and around public housing. *Journal of Developmental and Behavioral Pediatrics*, 1995;16(4): 233–237.

Durlak, J. A., Weissberg, R. P., Dymnicki, A. B., Taylor, R. D., & Schellinger, K. B. (2011). The impact of enhancing students' social and emotional learning: A meta-analysis of school-based universal interventions. *Child Development*, 82(1), 405–432.

Early, D., Barbarin, O., Bryant, D., Burchinal, M., Chang, F., Clifford, R., Crawford, G., Weaver, W., Howes, C., Ritchie, S., Kraft-Sayre, M., Pianta, R., & Barnett, W. S. (2006). Pre-Kindergarten in eleven states: NCEDL's multi-state study of pre-kindergarten & study of state-wide early education programs (SWEEP). FPG NCEDL Working Paper. https://fpg.unc.edu/sites/fpg.unc.edu/files/resources/reports-and-policy-briefs/NCEDL_PreK-in-Eleven-States_Working-Paper_2005.pdf

Eberhardt, J. L., Goff, P. A., Purdie, V. J., & Davies, P. G. (2004). Seeing Black: Race, crime, and visual processing. *Journal of Personality and Social Psychology*, 87, 876–893.

El-Sheikh, M., Buckhalt, J. A., Keller, P. S., Cummings, E. M., & Acebo, C. (2007). Child emotional insecurity and academic achievement: The role of sleep disruptions. *Journal of Family Psychology*, 21(1), 29–38. https://doi.org/10.1037/0893-3200.21.1.29

English, D., Lambert, S. F., Tynes, B. M., Bowleg, L., Zea, M. C., & Howard, L. C. (2020). Daily multidimensional racial discrimination among Black U.S. American adolescents. *Journal of Applied Developmental Psychology*, 66, 101068. https://doi.org/10.1016/j.appdev.2019.101068

Evans, G. W., Gonnella, C., Marcynyszyn, L. A., Gentile, L., & Salpekar, N. (2005). The role of chaos in poverty and children's socioemotional adjustment. *Psychological Science*, 16(7), 560–565. https://doi.org/10.1111/j.0956-7976.2005.01575.x

Evans, G. W., & Kim, P. (2013). Childhood poverty, chronic stress, self-regulation, and coping. *Child Development Perspectives*, 7(1), 43–48. https://doi.org/10.1111/cdep.12013

Farmer, A. D., Jr., Bierman, K. L., & The Conduct Problems Prevention Research Group. (2002). Predictors and consequences of aggressive-withdrawn problem profiles in early grade school. *Journal of Clinical Child and Adolescent Psychology*, 31(3), 299–311. https://doi.org/10.1207/153744202760082568

Fenning, P., & Rose, J. (2007). Overrepresentation of African American students in exclusionary discipline: The role of school policy. *Urban Education*, 42(6), 536–559.

Ferguson, A. A. (2001, revised 2020). *Bad boys: Public schools in the making of Black masculinity*. University of Michigan Press.

Ferguson, C. J. (2013). Spanking, corporal punishment and negative long-term outcomes: A meta-analytic review of longitudinal studies. *Journal of Family Psychology*, 27(4), 588–597.

Fontaine, K. L., Yang, C., Dodge, K. A., Pettit, G. S., & Bates, J. E. (2009). Developmental trajectories of African American and European American children's externalizing behaviors: Differences in risk, promotive, and protective factors. *Development and Psychopathology*, 21(2), 543–566.

Forehand, R. L., & Long, N. (2002). *Parenting the strong willed child: The clinically proven five-week program for parents of two- to six-year-olds.* Contemporary Books.

Frankenhuis, W. E., & de Weerth, C. (2013). Does early-life exposure to stress shape or impair cognition? *Current Directions in Psychological Science*, 22(5), 407–412. https://doi.org/10.1177/0963721413484324

García Coll, C., Lamberty, G., Jenkins, R., McAdoo, H. P., Crnic, K., Wasik, B. H., & Vázquez García, H. (1996). An integrative model for the study of developmental competencies in minority children. *Child Development*, 67, 1891–1914. http://dx.doi.org/10.2307/1131600

Gaylord-Harden, N. K., Barbarin, O. A., Tolan, P. H., & Murry, V. M. (2018). Understanding development of African American boys and young men: Moving from risks to positive youth development. *American Psychologist*, 73, 753–767.

Gaylord-Harden, N. K., Cunningham, J. A., & Zelencik, B. (2011). Effects of exposure to community violence on internalizing symptoms: Does desensitization to violence occur in African American youth? *Journal of Abnormal Child Psychology*, 39(5), 711–719. https://doi.org/10.1007/s10802-011-9510-x

Ge, X., Brody, G. H., Conger, R. D., & Simons, R. L. (2006). Pubertal maturation and African American children's internalizing and externalizing symptoms. *Journal of Youth and Adolescence*, 35, 528–537. 10.1007/s10964-006-9046-5

Gershoff, E. T. (2013). Spanking and child development: We know enough now to stop hitting our children. *Child Development Perspectives*, 7(3), 133–137.

Goff, P. A., Eberhardt, J. L., Williams, M. J., & Jackson, M. C. (2008). Not yet human: Implicit knowledge, historical dehumanization, and contemporary consequences. *Journal of Personality and Social Psychology*, 94(2), 292–306. https://doi.org/10.1037/0022-3514.94.2.292

Goff, P. A., Jackson, M. C., Di Leone, B. A., Culotta, C. M., & DiTomasso, N. A. (2014). The essence of innocence: consequences of dehumanizing Black children. *Journal of Personality and Social Psychology*, 106(4), 526–545. https://doi.org/10.1037/a0035663

Goings, T. C., Belgrave, F. Z., Mosavel, M., & Evans, B. R. (2023). An antiracist research framework: Principles, challenges, and recommendations for dismantling racism through research. *Journal of the Society for Social Work and Research*, 14, 101–128.

Goldsmith, H. H., & Campos, J. J. (1982). Toward a theory of infant temperament. In R. N. Emde & R. J. Harmon (Eds.), *The development of attachment and affiliative systems* (pp. 161–193). Plenum.

Greene, B. A. (1990). What has gone before: The legacy of racism and sexism in the lives of Black mother and daughters. In L. S. Brown & M. P. Root (Eds.), *Diversity and complexity in feminist therapy* (pp. 207–230). Haworth Press.

Gregory, A., & Weinstein, R. (2004). Connection and regulation at home and in school: Predicting growth in achievement for adolescents. *Journal of Adolescent Research*, 19, 405–427.

Gregory, A., & Weinstein, R. S. (2008). The discipline gap and African Americans: Defiance or cooperation in the high school classroom. *Journal Of School Psychology*, 46(4), 455–475. doi:10.1016/j.jsp.2007.09.001

Hall, D. M., Cassidy, E. F., & Stevenson, H. C. (2008). Acting "tough" in a "tough" world: An examination of fear among urban African American adolescents. *Journal of Black Psychology*, 34(3), 381–398. https://doi-org.proxy um.researchport.umd.edu/10.1177/0095798408314140

Halle, T., Forry, N., Hair, E., Perper, K., Wandner, L., Wessel, J., & Vick, J. (2009). *Disparities in early learning and development: Lessons from the early Childhood Longitudinal Study – Birth Cohort (ECLS-B)*. Executive summary, Child Trends. Council of Chief State School Officers.

Harrell, S. P. (1997). *The racism and life experiences scales*. Unpublished manuscript.

Harrell, S. P. (2000). A multidimensional conceptualization of racism-related stress: Implications for the well-being of people of color. *American Journal of Orthopsychiatry*, 70(1), 42–57. https://doi.org/10.1037/h0087722

Harris, J., Kruger, A. C., & Scott, E. (2022). "Sometimes I wish I was a girl, 'cause they do shit like cry": An exploration into black boys' thinking about emotions. *Urban Education*, 57(2), 224–250. https://doi.org/10.1177/0042085920933327

Hawkins, A. J., & Dollahite, D. C. (2017). Evaluating the effectiveness of fatherhood programs: Implications for practitioners. *Family Relations*, 66(4), 647–660. doi: 10.1111/fare.12263

Haye, J., & Buckner, M. M. (2013). *Bigger than me: How a boy conquered dyslexia to play in the NFL*. Haye Publishing.

Henderson, T. (2022, October 13) Black families fall further behind on home ownership. *Pew Stateline Article*. https://www.pewtrusts.org/en/research-and-analysis/blogs/statel ine/2022/10/13/black-families-fall-further-behind-on-homeownership#:~:text=In%202 022%2C%2074.6%25%20of%20 White,%2C%20a%2027%2 Dpoint%20gap

Hintsanen, M., Alatupa, S., Pullmann, H., Hirstio-Snellman, P., & Keltikangas-Jarvinen, L. (2010). Associations of self-esteem and temperament traits to self- and teacher-reported social status among classmates. *Scandinavian Journal of Psychology*, 51(6), 488–494.

Hirschi, T. (1969). *Causes of delinquency*. University of California Press.

Hoeve, M., Stams, G. J., van der Put, C. E., Dubas, J. S., van der Laan, P. H., & Gerris, J. R. (2012). A meta-analysis of attachment to parents and delinquency. *Journal of Abnormal Child Psychology*, 40(5), 771–785. https://doi.org/10.1007/s10802-011-9608-1

Hughes, D., Rodriguez, J., Smith, E. P., Johnson, D. J., Stevenson, H. C., & Spicer, P. (2006). Parents' ethnic-racial socialization practices: A review of research and directions for future study. *Developmental Psychology*, 42(5), 747. https://doi.org/10.1037/0012-1649.42.5.747

Idkowiak, J., Lavery, G. G., Dhir, V., Barrett, T. G., Stewart, P. M., Krone, N., & Arlt, W. (2011). Premature adrenarche: Novel lessons from early onset androgen excess. *European Journal of Endocrinology*, 165, 189–207.

Ialongo, N., McCreary, B. K., Pearson, J. L., Koenig, A. L., Schmidt, N. B., Poduska, J., & Kellam, S. G. (2004). Major depressive disorder in a population of urban, African-American young adults: Prevalence, comorbidity and unmet mental health service need. *Journal of Affective Disorders*, 79(1-3), 127–136. https://doi.org/10.1016/S0165-0327(02)00456-1

Izard, C. E., Ackerman, B. P., Schoff, K. M., & Fine, S. E. (2000). Self-organization of discrete emotions, emotion patterns, and emotion–cognition relations. In M. D. Lewis & I. Granic (Eds.), *Emotion, development, and self-organization: Dynamic systems approaches to emotional development* (pp. 15–36). Cambridge University Press.

James, S. A., Hartnett S., & Kalsbeek, W. D. (1983). John Henryism and blood pressure differences among Black men. *Journal of Behavioral Medicine*, 6(3), 259–278.

Jensen-Campbell, L. A., & Graziano, W. G. (2001). Agreeableness as a moderator of interpersonal conflict. *Journal of Personality*, 69 (2), 323–362. https://doi.org/10.1111/1467-6494.00148

Jessor, R., & Jessor, S. L. (1977). *Problem behavior and psycho-social development*. Academic Press.

Johnson, E. I., Planalp, E. M., & Poehlmann-Tynan, J. (2022). Parental arrest and child behavior: Differential role of executive functioning among racial subgroups. *Journal of Child and Family Studies*. https://doi.org/10.1007/s10826-022-02251-y

Kaiser Family Foundation. (2007). *Health insurance coverage in America, 2006 data update.* The Kaiser Family Foundation. Retrieved from http://www.kff.org/uninsured/upload/2006_DATA%20_UPDATE.pdf

Karpati, A. M., Rubin, C. H., Kieszak, S. M., Marcus, M., & Troiano, R. P. (2002). Stature and pubertal stage assessment in American boys: the 1988-1994 Third National Health and Nutrition Examination Survey. *Journal of AdolescentHhealth: Official publication of the Society for Adolescent Medicine,* 30(3), 205-212. https://doi.org/10.1016/s1054-139x(01)00320-2

Kessler, R. C. (1991-1992). *National Comorbidity Survey.* University of Michigan, Survey Research Center.

Kessler, R. C., Chiu, W. T., Demler, O., & Walters E. E, (2005). Prevalence, severity, and comorbidity of 12-month DSM-IV disorders in the National Comorbidity Survey Replication. Archives of General Psychiatry, 62(6), 617-627.

Khoury, B., Barbarin, O. Gutiérrez, G., Klicperova-Baker, M., Padakannaya, P., &Thompson, A. (2022). Disrupted mourning, Complicated grief during COVID-19. *International Perspectives in Psychology: Research, Practice, Consultation,* 11(3), 414-221. https://doi.org/10.1027/2157-3891/a000055

Kim, E. J., Pellman, B., & Kim, J. J. (2015). Stress effects on the hippocampus: A critical review. *Learning and Memory,* 22(9), 411-6. doi: 10.1101/lm.037291.114

Kistner, J. A., David, C. F., & White, B. A. (2003). Ethnic and sex differences in children's depressive symptoms: Mediating effects of perceived and actual competence. *Journal of Clinical Child and Adolescent Psychology,* 32(3), 341-350. https://doi-org.proxy-um.researchport.umd.edu/10.1207/S15374424JCCP3203pass:[_]0

Kistner, J. A., David-Ferdon C. F., Lopez, C. M., & Dunkel, S. B. (2007). Ethnic and sex differences in children's depressive symptoms. *Journal of Clinical Child & Adolescent Psychology,* 36, 171-181.

Kliewer, W., Cunningham, J. N., Diehl, R., Parrish, K. A., Jean, M., Atiyeh, C., Neace, B., Duncan, L., Taylor, K., & Mejia, R. (2004). Violence exposure and adjustment in inner-city youth: child and caregiver emotion regulation skill, caregiver-child relationship quality, and neighborhood cohesion as protective factors. *Journal of Clinical Child & Adolescent Psychology,* 33, 477-487. http://dx.doi.org/10.1207/s15374424jccp3303_5.

Klopack, E. T., Sutton, T. E., Simons, R. L., & Simons, L. G. (2020). Disentangling the effects of boys' pubertal timing: The importance of social context. *Journal of Youth and Adolescence,* 49(7), 1393-1405. https://doi-org.proxy-um.researchport.umd.edu/10.1007/s10964-019-01141-9

Kotlowitz, A. (1991). *There are no children here: The story of two boys growing up in the other America.* Doubleday.

Kraag, G., Zeegers, M. P., Kok, G., Hosman, C., & Abu-Saad, H. H. (2006). School programs targeting stress management in children and adolescents: A meta-analysis. *Journal of School Psychology,* 44(6), 449-472. https://doi.org/10.1016/j.jsp.2006.07.001.

Kraatz Keiley, M., Bates, J. E., Dodge, K. A., & Pettit, G. S. (2000). A cross-domain growth analysis: Externalizing and internalizing behaviors during 8 years of childhood. *Journal of Abnormal Child Psychology,* 28(2), 161-179. https://doi.org/10.1023/A:1005122814723

Kresovich, A., Reffner Collins, M. K., Riffe, D., & Carpentier, F. R. D. (2021). A content analysis of mental health discourse in popular rap music. *JAMA Pediatrics,* 175(3), 286-292. https://doi.org/10.1001/jamapediatrics.2020.5155

Labella, M. H. (2018). The sociocultural context of emotion socialization in African American families. *Clinical Psychology Review,* 59, 1-15. https://doi.org/10.1016/j.cpr.2017.10.006

Lanier, Y., Sommers, M. S., Fletcher, J., Sutton, M. Y., & Roberts, D. D. (2017). Examining racial discrimination frequency, racial discrimination stress, and psychological well-being among Black early adolescents. *Journal of Black Psychology,* 43(3), 219-229. https://doi.org/10.1177/0095798416638189

Larson, R. (2006). Positive youth development, willful adolescents, and mentoring. *Journal of Community Psychology*, 34(6), 677–689. https://doi.org/10.1002/jcop.20123

Larzelere, R. E., & Kuhn, B. R. (2014). Comparing child outcomes of physical punishment and alternative disciplinary tactics: A meta-analysis. *Clinical Child and Family Psychology Review*, 17(2), 131–157.

Last, C. G., & Perrin, S. (1993). Anxiety disorders in African-American and white children. *Journal of Abnormal Child Psychology*, 21, 153–164.

Lemery-Chalfant, K., Schreiber, J. E., Schmidt, N. L., Van Hulle, C. A., Essex, M. J., & Goldsmith, H. H. (2007). Assessing internalizing, externalizing, and attention problems in young children: Validation of the Macarthur HBQ. *Journal of the American Academy of Child and Adolescent Psychiatry*, 46(10), 1315–1323. doi:10.1097/chi.0b013e3180f616c6

Lerner, J. V., Hertzog, C., Hooker, K. A., Hassibi, M., & Thomas, A. (1988). A longitudinal study of negative emotional states and adjustment from early childhood through adolescence. *Child Development*, 59, 356–366.

Lewis, M. (2000). The emergence of human emotions. In M. Lewis & J. M. Haviland-Jones (Eds). *Handbook of emotions* (2nd ed., pp. 306–322). Guilford Press.

Lieberman, A. F. (1993). *The emotional life of the toddler*. Free Press.

Lindsey, M. A., Joe, S., & Nebbitt, V. (2010). Family matters: The role of mental health stigma and social support on depressive symptoms and subsequent help seeking among African American boys. *Journal of Black Psychology*, 36(4), 458–482. https://doi-org.proxy-um.researchport.umd.edu/10.1177/0095798409355796

Lindsey, M. A., Sheftall, A. H., Xiao, Y., & Joe, S. (2019). Trends of suicidal behaviors among high school students in the United States: 1991–2017. *Pediatrics*, 144(5), e20191187.

Loeber, R., & Farrington, D. P. (Eds.). (1998). *Serious & violent juvenile offenders: Risk factors and successful interventions*. Sage Press.

Loeber, R., Farrington, D. P., & Petechuk, D. (2003). *Child delinquency: Early intervention and prevention. (Juvenile Justice Bulletin)*. U.S. Office of Juvenile Justice and Delinquency Prevention (NCJ186182). https://www.ojp.gov/pdffiles1/ojjdp/186162.pdf

Luthar, S., Cicchetti, D., & Becker, B. (2000). The construct of resilience: A critical evaluation and guidelines for future work. *Child Development*, 71(3), 543–562.

Madigan, S., Fearon, R. M. P., van IJzendoorn, M. H., Duschinsky, R., Schuengel, C., Bakermans-Kranenburg, M. J., Ly, A., Cooke, J. E., Deneault, A.-A., Oosterman, M., & Verhage, M. L. (2023). The first 20,000 strange situation procedures: A meta-analytic review. *Psychological Bulletin*, 149(1-2), 99–132. https://doi.org/10.1037/bul0000388

Main, M., & Solomon, J. (1990). Procedures for identifying infants as disorganized/disoriented during the Ainsworth Strange Situation. In M. T. Greenberg, D. Cicchetti, & E. M. Cummings (Eds.), *Attachment in the preschool years: Theory, research, and intervention* (pp. 121–160). The University of Chicago Press.

Majors, R., & Billson, J. M. (1992). *Cool pose: The dilemma of Black manhood in America*. Lexington Books.

Maras, A., Laucht, M., Gerdes, D., Wilhelm, C., Lewicka, S., Haack, D., Malisova, L., & Schmidt, M. H. (2003). Association of testosterone and dihydrotestosterone with externalizing behavior in adolescent boys and girls. *Psychoneuroendocrinology*, 28, 932–940.

Masten, A. S., & Cicchetti, D. (2016). Resilience in development: Progress and transformation. In D. Cicchetti (Ed.), *Developmental psychopathology: Risk, Resilience, and Intervention* (3rd ed., Vol. 4, pp. 271–333). John Wiley & Sons. https://doi.org/10.1002/9781119125556.devpsy406

Masten, A. S., & Coatsworth, J. D. (1998). The development of competence in favorable and unfavorable environments: Lessons from research on successful children. *American Psychologist*, 53, 205–220.

Masten, A. S., & Tellegen, A. (2012). Resilience in developmental psychopathology: Contributions of the project competence longitudinal study. *Developmental Psychopathology*, 24, 345–361.

BIBLIOGRAPHY 247

Matthews, J. S., Kizzie, K. T., Rowley, S. J., & Cortina, K. (2010). African Americans and boys: Understanding the literacy gap, tracing academic trajectories, and evaluating the role of learning-related skills. *Journal of Educational Psychology*, 102(3), 757–771. https://doi.org/10.1037/a0019616

McGhee, H. (2021). *The Sum of Us: What racism costs everyone and how we can prosper together*. Penguin Random House.

McLeod, J. D., & Shanahan, M. J. (1996). Trajectories of poverty and children's mental health. *Journal of Health Social Behavior*, 37(3), 207–220.

McLoyd, V. C. (1998). Socioeconomic disadvantage and child development. *The American Psychologist*, 53(2), 185–204. https://doi.org/10.1037//0003-066x.53.2.185

Mendez, D. D., & Hillman, J. B. (2015). Timing of puberty in African American boys as a result of early life exposure to racism. *Pediatrics*, 135(6), 1–8. https://doi.org/10.1542/peds.2014-3889

Mendez, J. L., Fantuzzo, J., & Cicchetti, D. (2002). Profiles of social competence among low-income African American preschool children. *Child Development*, 73(4), 1085–1100. https://doi.org/10.1111/1467-8624.00459

Miner, J. L., & Clarke-Stewart, K. A. (2008). Trajectories of externalizing behavior from age 2 to age 9: Relations with gender, temperament, ethnicity, parenting, and rater. *Developmental Psychology*, 44, 771–786.

Mitchell C., Hobcraft, J., McLanahan, S. S., Rutherford Siegel, S., Berg, A., Brooks-Gunn, J., Garfinkel, I., & Notterman, D. (2014). Social disadvantage, genetic sensitivity, and children's telomere length. *Proceedings of the National Academies of Science*, 111, 5944. https://doi.org/10.1073/pnas.1404293111

Molgaard, V., & Spoth, R. (2001). The Strengthening Families Program for young adolescents: Overview and outcomes. *Residential Treatment for Children and Youth*, 18(3), 15–29.

Moore, W. (2010). *The other Wes Moore*. One World Publishers.

Mrug, S., King, V., & Windle, M. (2016). Brief report: Explaining differences in depressive symptoms between African American and European American adolescents. *Journal of Adolescence*, 46, 25–29. https://doi.org/10.1016/j.adolescence.2015.10.017

Mulligan, G. M., & Flanagan, K. D. (2006). *Age 2: Findings from the 2-year-old follow-up of the early childhood longitudinal study, birth cohort (ECLS-B)* (NCES 2006-043). U.S. Department of Education, National Center for Education Statistics.

Mundy, L. K., Romaniuk, H., Canterford, L., Hearps, S., Viner, R. M., Bayer, J. K., Simmons, J. G., Carlin, J. B., Allen, N. B., & Patton, G. C. (2015). Adrenarche and the emotional and behavioral problems of late childhood. *Journal of Adolescent Health: Official Publication of The Society for Adolescent Medicine*, 57, 608–616. doi: 10.1016/j.jadohealth.2015.09.00

Murray, A. D., & Hornbaker, A. V. (1997). Maternal directive and facilitative interaction styles: Associations with language and cognitive development of low risk and high risk toddlers. *Development and Psychopathology*, 9(3), 507–516. https://doi.org/10.1017/S0954579497001272

Murry, V. M., Berkel, C., Simons, R. L., Simons, L. G., & Gibbons, F. X. (2014). A twelve-year longitudinal analysis of positive youth development among rural African American males. *Journal of Research on Adolescence*, 24(3), 512–525.

Murry, V. M., Simons, R. L., Simons, L. G., & Gibbons, F. X. (2013). Contributions of family environment and parenting processes to sexual risk and substance use of rural African American males: A 4-year longitudinal analysis. *American Journal of Orthopsychiatry*, 83(2-3), 299–309. https://doi.org/10.1111/ajop.12035

National Academies of Sciences, Engineering, and Medicine. 2002. *Scientific research in education*. The National Academies Press. https://doi.org/10.17226/10236

National Center for Education Statistics. (2023). *Annual earnings by educational attainment*. https://nces.ed.gov/programs/coe/pdf/2023/cba_508.pdf

National Center for Health Statistics. (2020). *National health interview survey, 2019.* Public-use data file and documentation. https://www.cdc.gov/nchs/nhis/data-questionnaires-documentation.htm

Negriff, S., Blankson, A. N., & Trickett, P. K. (2015). Pubertal timing and tempo: Associations with childhood maltreatment. *Journal of Research on Adolescence,* 25(2), 201–213. doi: 10.1111/jora.12128

Nelson, J. A., Leerkes, E. M., Perry, N. B., O'Brien, M., Calkins, S. D., & Marcovitch, S.; New York State Department of Education. (2014). *NY State's plan to ensure equitable access to the most effective educators 2014–15.* Report prepared for the US Department of Education https://s3.documentcloud.org/documents/2094487/finalnysequityplan.pdf

New York State Department of Education. (2018). *Mental health education literacy in schools: Linking to a continuum of well-being: Comprehensive guide.* Author. Retrieved from www.nysed.gov/sites/default/files/programs/curriculum-instruction/educationliteracyinschoolsfinal.11.2018.pdf

Nyborg, V. M., & Curry, J. F. (2003). The impact of perceived racism: Psychological symptoms among African American boys. *Journal of Clinical Child and Adolescent Psychology,* 32(2), 258–266. https://doi.org/10.1207/S15374424JCCP3202_11

Okonofua, J. A., & Eberhardt, J. L. (2015). Two strikes: Race and the disciplining of young students. *Psychological Science,* 26, 617–624.

Olson, S. L., Sameroff, A. J., Lansford, J. E., Sexton, H., Davis-Kean, P., Bates, J. E., Pettit, G. S., & Dodge, K. A. (2013). Deconstructing the externalizing spectrum: Growth patterns of overt aggression, covert aggression, oppositional behavior, impulsivity/inattention, and emotion dysregulation between school entry and early adolescence. *Development and Psychopathology,* 25, 817–842.

Onyeka, O., Richards, M., Tyson McCrea, K., Miller, K., Matthews, C., Donnelly, W., Sarna, V., Kessler, J., & Swint, K. (2021). The role of positive youth development on mental health for youth of color living in high-stress communities: A strengths-based approach. *Psychological Services,* 10.1037/ser0000593. Advance online publication. https://doi.org/10.1037/ser0000593

Owens, E. B., & Shaw, D. S. (2003). Predicting growth curves of externalizing behavior across the preschool years. *Journal of Abnormal Child Psychology,* 31, 575–590. doi: 10.1023/A:1026254005632

Oyserman, D., & Yoon, K. (2009). Neighborhood effects on racial–ethnic identity: The undermining role of segregation. *Race and Social Problems,* 1(2), 67–76.

Parks, C. (2021, September 7). The tragedy of America's rural schools. *The Education Issue, New York Times.* Updated 9/9/2021. https://www.nytimes.com/2021/09/07/magazine/rural-public-education.html

Petersen, I. T., Bates, J. E., & Staples, A. D. (2015). The role of language ability and self-regulation in the development of inattentive-hyperactive behavior problems. *Development and Psychopathology,* 27 (1), 221–237. https://doi.org/10.1017/S0954579414000698

Pierce, C. (1995). Stress analogs of racism and sexism: Terrorism, torture, and disasters. In C. V. Willie (Ed.), *Mental health, racism and sexism.* Routledge.

Rattan, A., & Eberhardt, J. L. (2010). The role of social meaning in inattentional blindness: When the gorillas in our midst do not go unseen. *Journal of Experimental Social Psychology,* 46(6), 1085–1088. https://doi.org/10.1016/j.jesp.2010.06.010

Rhodes, J., & Dubois, D. (2008). Mentoring relationships and programs for youth. *Current Directions in Psychological Science,* 17. 10.1111/j.1467-8721.2008.00585.x

Rice, F., Jones, I., Thapar, A., & the PGS Consortium. (2018). An observational study of the association between childhood depressive symptoms and pubertal timing. *Journal of Child Psychology and Psychiatry,* 59(10), 1069–1078. https://doi.org/10.1111/jcpp.12907

Ridley, C. R. (1984). Clinical treatment of the nondisclosing black client: A therapeutic paradox. *American Psychologist,* 39(11), 1234–1244.

Riessman, F. (1965). The "Helper" therapy principle. *Social Work,* 10(2), 27–32.

Roberts, Y. H., Snyder, F. J., Kaufman, J. S, Finley, M. K., Griffin, A., Anderson, J., Marshall, T., Radway, S., Stack, V., & Crusto, C. A. (2014). Children exposed to the arrest of a family member: Associations with mental health. *Journal of Child and Family Studies*, 23(2), 214–244. doi: 10.1007/s10826-013-9717-2

Robinson, M., Whitehouse, A. J. O., Jacoby, P., Mattes, E., Sawyer, M. G., Keelan, J. A., & Hickey, M. (2013). Umbilical cord blood testosterone and childhood internalizing and externalizing behavior: A prospective study. *PLoS ONE*, 8, 1–8.

Rogeness, G. A., & Badner, R. A. (1973). Teenage helper: A role in community mental health. *American Journal of Psychiatry*, 130, 933–936.

Rogoff, B. (2003). *The cultural nature of human development*. Oxford University Press.

Rosenthal, L., Earnshaw, V. A., Moore, J. M., Ferguson, D. N., Lewis, T. T., Reid, A. E., Lewis, J. B., Stasko, E. C., Tobin, J. N., & Ickovics, J. R. (2018). Intergenerational consequences: Women's experiences of discrimination in pregnancy predict infant social-emotional development at 6 months and 1 year. *Journal of Developmental and Behavioral Pediatrics*, 39(3), 228–237. https://doi.org/10.1097/DBP.0000000000000529

Rosenthal L., & Lobel, M. (2018). Gendered racism and the sexual and reproductive health of Black and Latina women. *Ethnicity & Health*, 23, 1–26. doi:10.1080/13557858.2018.1439896

Rubin, K. H., Bukowski, W. M., & Parker, J. G. (2006). Peer interactions, relationships, and groups. In N. Eisenberg, W. Damon, & R. M. Lerner (Eds.), *Handbook of child psychology: Social, emotional, and personality development* (pp. 571–645). John Wiley & Sons.

Saarni, C. (1999). *The development of emotional competence*. Guilford Press.

Sampson, R. J. (2019). Neighbourhood effects and beyond: Explaining the paradoxes of inequality in the changing American metropolis. *Urban Studies*, 56(1), 3–32.

Sampson, R. J., & Laub, J. H. (2005). A life-course view of the development of crime. *Annals of the American Academy of Political and Social Science*, 602, 12–45. https://doi.org/10.1177/0002716205280075

Sampson, R. J., Raudenbush, S., & Earls, F. (1997). Neighborhood and violent crime: A multilevel study of collective efficacy. *Science*, 277, 918–924.

Sánchez, B., Colón, Y., Esparza, D., & González, M. (2012). The effectiveness of a positive youth development program for preventing substance use and violence in a longitudinal study of Latino youth. *Journal of Primary Prevention*, 33(5-6), 251–259. doi: 10.1007/s10935-012-0289-y

Sandler, I. (2001). Quality and ecology of adversity as common mechanisms of risk and resilience. *American Journal of Community Psychology*, 29, 19–61. DOI: 10.1023/A:1005237110505

Santos, C. E., Galligan, K., Pahlke, E., & Fabes, R. A. (2013). Gender-typed behaviors, achievement, and adjustment among racially and ethnically diverse boys during early adolescence. *American Journal of Orthopsychiatry*, 83(2–3), 252–264. https://doi.org/10.1111/ajop.12036

Seaton, E. K., Caldwell, C. H., Sellers, R. M., & Jackson, J. S. (2008). The prevalence of perceived discrimination among African American and Caribbean Black youth. *Developmental Psychology*, 44, 1288–1297. 10.1037/a0012747

Selman, R. L. (2003). *Promotion of social awareness: Powerful lessons for the partnership of developmental theory and classroom practice*. Russell Sage Foundation. http://www.jstor.org/stable/10.7758/9781610444897

Serwatka, T. S., Deering, S., & Grant, P. (1995). Disproportionate representation of African Americans in emotionally handicapped classes. *Journal of Black Studies*, 25(4), 492–506.

Shonkoff, J. P., Boyce, W. T., & McEwen, B. S. (2009). Neuroscience, molecular biology, and the childhood roots of health disparities: Building a new framework for health promotion and disease prevention. *Journal of the American Medical Association*, 301(21), 2252–2259. doi:10.1001/jama.2009.754

Shonkoff J. P. (2010). Building a new biodevelopmental framework to guide the future of early childhood policy. *Child Development*, 81(1), 357–367. https://doi.org/10.1111/j.1467-8624.2009.01399.x

Shonkoff, J. P., Garner, A. S., Siegel, B. S., Dobbins, M. I., Earls, M. F., et al. (2012). The lifelong effects of early childhood adversity and toxic stress. *Pediatrics*, 129(1), 232–246.

Shrider, E. A., Kollar, M., Chen, F., & Semega, J. (September 2021). *Income and Poverty in the United States: 2020*. U.S. Census Bureau, Report Number P60-273.

Sibley, C. G., & Duckitt, J. (2008). Personality and prejudice: A meta-analysis and theoretical review. *Personality and Social Psychology Review*, 12(3), 248–279. https://doi.org/10.1177/1088868308319226

Silverman, W. K., & Albano, A. M. (1996). *The anxiety disorders interview schedule for children and parents—DSM-IV version*. Graywind.

Silverman, W. K., La Greca, A. M., & Wasserstein, S. (1995). What do children worry about? Worries and their relation to anxiety. *Child Development*, 66(3), 671–686. https://doi.org/10.2307/1131942

Simpson, J. A., Griskevicius, V., Kuo, S. I., Sung, S., & Collins, W. A. (2012). Evolution, stress, and sensitive periods: The influence of unpredictability in early versus late childhood on sex and risky behavior. *Developmental Psychology*, 48(3), 674–686. doi: 2012-03330-001

Skiba, R. J., Horner, R. H., Chung, C. G., Rausch, M., May, S. L., & Tobin, T. (2011). Race is not neutral: A national investigation of African American and Latino disproportionality in school discipline. *School Psychology Review*, 40, 85–107.

Skiba, R. J., Peterson, R. L., & Williams, T. (1997). Office referrals and suspension: Disciplinary intervention in middle schools. *Education and Treatment of Children*, 20(3), 295–315.

Slaughter, D. T., & Epps, E. G. (1987). The home environment and academic achievement of Black American children and youth: An overview. *Journal of Negro Education*, 56, 3–20.

Smith, C. D., & Hope, E. C. (2020). "We just want to break the stereotype": Tensions in Black boys' critical social analysis of their suburban school experiences. *Journal of Educational Psychology*, 112(3), 551–566. https://doi.org/10.1037/edu0000435

Smithsonian National Museum of African American History and Culture. (2018). *Conflict and compromise in history*. Author.

Spencer, M. B. (2006). Phenomenology and ecological systems theory: Development of diverse groups. In W. Damon & R. Lerner (Eds.), *Handbook of child psychology*, Vol. 15. *Theory* (6th ed., pp. 829–893). Wiley.

Spencer, M. B., Dupree, D., & Hartmann, T. T. (1997). A phenomenological variant of ecological systems theory (PVEST): A self-organization perspective in context. *Development and Psychopathology*, 9, 817–833.

Spieker, S. J., Larson, N. C., Lewis, S. M., Keller, T. E., & Gilchrist, L. (1999). Developmental trajectories of disruptive behavior problems in preschool children of adolescent mothers. *Child Development*, 70(2), 443–458. https://doi.org/10.1111/1467-8624.00032

Sroufe L. A. (2021). Then and now: The legacy and future of attachment research. *Attachment and Human Development*, 4, 396–403. doi: 10.1080/14616734.2021.1918450

Sroufe, L. A., Coffino, B., & Carlson, E. A. (2010). Conceptualizing the role of early experience: Lessons from the Minnesota longitudinal study. *Developmental Review*, 30(1), 36–51. https://doi.org/10.1016/j.dr.2009.12.002

Steele, R. G., Little, T. D., Ilardi, S. S., Forehand, R., Brody, G. H., & Hunter, H. L. (2006). A confirmatory comparison of the factor structure of the Children's Depression Inventory between European American and African American youth. *Journal of Child and Family Studies*, 15, 779–794.

Stevenson, H. C. (1997). "Missed, dissed, and pissed": Making meaning of neighborhood risk, fear and anger management in urban Black youth. *Cultural Diversity and Mental Health*, 3, 37–52.

Stewart, E. A., & Simons, R. L. (2010). Race, code of the street, and violent delinquency: A multilevel investigation of neighborhood street culture and individual norms of violence.

Criminology: An Interdisciplinary Journal, 48(2), 569–605. https://doi.org/10.1111/j.1745-9125.2010.00196.x

Strohschein. L., & Gauthier A. H. 2018. Poverty dynamics, parenting and child mental health in Canada. *Society and Mental Health* 8(3), 231–247.

Strong, R. K., & Dabbs, J. M. (2000). Testosterone and behavior in normal young children. *Personality and Individual Differences*, 28(5), 909–915. DOI:10.1016/S0191-8869(99)00149-X

Tashjian, S. M., Rahal, D., Karan, M., Eisenberger, N., Galván, A., Cole, S. W., & Fuligni, A. J. (2021). Evidence from a randomized controlled trial that altruism moderates the effect of prosocial acts on adolescent well-being. *Journal of Youth and Adolescence*, 50(1), 29–43. https://doi-10.1007/s10964-020-01362-3

Taylor, C. A., Manganello, J. A., Lee, S. J., & Rice, J. C. (2010). Mothers' spanking of 3-year-old children and subsequent risk of children's aggressive behavior. *Pediatrics*, 125(5), e1057–e1065.

Thomas, D. E., Coard, S. I., Stevenson, H. C., Bentley, K., & Zamel, P. (2009). Racial and emotional factors predicting teachers' perceptions of classroom behavioral maladjustment for urban African American male youth. *Psychology in the Schools*, 46, 184–196.

Thompson, J. E., & Twibell, K. K. (2009). Teaching hearts and minds in early childhood classrooms: Curriculum for social and emotional development. In O. A. Barbarin & B. Wasik (eds.), *Handbook of child development and early education: Research to practice* (pp. 199–222). Guilford Press.

Thulin, E. J., Lee, D. B., Eisman, A. B., Reischl, T. M., Hutchison, P., Franzen, S., & Zimmerman, M. A. (2022). Longitudinal effects of youth empowerment solutions: Preventing youth aggression and increasing prosocial behavior. *American Journal of Community Psychology*, 70(1-2), 75–88. https://doi.org/10.1002/ajcp.12577

Todd, A. R., Simpson, A. J., Thiem, K. C., & Neel, R. (2016). The generalization of implicit racial bias to young Black boys: Automatic stereotyping or automatic prejudice? *Social Cognition*, 34(4), 306–323. https://doi.org/10.1521/soco.2016.34.4.306

Todd, A. R., Thiem, K. C., & Neel, R. (2016). "Does seeing faces of young black boys facilitate the identification of threatening stimuli?": Corrigendum. *Psychological Science*, 27(12), 1673. https://doi.org/10.1177/0956797616678204

Tolan, P. H., Gorman-Smoth, D., & Henry, D. B. (2003). The developmental ecology of urban males' youth violence. *Developmental Psychology*, 39(2), 274–291. DOI: 10.1037/0012-1649.39.2.274

Tremblay, R. E., Hartup, W. H., & Archer, J. (2005). *Developmental origins of aggression*. Guilford Press.

UNDP. (1996). *Human development report 1996: Economic growth and human development*. Oxford University Press.

U.S. Census Bureau. (2023). *Current Population Survey*. https://www.census.gov/programs-surveys/cps.html

U.S. Department of Education. (2015). *Early childhood longitudinal study, kindergarten class of 2010–11 (ECLS-K:2011), User's Manual for the ECLS-K:2011 Kindergarten–First Grade Data File and Electronic Codebook, Public Version (NCES 2015-078)*. U.S. Department of Education.

U.S. Department of Education Office for Civil Rights. (2016). *2013–2014 Civil rights data collection: A first look*. U.S. Department of Education, Office for Civil Rights.

U.S. Department of Education, Office of Special Education and Rehabilitative Services. (2021). *Supporting child and student social, emotional, behavioral, and mental health needs*. Retrieved from https://www2.ed.gov/documents/students/supporting-child-student-social-emotional-behavioral-mental-health.pdf

van Goozen, S. H. M., Matthys, W., Cohen-Kettenis, P. T., Thijssen, J. H. H., & van Engeland, H. (1998). Adrenal androgens and aggression in conduct disorder prepubertal boys and normal controls. *Biological Psychiatry*, 43, 156–158. doi: 10.1016/S0006-3223(98)00360-6 van Goozen, S. H. M., van den Ban, E., Matthys, W., Cohen-Kettenis, P. T., Thijssen, J. H. H., & van Engeland, H. (2000). Increased adrenal androgen functioning in children with oppositional defiant disorder: A comparison with psychiatric and normal controls. *Journal of the American Academy of Child & Adolescent Psychiatry*, 39, 1446–1451. doi: 10.1097/00004583-200011000-00020

Vernon-Feagans, L., & Cox, M. (2013). The Family Life Project: An epidemiological and developmental study of young children living in poor rural communities: I. Poverty, rurality, parenting, and risk: An introduction. *Monographs of the Society for Research in Child Development*, 78(5), 1–23. https://doi.org/10.1111/mono.12047

Voight A., Hanson T., O'Malley M., & Adekanye, L. (2015). The racial school climate gap: Within-school disparities in students' experiences of safety, support, and connectedness. *American Journal of Community Psychology*, 56(3/4), 252–267.

Wade, M., Fox, N. A., Zeanah, C. H., Nelson, C. A., & Drury, S. S. (2020). Telomere length and psychopathology: Specificity and direction of effects within the Bucharest early intervention project. *Journal of the American Academy of Child and Adolescent Psychiatry*, 59(1), 140–148.e3. https://doi.org/10.1016/j.jaac.2019.02.013

Wallace, J. M., Goodkind, S., Wallace, C. M., & Bachman, J. G. (2008). Racial, ethnic, and gender differences in school discipline among U.S. high school students: 1991–2005. *The Negro Educational Review*, 59(1-2), 47–62.

Werner, E. E., & Smith, R. S. (1982). *Vulnerable but invincible: A longitudinal study of resilient children and youth*. McGraw-Hill.

Wight, R. G., Aneshensel, C. S., Botticello, A. L., & Sepúlveda, J. E. (2005). A multilevel analysis of ethnic variation in depressive symptoms among adolescents in the United States. *Social Science & Medicine*, 60(9), 2073–2084. https://doi.org/10.1016/j.socscimed.2004.08.065

Wilkerson, I. (2021). *Caste: The origins of our discontents*. Thorndike Press.

Woody, M., Bell, E., Cruz, N., Wears, A., Anderson, R., & Price, R. (2022). Racial stress and trauma and the development of adolescent depression: A review of the role of vigilance evoked by racism-related threat. *Chronic Stress*, 6. https://doi.org/10.1177/24705470221118574

Worden, J. W. (2009). *Grief counseling and grief therapy: A handbook for the mental health practitioner* (4th ed.). Springer.

Yoshikawa, H., Aber, J. L., & Beardslee, W. R. (2012). The effects of poverty on the mental, emotional, and behavioral health of children and youth. *American Psychologist*, 67(4), 272–284.

Zimmerman, M. A., Stoddard, S. A., Eisman, A. B., Caldwell, C. H., Aiyer, S. M., & Miller, A. (2013). Adolescent resilience: Promotive factors that inform prevention. *Child Development Perspectives*, 7(4), 215–220. https://doi.org/10.1111/cdep.12042

Zimmerman, R. S., Khoury, E. L., Vega, W. A., Gil, A. G., & Warheit, G. J. (1995). Teacher and parent perceptions of behavior problems among a sample of African American, Hispanic, and Non-Hispanic White students. *American Journal of Community Psychology*, 23, 18.

Index

For the benefit of digital users, indexed terms that span two pages (e.g., 52–53) may, on occasion, appear on only one of those pages.

Tables, figures, and boxes are indicated by an italic *t, f,* and *b* following the page number.

3-legged stool, 3*f*, 7–8
   social assets, 188–89
   wobbly, serious behavior problems, 8–9
4H clubs, 226
100 Black Fathers, 213

academic success, promoting, 223–24
acceptance
   of adult authority, 82–83
   of adversity, 178–79, 180
   of differences, 15–16, 70–72
   maternal, 192–93
   need for, 170
   peer, 20
   self- (*see* self-acceptance)
   social, preschool, 25
   of wrongdoer by school community, 221
accommodation
   to adversity, 178–79
   to difficult circumstances, 196
   to kindergarten culture, 218–19
   parent modeling, 194
   PLAAY for, 223
   to schooling, 93, 122–23
   by schools, to children who fall behind, 190
   self-regulation, 92–93
   social, middle childhood, 82–83
   socio-emotional competence, 185–86
   temperament, 57, 58
   to violence, 34
achievement gaps, 38–39, 160, 217
Ackerman, B. P., 42–43
active temperament, 57–58
adaptability, 57, 59–60, 82, 84–85
adrenarche
   adultlike roles and responsibilities, 104
   cortisol elevation and early onset, 101–2
adulthood
   reflections about, 169
   transition to, 167–68

adultification, 105–7, 108, 155–56
adults, relations with
   caring, 165–69
   implicit bias on, 42–43
adverse childhood events (ACEs)
   loss from, 113
   poverty, 31–32
   problem behavior, 113
   racism and poverty, 47–48
adversity
   early life, 113
   on executive function, 109, 192
   family, 98–99, 120–21
   material disadvantage and, 5–6
   preparation for, 203–14 (*see also* preparation, for racism and adversity)
   resilience, 6–7
   risks, protection against, 6–7
   schools, buffering effects, 217
   self-awareness and emotional resilience
      accepting and accommodating, 178–79
      reframing, 179–80
   self-protective responses, 144–54, 155–56 (*see also* self-protective responses to adversity)
   social assets
      for protection, 191–92
      for recovery, 191
      without, 138
   social environments, 188
   trauma, stress and, 99–101
affection
   expression, separation and loss on, 113
   statements, 221
affirmation, 181–82, 184
   classroom instruction, culturally responsive, 217–18
   cultural beliefs and practices, 189–90
   lack, 145

affirmation, *(cont.)*
   of masculinity, 86
   school programs, expanding, 223
   secure attachment, 63
   self-awareness, 68
   self-worth and personal efficacy, 175–77
   from teachers, 224–25
aggression, 91–93, 96–97
   adolescence, racial differences, 90–91
   adverse childhood events, 31–32
   adversity, trauma, and stress, 99
   anger and, 133
   controlling, strategies, 178
   cortisol and early adrenarche, 101–2
   as defensive reaction, 150
   kindness and service on, 182
   loss and trauma, 122–23
   middle childhood, decreased, 81, 88–89
   peer relationships, 70–72
   poverty, 49, 51
   Preventing Long-term Anger and Aggression in Youth, 223
   redirecting, 179
   separation and loss, 119
   social environments, adverse, 5–6
   toxic masculinity, 148–49
altruism, 68–69, 70, 82, 179, 182–83, 227–28
amygdala, 48–49
anger, 42–43, 132–33
   arousal, 132
   cause
      serious, 133
      trivial, 132–33
   control of, mother modeling, 194
   danger, 130
   definition, 132
   expression, parental suppression, 194
   poverty, 51
   Preventing Long-term Anger and Aggression in Youth, 223
   racism and poverty, 43–44
   separation and loss, 113
antisocial behavior, 125, 192, 208
   feelings, redirecting, 160
   knucklehead, 157–58
   knucklehead pathway, 158
   poverty, 46
   puberty, early, 103
   trauma, early, 65–66
antisocial peers, 116, 120, 162–63, 165–66, 170, 192–93, 195, 208, 229–30, 233–34
anxiety, 127–29, 128*t*, 130–32
   about safety, 130

   biases, 234–35
   cortisol and chronic stress, 101
   disorders, 127–28
   economic worry, 31
   emotional regulation, 194
   middle childhood, 93–94
   misbehavior with, 130–32
   poverty, 46, 50
   redirecting, 179, 180
   sadness and, 133–34, 178
   separation, 56
   socio-emotional competencies, 70–72
   teasing, 19–20
   violence exposure, 31–32, 50
Argabright, S. T., 102–3
arousal
   adversity, trauma, and stress, 99
   anger, 132
   avoidance, 180–81
   coping strategies, 184
   danger, 130
   hip-hop music, 184–85
   managing, 67, 70, 186, 188–89, 192–93, 196–97, 204
   racism, 40–41
   secure attachments, 62
arts and culture programs, 226
attachment, 60–65
   avoidant, 118
   disorganized, 60
   secure (*see* secure attachment)
   styles, 60–61
attribution bias, hostile, 88–89
attributions
   paradoxical 207
avoidance
   of arousal, 180–81
   of danger, 180–81
   of internalizing, 184
   of sadness, 180–81
avoidant attachment, 118

Bad Boys: Public Schools in the Making of Black Masculinity (Ferguson), 123
Baldwin, J., "The Use of the Blues," 205–6
Barbarin, O., 25, 72, 91–92
behavior
   development, 96
      fast, 96–109 (*see also* growing up fast)
   overcompensation, 146–47
      as self-protective response, 146–47

INDEX

positive
    encouraging, 220, 227
    positive youth development, 225–28
  preschool trajectories, 92–93
  racism and family instability, 40
  regulation, 48–49, 74, 217–18
  self-control, limits to augment, 192–93
behavior, problems
  adversity, early life, 113
  anxiety, fear and, 130–32
  conduct, 40–41, 73–74, 81, 89, 90f, 90, 92–93, 114, 160, 210–11, 217
  decline, typical, 88
  emotions, troubled, 129–34
  infractions, minor, 159–60
  loss, trauma, and, 113–26
  middle childhood, decline, 81, 88–89
  serious, wobbly stools, 8–9
  See also discipline; knucklehead, becoming
bias, implicit, 21, 40–41
  definition, 21
  development and, 4
  middle childhood, 125–26
  preparing for, strategies, 203–4, 211
  punishment, harsh, 23–24
  racism and financial adversity, 97f
  restorative justice practices, 221
  school, middle class minorities, 38
  stereotypes and unfair discipline, 21–22
  stigma and scapegoating, 25
  subtle, 40–41
  teachers and adults, 19, 21, 42–43
  violence and harsh punishment, 23–24
bias, racial, 4
  overcoming, 234–36
  See also bias, implicit; discrimination; racism
Bigger Than Me (Haye), 146
Biggie Smalls. *See* Notorius B.I.G.
"big man," 149, 155–56
biological memories, 100
The Black Dad Initiative, 213
Black Dad Initiative, The, 213
Black Fathers Rock, 213
Black Parenting Strengths and Strategies (BPSS), 210–11
Borges, J., 102–3
Bowlby, J., 115–16
Boys Clubs, 226
brain development, racism and poverty on, 48–49
bravado, 108–9, 125–26, 146, 150–51
Brown, J., 46

bullying, 19–20, 49–50, 98, 123, 133
Butler, The, 148

caregivers
  loss and trauma, problem behavior, 113–26 (*see also* loss, trauma, and behavior problems)
  positivity, 64
  solo, misbehavior from separation and loss, 116–17
  See also father; mother; parents
caring adults, relations with, 165–69
caring networks, 6–7, 229–31
cautious temperament, 58
church, participation, 183–84
classroom
  culturally responsive instruction, 217–18
  kindergarten, transitional, 219–20
  pedagogy, transforming, 216–17
  socio-emotional development, 216–17
  See also schools
cognitive capacities, social competence, 67–70
  self-awareness, 68
  self-regulation, 69–70
  social awareness, 68–69
Colarusso, C. A., 81
community
  poverty, 33
  spiritual, resilience from, 183–84
competence/competencies
  developing, 227
  minority children, factors, 2–3, 3f
  social, 67–76 (*see also* social competence/competencies)
  socio-emotional (*see* socio-emotional competencies)
concealing feelings, 147–49
concealment
  cost, 154–56
  feelings and emotions, 143–44, 147–49, 158, 176, 178, 184, 194
  posturing, 152
  weaknesses, 68
conduct problems, 40–41, 73–74, 81, 89, 90f, 90, 92–93, 114, 160, 210–11, 217. *See also* behavior, problems; loss, trauma, and behavior problems
confrontation, 177
control, external, 207
control, personal
  family strategies, 204–5
  self-affirming expectations, fostering, 206–7

control structures, 229–30, 231–32
    for redirecting, 231–32
    for self-regulation, 231–32
    social assets, 189–90
Cooke, C. L., 42–43
coping, 175
    adultification, 155–56
    case example, 135–36
    concealment, 155–56 (*see also* concealment)
    effective strategies, resilience from, 184
    hip-hop music for, 184–85
    loss with, 136–37
    social assets, 192
    social competencies for, 184, 185–86, 188
cortisol elevation
    adrenarche, early onset, 101–2
    stress, chronic, 101
cortisol stress response
    executive function, 47
    racism and poverty, 47
Cox, J. W., 134
Crawford, G., 25
cultural beliefs and practices
    comfort and affirmation, 189–90
    as social assets, 189–90
culturally informed and affirming school programs, expanding, 223
cultural mistrust, 153–54
cultural practices, 208
culture programs, 226
Cunningham, M., 150

danger
    anger, arousal, and fear, 130
    avoiding, 180–81
Daye, Lucky, "Over," 152–53
death, friend/family
    emotional numbing, 144
    hyper-masculinity, 149
DelGiudice, M., 81, 102
delinquency
    drugs, selling/dealing, 114, 160–61, 162
    on family/self, realizing impact, 168–69
    petty crimes, dabbling, 160–62
    shoplifting, 107, 160
    stealing, 49, 114, 115, 160, 163
    weed, smoking, 124, 159–60, 162, 163
    See also knucklehead, becoming
depression
    racism, 17
    stress, 133–34
depressive symptoms
    middle childhood, 91–92, 93–94

paternal support on, 191
puberty, early, 103
deprivation, neighborhood, poverty and, 34
desperation
    poverty, 50
    separation and loss, 113
detachment, separation and loss, 113
development
    behavior, 96
        fast, 96–109
    brain, racism and poverty on, 48–49
    emotional, 55–66 (*see also* emotional development)
    implicit bias on, 4
    juvenile offenders, understanding, 90–91
    positive youth, 225–28
    preschool path, 99
    socio-emotional, 216–17
    trajectory, redirecting, 189–90
DHEA, 101
DHEA-S, 101–2
discipline
    disparate, 21–22, 98, 220
    unfair, stereotypes and, 21–23
    See also behavior, problems
discipline, parental/family
    consistency, 210, 214
    harsh, 51
    partnering, 221–22
discipline, schools
    criminalizing, 18
    empathic shift, making, 7–8, 219–21
    fair, 216
    fights, unfair, 108
    racial disparities, 15, 24–26, 98, 143
    respect and support, 225
    teacher decisions, 21
discrimination, 2, 4
    resisting, 177–78
    school, 19
    vicarious, 16b
    See also racism
disorganized attachment, 60
disparagement, 19, 24, 180. *See also* teasing
disparities, racial
    discipline, school, 15, 21–22, 24–26, 98, 143, 220
    income, 30
    suspensions, school, 21–23, 24–25, 89, 123, 155, 162, 219–20
dissociation
    cost, 154–56
    physical, 145–46

INDEX

distress, emotional, 127–38
  adversity, without social assets, 138
  case study
    loss, coping with, 136–37
    sadness, 134–36
  consequences, 127
  discrete emotions, 40
  maternal, 46
  middle childhood, heightened, 91–92
  racism and poverty, 43–44
  troubled behaviors and troubling
      emotions, 129–33
    anger and resentment, 132–33
    anxiety and fear, 130–32
    fundamentals, 129–34
    sadness, 133–34
distrust, hypervigilance and, 153. *See also*
      hypervigilance
divorce, parent
  as adverse childhood event, 31–32, 47–48
  father absence, 116–17
  poverty, 113
  socio-economic status, 40
Dodge, K. A., 51
drugs, selling/dealing, 114, 160–61, 162
DuBois, W. E. B., *The Souls of Black Folk*, 92
Duncan, G. J., 234
dyadic mutuality, 64–65

Early Childhood Longitudinal Study-Birth
    Cohort (ECLS-B), 58–59, 63–64
Early Childhood Longitudinal Study-
    Kindergarten (ECLS-K), 72
easy-going temperament, 57
Eberhardt, J. L., 22–23
economic disadvantage 31
economics
  inequalities, talking about in families, 205
  status (*see* socio-economic status)
Edwards, John, 127
efficacy, personal
  acknowledging, 176–77
  beliefs, 45–46, 70, 175–77, 185, 204, 209,
    210, 235–36
embarrassment, poverty and, 51
emotional development, 55–66
  attachment, 60–65
    secure, 61, 62–65 (*see also* secure
      attachment)
  attachment, styles, 60–61
  definition, 55
  individuation, 56–57
  infants, 55–56

  positive, middle childhood, 84–88
    self-awareness, 85–86
    self-regulation, 87–88
    social awareness, 87
  separation anxiety, 56
  sleep, irritability, adaptability and reactivity
      to others, 59–60
  support, on resilience, 65–66
  temperament, 57–59
emotional distress
  maternal, 46
  middle childhood, heightened, 91–92
  racism and poverty, 43–44, 50
emotionally responsive instruction, 217–18
emotional regulation
  middle childhood, building blocks, 87–88
  modeling and demonstrating, 193–94
emotional resilience, 175–86, 197–98, 198*t*
  building, 233–36
    poverty, robustly combating, 234
    stereotypes and bias, overcoming, 234–36
  definition, 175
  hip-hop music for, 184–85
  neighborhood supports, 225–28
  progress toward, 186
  prosocial skills, 175
  schools, 225
  self-awareness and, 175–80
    adversity, accepting and
      accommodating, 178–79
    adversity, reframing, 179–80
    feelings, redirecting, 179
    pain, acknowledging, 176
    racism stereotypes and discrimination,
      resisting, 177–78
    self-worth and personal efficacy,
      acknowledging, 176–77
  social assets, 2–3, 3*f*, 188–98 (*see also* social
      assets)
  social awareness, 180–84
    danger, avoiding, 180–81
    help, accepting, 181–82
    helping others, 182–83
    social ties, developing positive, 67,
      181, 226
    spiritual community,
      participation, 183–84
  social competence and effective coping, 184
  socio-emotional competence, 185–86
  socio-emotional skills, 175
emotions
  expressing as weakness, 143–44
  processing, racism and poverty, 48–49

emotions, (cont.)
  stress on, chronic, 43
  troubling, in troubled behavior, 129–34
  wounds, 113
emotions, denying, 143–56
  fundamentals, 143–44
  self loss from, 154–56 (see also self, losing)
  self-protective responses to adversity, 144–54, 155–56
    concealing feelings, 147–49
    dissociation, physical, 145–46
    fronting, 149–53, 235–36
    hypervigilance and distrust, 153
    indifference and passivity, feigning, 149–50
    mistrust, cultural, 153–54
    numbing, emotional, 144–45
    overcompensation, behavioral, 146–47
emotions, regulation, 48–49, 73, 75, 129, 193–94, 203
  anxiety, 194
  concealing feelings, 147–49
  numbing, 144–45
  redirecting feelings, 179
  stress on, chronic, 43
Engaging, Managing, and Bonding through Race (EMBRace), 211–12
environments, social, 229–30
  adverse, risks, 5–6, 188
  alteration, family strategies, 208–9
  auspicious, for resilience, 7
  changing, 166–67
"Everyday Struggles" (Notorius B.I.G.), 151
exclusion
  from defensive strategies, 155
  implicit bias, 42–43
  microaggressions, 26
  poverty, 29
  schools
    discipline, empathic shift, 219–20, 221
    punishment, 24–25, 219–20 (see also expulsion, school; suspension, school, disparities)
  social, 19, 20
executive function
  adversity, protection from, 192
  cortisol stress response, 47
  racism and poverty, 47, 48–49
  schools on, 216–17
  self-regulation and, 69–70, 125–26
  stress and adversity, 109
experience
  on resilience, 65–66

See also adverse childhood events (ACEs); trauma
expulsion, school, 21–22, 24–25, 89, 219–20
extended family networks, 208
externalizing behavior
  cortisol and adrenarche early onset, 101–2
  middle childhood, 82, 88–89, 90f, 92–93
  resilience, 51
external locus of control, 207

family
  networks, extended, 208
  school partnering with, 221–22
family life
  adversity, 98–99, 120–21
  instability, racism, and behavior problems, 40
  poverty on
    disruptions, 31
    material hardship, 30
  separation and loss, 116–20
Family Life Study, 47, 72, 74
family strategies, racism and adversity preparation, 203–9
  cultural practices, spiritual values, and extended family networks, 208
  environment, altering, 208–9
  fundamentals, 203–9
  personal control, fostering self-affirming expectations, 206–7
  personal responsibility, instilling paradoxical beliefs about, 207
  racism and economic inequalities, talking about, 205
  self-acceptance and racial identity, 205–6
  support, monitoring, and control, 204–5
father, absence, 31–32, 113, 116–20
father, death
  family change, 117–18
  sadness from
    ambivalent, 137
    case study, 134–36
fatherhood programs, 212–14
  100 Black Fathers, 213
  The Black Dad Initiative, 213
  Black Dads Matter, 214
  Black Fathers Rock, 213
fear, 42–43, 127–28
  about safety, 130
  danger, 130
  infant, 55–56
  misbehavior with, 130–32
  police encounter, 164–65
  poverty, 51

self-awareness, 85
vigilance, 130
feelings
  concealing, 143–44, 147–49, 158, 176, 178, 184, 194
  See also emotions
feelings, redirecting, 179
  antisocial behavior, 160
  emotional resilience and self-awareness, 179
  kindness, 179
  teasing, 148
feisty temperament, 57–58
Ferguson, A. A., *Bad Boys: Public Schools in the Making of Black Masculinity*, 123
financial hardship
  meaning, 50–51
  racism and poverty, 97f, 97–98
  See also poverty
food insecurity, 32, 73–74
4H clubs, 226
frame
  definition, 179
  See also reframing
Frankenhuis, W. E., 195–96
fronting, 149–53, 235–36

García Coll, C., 2–3
gender identity, 70, 81, 87
Girls Clubs, 226
Goff, P. A., 23–24
Golden Age. *See* middle childhood
growing up fast, 96–109
  adultlike roles and responsibilities, assumption, 105–7
  adversity
    family life, 98–99
    trauma, stress and, 99–101
  cortisol elevation
    adrenarche, early onset, 101–2
    stress, chronic, 101
  fundamentals, 96–98, 97f
  independence, seeking and gaining, 107
  innocence, loss, 108–9
  pubertal timing, early, 102–3
  self-reliance, 107–8
  self-reliance and independence of action, premature, 105–7
  weathering, 103–4

hardship, material, 30
Haye, Jovan, *Bigger Than Me*, 146
health, racism and poverty
  on, 40–41, 41b

help
  accepting, 181–82
  offering, 182–83
Hillman, J. B., 102–3
hip-hop music, for emotional coping, 184–85
hippocampus, 48–49, 129
homelessness, 1, 8–9, 32, 33, 40, 117, 229–30, 234
Hope, E. C., 177–78
hostile attribution bias, 88–89
housing
  affordable, 234
  insecurity, 1, 8–9, 32–33, 40, 117, 229–30, 234
human, less that, 15–27. *See also* racism
hyper-masculinity, 148–51
hypervigilance, 44, 99, 143–44, 229–30
  cost, 154–56
  cultural mistrust/paranoia, 153–54
  distrust and, 153
hypothalamic-pituitary-adrenal (HPA) axis, 47

implicit bias. *See* bias, implicit
income
  economic inequalities, talking about in families, 205
  racial disparities, 30
  See also poverty; socio-economic status
independence
  of action, premature, 105–7
  seeking and gaining, 107
indifference, feigning, 149–50
individuation, 56–57
inequalities
  economic, talking about in families, 205
  racial, on economic status, 4
infants
  emotions, 55–56
  separation anxiety, 56
inflection points, 9, 163–69
  adult status, transition to, 167–68
  caring adults, relations with, 165–69
  delinquency on family/self, realizing impact, 168–69
  environments, changing, 166–67
  examples, 163–64
  management, effective, 164
  police encounter, frightening, 164–65
innocence, loss, 108–9
  racism, 113
institutional racism, 16b, 17–18
internalizing
  avoiding, 184
  negative messages, 5, 177
  problems, 46, 91–92, 127–28

interpersonal racism, 16b
interpretive frameworks, 6–7, 45, 189–91, 232–33
intimate partner violence, parental, 119
irritability, 42–43, 49–50, 57, 59–60, 64, 91–92, 129–30, 136
Izard, C. E., 42–43

James, Sherman, 147
John Henryism, 146
juvenile offenders, understanding development, 90–91
    loss, trauma, and (*see* loss, trauma, and behavior problems)

kindergarten transition
    problems, schools addressing, 219–21
    socio-emotional functioning, 218–19
    transitional classrooms, 219–20
kindness
    acts, 182
    caring networks, 230–31
    cultural practices, 208
    redirecting feelings, 179
knucklehead, becoming, 157–71
    antisocial pathway, 158
    antisocial peers, imitating, 162–63
    definition, 157
    inflection points, 163–69
        adult status, transition to, 167–68
        caring adults, relations with, 165–69
        delinquency on family/self, realizing impact, 168–69
        environments, changing, 166–67
        police encounter, frightening, 164–65
    infractions, minor, 159–60
    petty crimes, dabbling, 160–62
    prevalence, 158
    process, 157–58
    wisdom comes late, 169–71
Kotlowitz, A., *There Are No Children Here*, 99–100

labeling, 92–94
    troublemakers, 22–23, 108–9, 234–35
    See also bias, implicit; stereotypes
Loeber, R., 158
loneliness, 181
    juvenile offenders, 114, 116
    parental absence, 114
    poverty, 46, 50
    social connections, antisocial peers/gangs, 98, 163, 170
loss
    adversity, early life, 113

    aggression and, 119, 122–23
    coping with, 136–37
    family adversity as, 120–21
    family life, 116–20
    of innocence, 108–9
    neighborhoods, 123–24, 125
    psychological effects, 115
    from racism, poverty, and adverse childhood experience, 113
    of self, denying emotions, 154–56 (*see also* self, losing)
    on self-regulation, 125–26
    of social supports, from disassociation, concealment, hypervigilance, and mistrust, 155
    traumatic, socio-emotional competencies on, 136–37
    from violence, 98
loss, trauma, and behavior problems, 113–26
    Black boys' perspectives, 116–21
        family adversity, 120–21
        home, separation and loss, 116–20
    case story: loss, trauma and redemption, 121–22
    fundamentals, 113–15
    outside home, loss and trauma, 122–26
    separation and loss, psychological effects, 115

masculinity
    affirmation, 86
    hyper-/toxic, 148–51
material disadvantage. *See* poverty
material hardship
    family life and, 30
    See also poverty
Mendez, D. D., 102–3
mental health
    emotional problems, racism and poverty, 50
    poverty on, 46
    racism on, 17
mentors, adult, 6–8, 227, 229–30
    drug-dealing, exploitation, 161
    fatherhood programs, 212–14
    inflection points, 9
    limits augmenting behavior self-control, 192–93
    protection from adversity, 191
    resilience, culturing, 52
    social assets, 188–90
    social awareness, instilling, 194–95
    unrecognized strengths, fostering self-awareness, 195–96
microaggressions, 4, 26–27, 40–41
    definition, 26

INDEX

implicit bias, 42–43
  on self-confidence, 113
middle childhood, 81–94, 229–30
  bypassing, 88–90, 90f
  critical period, 9–10
  emotional development, positive, 84–88
    self-awareness, 85–86
    self-regulation, 87–88
    social awareness, 87
  emotional distress, heightened, 91–92
  growth, substantial, 81
  juvenile offenders, understanding development as, 90–91
  labeling, 92–94
  misbehavior, decline, 88
  residential camps, 83
  social competence, 82–84
misbehavior. *See* behavior, problems
mistrust
  cost, 154–56
  cultural, 153–54
monitoring, family strategies, 204–5
Moore, Wes, 1–2
  caring network, 230–31
  control structures, 231–32
  environment, 208–9
  interpretive frameworks, 233
  Other Wes Moore, The, 104–5, 164–65, 167
  racism and poverty, 233–34
  reimagining, 235
  social assets, 196–97, 229–30
  socio-emotional development, 48–49
mother
  acceptance by, 192–93
  emotional distress, 46
  modeling by
    on anger control, 194
    of emotional regulation, 193–94
  relationship with, strong/supportive, 192–93
  on self-regulation, 192–93
murder, friend/family, 119, 120
  emotional numbing, 144–45
  gang/neighborhood violence, 131–32, 135–36, 144–45
  hyper-masculinity, 149
  hypervigilance and distrust, 153
mutuality, dyadic, 64–65
"My Brother's Keeper," 4–5

negativity, child, 64
neighborhoods
  loss and trauma, 123–24, 125
  poverty, deprivation and volatility, 34
neighborhoods, strengthening, 225–28
  4H clubs, 226
  arts and culture programs, 226
  Boys and Girls Clubs, 226
  emotional resilience supports, 225–28
  service-learning programs, 226
  sports and recreation programs, 226
neuro-endocrine system, 96–97
Notorius B.I.G.
  "Everyday Struggles," 151
  "Suicidal Thoughts," 151–52
numbing, emotional, 144–45

Okonofua, J. A., 22–23
100 Black Fathers, 213
online racism, 16b, 19
open-ended questions, 221
optimism, 1–2, 125–26, 229–30, 235–36
  3-legged stool, 7–8, 214
  emotional resilience, 186
  family intervention programs, 207, 214
  parental, 205
  social assets, 7
  social competence, 185
Other Wes Moore, The (Moore), 104–5, 164–65, 167
"Over" (Daye), 152–53
overachieving, 146
overcompensation, behavioral, 146–47

pain
  acknowledging, 176
  denying/concealing, 143
Parenting the Strong-Willed Child (PSWC) program, 211
parents
  conflict/separation/divorce (*see also* divorce, parent)
    loss and trauma, problem behavior, 113–26 (*see also* loss, trauma, and behavior problems)
    poverty, 113
  solo, child behavior problems, 116–17
  See also father; mother
Parks, C., 35–37
passivity, feigning, 149–50
pedagogy, transforming classroom, 216–17
personal efficacy. *See* efficacy, personal
perspective taking, social, 68–69
petty crimes, dabbling, 160–62
physical characteristics, testing, 19–20
physical dissociation, 145–46
physical threats, 20–21
Pierce, C., 26
police encounter, frightening, 164–65
Positive Behavior Interventions and Supports (PBIS), 220

262 INDEX

positive youth development (PYD), 225–28
positivity, caregiver, 64
post-traumatic stress disorder (PTSD), 127–28
poverty, 29–39
  adverse child events, 31–32
  adversity and, 5–6
  combating, robustly, 234
  consequences, 46
  facets, 29
  family life
    disruptions, 31
    material hardship, 30
  financial hardship
    meaning, 50–51
    racism, 97f, 97–98
  food insecurity, 32, 73–74
  loss from, 113
  neighborhood deprivation and volatility, 34
  from parental conflict, separation, and divorce, 113
  problem behavior, 113, 114
  race, salience of, 37–39
  racism, 38–39
  residential insecurity, 32–33
  schools and communities, 33
  socio-economic status, 29–30
  traumatic experiences, 49–50
  See also financial hardship
poverty and racism, 40–52. *See also* racism and poverty
preparation, for racism and adversity, 203–14
  family strategies, 203–9
    cultural practices, spiritual values, and extended family networks, 208
    environment, altering, 208–9
    fundamentals, 203–9
    personal control, fostering self-affirming, 206–7
    personal responsibility, instilling paradoxical beliefs, 207
    racism and economic inequalities, talking about, 205
    self-acceptance and racial identity, 205–6
    support, monitoring, and control, 204–5
  programs to help families support sons, 209–14
    Black Parenting Strengths and Strategies, 210–11
    Engaging, Managing, and Bonding through Race, 211–12
    fatherhood programs, 212–14
    fundamentals, 209–14

    Strong African American Families Program, 209–10
preschool
  behavioral trajectories, 92–93
  developmental path, 99
  scapegoating, 25–26
  self-awareness, 85–86
  social competence, 67–68
  suspensions and expulsions, 21–22, 24
preschool-to-prison pipeline, 123
Preventing Long-term Anger and Aggression in Youth (PLAAY), 223
Promoting Academic Success for Boys of Color (PAS) project, 223–24
prosocial skills, 175
psychology, racism and poverty on, 40–41, 41b
puberty, early, 102–3
punishment
  exclusionary, 24–25, 219–20 (*see also* expulsion, school; suspension, school, disparities)
  harsh, implicit bias, 23–24
purpose, from interpretive frameworks, 232–33

questions, open-ended, 221

race salience, poverty, 37–39
racial disparities. *See* disparities, racial
racial identity, family strategies, 205–6
racial inequality, economic status and, 4
racism, 4, 15–27
  anger and emotional distress, 43–44
  depression, 17
  on developmental competencies, 5
  disobedience as reaction to, 17
  exposure to, minimizing, 208–9
  health and psychological consequences, 40–41, 41b
  institutional, 16b, 17–18
  interpersonal, 16b
  less than human, 15
  loss from, 113
  online, 16b, 19
  poverty and, 38–39 (*see also* poverty)
  preparation for, 203–14 (*see also* preparation, for racism and adversity)
  problem behavior, 113, 114
  stereotypes, resisting, 177–78
  structural, 4
  talking about, in families, 205
  transgenerational, 16b, 17
  vicarious, 15–17, 16b
  vicarious discrimination, 16b

racism, seen and felt, 18–27
　discipline at school, disparities, 24–25
　implicit bias, 21
　　violence and harsh punishment, 23–24
　microaggressions, 26–27
　physical characteristics, testing, 19–20
　physical threats, 20–21
　preschool, scapegoating, 25–26
　social exclusion, 19, 20
　stereotypes, 18
　　unfair discipline and, 21–23
racism and poverty, 40–52
　adverse childhood events, 47–48
　anger and emotional distress, 43–44
　behavior problems and family instability, 40
　brain development, 48–49
　cortisol stress response, 47
　emotional problems, 50
　financial hardship, 50–51, 97f, 97–98
　health and psychology, 40–41, 41b
　personal efficacy beliefs, 45–46
　poverty, consequences, 43–44
　resilience, 51–52
　teacher/adult relations and implicit bias, 42–43
　traumatic experiences, 49–50
reaching out, 154, 180, 181–82
reaction
　defensive, aggression as, 150
　to racism, disobedience as, 17
reactivity
　to others, 59–60
　temperament, 57
　testosterone, 101
recreation programs, 226
redirecting
　adult relations, caring, 166
　control structures, 231–32
　developmental trajectory, 189–90
　feelings, 179, 217–18
　inflection points, 164
reframing
　adversity, 179–80, 190
　sadness, 183
　societal messages, 205–6
reimagining Black youth and boys, 229–36
　caring networks, 6–7, 229–31
　control structures, 231–32
　emotional resilience, 233–36
　　poverty, robustly combating, 234
　　stereotypes and bias, overcoming, 234–36
　interpretive frameworks, 6–7, 45, 189–91, 232–33

rejection, 20, 184
　fear of, 130
　hypersensitivity to, 150
　parental, 229–30
　peer, 70–72, 178, 180
　protection from, 68
　racism, 205
relationships, building positive, 67, 181, 226
religious community, participation, 183–84
resentment, 40–41, 121, 132–33, 224
residential insecurity, 32–33
resilience
　adversity with, 6–7
　auspicious environments and social assets, 7
　definition, 155–56
　emotional (*see* emotional resilience)
　essence, 175
　examples, 196–97
　fostering, 226
　racism and poverty, 51–52
　self-knowledge, 155–56
　social assets, 192
　social support, 136–37, 155–56
　support on, 65–66
responsibility
　adultlike, adrenarche, 104
　personal, instilling paradoxical beliefs about, 207
Restorative Justice Practices (RJP), 220–21
Rice, F., 102–3
Rubin, K. H., 70–72

sadness, 127–29, 133–34, 135–36
　acknowledging, 176
　adversity, reframing, 180, 183
　avoidance, 180–81
　case study, 134–36
　causes, 143
　concealing, 147–48
　coping strategies, 175
　infant, 55–56
　irritability and, 129–30
　loss, traumatic, 120–21
　numbing, emotional, 144
　parent death, 137, 152
　redirecting, 179
　regulation of, parental modeling, 193–94
　self-awareness, 85
　separation and loss, 113, 116–17, 121–22
　socio-emotional learning, 220
safety
　anger suppression for, 147–48
　anxiety and fear about, 130

safety (*cont.*)
  attachment, 60
  caregiving and monitoring systems, 116
  caring networks, 230–31
  gangs, illusion, 99–100
  hypervigilance and distrust, 153
  parent/family concerns and protection, 34, 107–8, 191–92, 204
  protective factors, 7–8
  psychological, at school, 42–43
  in schools, 113, 123, 223–24
  secure attachment, 62, 63, 115
  separation anxiety, 56
  social assets, 188–89, 190
  social ties, positive, 181
Santos, C. E., 150
scapegoating
  definition, 25
  preschool, 25–26
  school, 21–22, 42–43
scars, emotional, 113
schools
  discipline (*see* discipline, schools)
  discrimination, 19 (*see also* discrimination; racism)
  exclusionary punishment, 24–25, 219–20 (*see also* exclusion)
  expulsion, 21–22, 24–25, 89, 219–20
  loss and trauma, 122–23, 124–25
  poverty
    lower quality, 33
    struggling, 34–37
  racism, 19 (*see also* racism)
  on social competence, 75
  suspension, disparities, 21–23, 24–25, 89, 123, 155, 162, 219–20
schools, strengthening, 216–25
  academic success, promoting, 223–24
  classroom pedagogy, transforming, 216–17
  culturally informed and affirming programs, 223
  discipline, making empathic shift, 219–21
  emotionally responsive instruction, 217–18
  emotional resilience, 225
  families, partnering with, 221–22
  kindergarten transition, addressing problems, 218–21
  Promoting Academic Success for Boys of Color, 223–24
  socio-emotional learning, 216–17
  teachers, support for, 224–25
school-to-prison pipeline, 18, 123
secure attachment, 61, 63, 189–90

Black boys, 63–65
  development, 62–63
  lack, psychological effects, 115
  as protection against adversity, 191
self, losing, 154–56
self-acceptance, 185
  Notorius B.I.G., 151
  racial identity and, 205–6
  social competence, 67
self-affirmation, 184
  cultural beliefs and practices, 189–90
self-awareness, 68
  emotional resilience and, 175–80
    adversity, accepting and accommodating, 178–79
    adversity, reframing, 179–80
    feelings, redirecting, 179
    pain, acknowledging, 176
    racism stereotypes and discrimination, resisting, 177–78
    self-worth and personal efficacy, acknowledging, 176–77
  of fear, 85
  middle childhood, positive emotional development, 85–86
  preschool, 85–86
  of sadness, 85
  social competence, 68
  of unrecognized strengths, fostering, 195–96
self-blame, 10–11, 178, 206–7
self-confidence, 207
  attachment quality, 62–63
  microaggressions, 113
self-knowledge, 155–56
self-protective responses to adversity, 144–54, 155–56
  concealing feelings, 147–49
  dissociation, physical, 145–46
  fronting, 149–53, 235–36
  hypervigilance and distrust, 153
  indifference and passivity, feigning, 149–50
  mistrust, cultural, 153–54
  numbing, emotional, 144–45
  overcompensation, behavioral, 146–47
self-regulation, 69–70, 74–75, 229–30
  acquisition, racism on, 97–98
  biological memories on, 100
  capacity, 92–93
  control structures, 231–32
  coping strategies, 178
  deficits, 217
  emotional resilience, 175
  executive functioning, 47

losses on, 125–26
middle childhood, 84, 87–89
mother on, 192–93
peer relationships, 70–72
poverty, 40
research, 72
school adjustment, 70
secure attachment, 62
social assets, 188–89, 192, 196, 198*t*
socio-emotional competence, 67–68, 185–86
wisdom, late, 169–70
self-reliance, 107–8
premature, 97–98, 105–7
self-worth, 52
affirmation, 175–77
racial identity, 205–6
separation, parental
accepting and accommodating, 178
father absence, 116–17, 118
psychological effects, 115
separation anxiety, 56
service-learning programs, 226
shame, poverty and, 51
Shonkoff, J. P., 100
shoplifting, 107, 160
skills, developing, 227
sleep, 31, 59–60, 91–92, 130
Smith, C. D., 177–78
social assets, 2–3, 3*f*, 188–98, 229–30
for adversity
protection against effects of, 191–92
recovery from effects of, 191
adversity without, 138
auspicious environments for resilience, 7
behavior self-control, limits for augmenting, 192–93
benefits and roles, 189–90
definition and elements, 188–90
effects, 196–97
emotional regulation, modeling and demonstrating, 193–94
emotional resilience, 197–98, 198*t*
fundamentals, 188
as networks of caring, 189–90
for resilience, 188–89, 192
roles, 190
schools and neighborhoods, 216–28 (*see also* neighborhoods, strengthening; schools, strengthening)
self-awareness of unrecognized strengths, fostering, 195–96
social awareness, 194–95
social awareness, 68–69

instilling, 194–95
middle childhood, 87
social awareness and emotional resilience, 180–84
danger, avoiding, 180–81
help, accepting, 181–82
helping others, 182–83
social ties, developing positive, 67, 181, 226
spiritual community, participation, 183–84
social competence/competencies, 3*f*, 4–5, 67–76, 185–86
anxiety, 70–72
Black boys *vs.* girls, 74
cognitive capacities, 67–70
self-awareness, 68
self-regulation, 69–70
social awareness, 68–69
definition, 67
description, 70–72, 71*t*
importance, 70
kindergarten, behavioral regression, 74–75
middle childhood, growth, 82–84
pre-K programs, 67–68, 74
research, 72–76
resilience from, 184
school on, 75
teasing, 71*t*, 73–74
social environments. *See* environments, social
social exclusion, 19, 20. *See also* exclusion
social perspective taking, 68–69
social sciences, in divergent outcomes, 2–3
social supports, 155–56
loss, from disassociation, concealment, hypervigilance, and mistrust, 155
for resilience, 136–37, 188
for stress, 136–37
social ties
peer relations, 70–72
positive, developing, 67, 181, 226
socio-economic status
Black families, 29–30
factors, key, 40
racial inequality, 4
racism, 38–39
socio-emotional competencies, 185–86
adversity on, 175
case study, 84–85
cognitive capacities for, 67–68
importance, 70
lack, effects, 70–72
PLAAY for, 223
on traumatic loss, 136–37
socio-emotional deprivation, school bias, 42–43

socio-emotional development, 10–11
  adverse childhood events on, 47–48
  adverse conditions on, 5
  classroom pedagogy, 216–17
  as collective, 192
  cortisol and neurohormones on, 96–97
  deprivation on, 138
  middle childhood, 102
socio-emotional functioning, 3f
  kindergarten, transition to, 218–21
  temperament, 57–59
socio-emotional learning (SEL), in schools, 190, 216–17
Socio-Emotional Learning (SEL) programs, 220
socio-emotional skills, 58–59, 65–66, 70, 175
Soler, R., 91–92
solo caregivers, child behavior problems, 116–17
somatic symptoms, 91–92, 130
Souls of Black Folk, The (DuBois), 92
spiritual community, participation, 183–84
spiritual values, 208
sports programs, 226
Sroufe, L. A., 163
stealing, 49, 114, 115, 160, 163
stereotypes, 2, 18
  overcoming, 234–36
  racism, resisting, 177–78
  at school, 45
  unfair discipline and, 21–23
  See also bias, implicit; labeling
stigma, 15, 21–22
  countering/rejecting, 175–76, 184, 186
  definition, 25
  on emotion expression, 147–48
  preschool, scapegoating, 25
  racial disparities, 24
  stereotypes and unfair discipline, 21–22
stigma, adversity, and worry, 1–12
  adversity risks, protection against, 6–7
  economic status and racial inequality, 4
  focus of book, 10–11
  implicit bias and development, 4
  inflection points, 9
  material disadvantage and adversity, 5–6
  middle childhood, critical period, 9–10
  racism, 4
  social assets, 7
  social sciences, divergent outcomes, 2–3
  thesis, principal, 11–12
  3-legged stool, 7–8

wobbly stool, serious behavior problems, 8–9
stool, 3-legged, 7–8
  social assets, 188–89
  wobbly, serious behavior problems, 8–9
strengths, unrecognized, fostering self-awareness of, 195–96
stress, 184
  extraordinary, 127–38 (*see also* distress, emotional)
  family adversity with, as loss, 120–21
  social support for, 136–37
stress, adversity and
  on executive function, 109
  family, as loss, 120–21
  trauma with, 99–101
stress, chronic, 127–38
  anxiety, cortisol and, 101
  consequences, 127–28
  cortisol elevation, 101
  on emotions, 43
stress response, cortisol
  executive function, 47
  racism and poverty, 47
Strong African American Families Program (SAAF), 209–10
substance abuse, parental, child behavior problems with, 117–18
suicidal ideation, 151–52, 191
"Suicidal Thoughts" (Notorius B.I.G.), 151–52
suicide, 31–32, 91–92, 93–94, 127, 152
support
  family strategies, 204–5
  on resilience, 65–66
  for sons, programs, 209–14 (*see also under* preparation, for racism and adversity)
suspension, school, disparities, 21–23, 24–25, 89, 123, 155, 162, 219–20

"Talk, the," 192–93, 198*t*, 205
Tashjian, S. M., 182
teachers
  affirmation from, 224–25
  discipline, 21
  implicit bias, 19, 21, 42–43
  support for, 224–25
  See also schools
teasing, 19
  feelings, concealing, 148
  indifference, feigning, 149
  physical characteristics, 19–20
  social competence and, 71*t*, 73–74
  social exclusion, 20

telomeres, premature aging, 103–4
temperament
    active/feisty, 57–58
    cautious, 58
    Early Childhood Longitudinal Study-Birth Cohort, 58–59
    easy-going, 57
    styles, 57–58
testosterone, 101
There Are No Children Here (Kotlowitz), 99–100
thesis, principal, 11–12
threats, physical, 20–21
3-legged stool, 3*f*, 7–8
    social assets, 188–89
    wobbly, serious behavior problems, 8–9
Toddler Attachment Sort-45 (TAS-45), 63–64
toxic masculinity, 148–51
transgenerational racism, 16*b*, 17
transitional kindergarten classrooms, 219–20
trauma
    adversity, stress and, 99–101
    aggression, arousal, and, 99
    bullying, 19–20, 49–50, 98, 123, 133
    early experience, antisocial behavior, 65–66
    emotional problems, 50
    exposure, 31–32, 50
    loss, socio-emotional competencies on, 136–37
    racism and poverty, 49–50

troublemakers, 22–23, 108–9, 234–35
trust
    hypervigilance and, 153
    See also mistrust
turning points. *See* inflection points

"The Use of the Blues" (Baldwin), 205–6

vicarious discrimination, 16*b*
vicarious racism, 15–17, 16*b*
vigilance
    fear, 130
    See also hypervigilance
violence
    accommodation, 34
    bullying, 19–20, 49–50, 98, 123, 133
    exposure, 31–32, 50
    implicit bias, 23–24
    loss from, 98
    parental, 119
    police, hypervigilance and distrust, 153
volatility, neighborhood, poverty and, 34

weathering, 103–4
weed, smoking, 124, 159–60, 162, 163
Wilkerson, I., 51
wisdom, late, 169–71
wounds, emotional, 113

Yoshikawa, H., 46